THE DICTIONARY OF
LABOUR
QUOTATIONS

THE DICTIONARY OF
LABOUR
QUOTATIONS

— *Stuart Thomson* —

Biteback Publishing

First published in Great Britain in 2013 by
Biteback Publishing Ltd
Westminster Tower
3 Albert Embankment
London SE1 7SP

ISBN 978-1-84954-537-2

10 9 8 7 6 5 4 3 2 1

A CIP catalogue record for this book is available from the British Library.

Set in Perpetua by Duncan Brack

Printed and bound in Great Britain by
CPI Group (UK) Ltd, Croydon CR0 4YY

This book is dedicated to
Alex, Will, Callum and Elenya

Introduction

Being asked to update the *Dictionary of Labour Quotations* took me back to compiling the original, over ten years ago. At that time, I spent many hours visiting libraries, writing out quotes and then typing them up at home. The process this time was very different – I could search online, chase down thoughts and memories about particular issues and individuals. This type of online research, though, brought with it a different set of challenges in sourcing the quotes: many things that are supposedly said are then repeated as fact but turn out not to be entirely accurate. Really getting to the source of the quote proved a challenge on many occasions.

I have tried not to concentrate solely on Labour Party politicians in this book. While they are of course important, there are plenty of other people who make a significant contribution to Labour thinking and that of the wider left. Influences come in many shapes and forms and from many different places and I hope I have captured a good sample of them. The book brings together people who may not think that they ever had anything to do with left-wing politics.

While I would like to thank wikiquotes, brainyquote.com, YouTube, Google, and online versions of newspapers as key tools this time around, the basis of the book remains the work put in over ten years ago and books by Donald Sassoon (*One Hundred Years of Socialism*), Tony Wright (*Socialisms: Old and New*), Geoffrey Foote (*The Labour Party's Political Thought*), Eric Shaw (*The Labour Party Since 1945*, *The Labour Party Since 1979*), Iain Dale (*The Blair Necessities: The Tony Blair Book of Quotations*) and R. Stewart (*A Dictionary of Political Quotations*). The *Oxford Essential Quotations* edited by Susan Ratcliffe also proved invaluable for this new version.

I would like to thank everyone at Bircham Dyson Bell who has supported me over the years, and Iain Dale and the team at Biteback Publishing who were happy to let me have another go at bringing the quotes together.

I have the love and support of a wonderful family – my wife, Alex, and our children, Will, Callum and Elenya. Somehow, I managed to find the time to complete the book! Also, my mum (Maureen), dad (William) and brother (Iain): I needed to write another book to show you that I don't just drink coffee all day!

Stuart Thomson
July 2013

A

Diane Abbott

b. 1953; Labour Party politician, shadow Minister for Public Health 2010–

Tony Blair walks on water. Tony Blair walks on water. Tony Blair walks on water.

Explaining New Labour, April 1997

The law was used in the miners' strike as it has been used in Ireland, used against the black community, used in colonial struggles since time immemorial, as a weapon of the British state against working class people.

Speech to Labour Party Conference, 2 October 1985

People wring their hands and say, 'How un-British to see policemen rushing into people's homes and shooting them down.' Black people know it's not un-British. We know it is *intrinsically* British. We know it's the way the British state has always operated.

Why Women Demand Power (1986)

If they came for *Militant* in the morning, they'll come for the rest of us in the afternoon.

Cited in A. Roth, *Parliamentary Profiles*

White people love playing 'divide & rule'. We should not play their game.

Tweet, 4 January 2012, for which Abbott later apologised

I'm a West Indian mum and West Indian mums will go to the wall for their children.

Interview, *Daily Mirror*, 'Diane Abbott: I sent my son to private school so he wouldn't end up in a gang', 21 June 2010

In politics, the people I most despise are those who have no values.

Q&A, *The Guardian*, 22 January 2011

Private schools prop up the class system in society. It is inconsistent, to put it mildly, for someone who believes in a fairer and more egalitarian society to send their child to a fee-paying school. But I had to choose between my reputation as a politician and my son.

Interview, BBCTV, *This Week*, October 2003

I put being a mother ahead of being a politician.

Quoted in BBC online, Profile: Diane Abbott, 5 January 2012

Leo Abse
1917–2008; former Labour Party politician

As Blair and his impertinent young political pups wage war on old Labour ... as they seek to kill off their fathers, these political adolescents boost themselves with a dangerous amnesia and, thus drugged, the courageous volunteers, manned with piss-proud erections, dare to obliterate the reality that the most radical and 'regenerative Labour government', that brought us the welfare state, was led by old men.

The Man Behind the Smile: Tony Blair and the Politics of Perversion (1998)

First Baron Acton
1834–1902; politician and historian

The danger is not that a particular class is unfit to govern. Every class is unfit to govern.

Letter to Mary Gladstone, 1881

Power tends to corrupt, and absolute power corrupts absolutely. Great men are almost always bad men … There is no worse heresy than that the office sanctifies the holder of it.
  Letter to Bishop Mandell Creighton, 1887

Andrew Adonis
b. 1963; Labour Party politician, Secretary of State for Transport 2009–10

High-speed has well and truly arrived in Britain.
  'High speed rail has well and truly arrived in Britain', *The Guardian*,
  5 August 2009

We have had a massive national aversion to long-term transport planning. We had this view that high-speed trains might be suitable for France and Japan but these were highly exceptional. While we were busy conducting ideological experiments in rail privatisation most of the rest of Europe was getting on with the serious job of building high-speed railway lines astonishingly fast.
  'High speed rail has well and truly arrived in Britain', *The Guardian*,
  5 August 2009

I propose that all underperforming schools – primary as well as secondary – should become academies. Every successful state and private school, and every university, should sponsor an academy, taking full responsibility for the management of a failing school. This would hugely boost the number of successful academies. It would also help to bridge the Berlin Wall between state and private education and promote far stronger links between state schools and higher education.
  Mumsnet, Guest Blog, 21 September 2012

Every child needs a decent education, every teenager who works hard should have good opportunities, and no parent should have to worry that the schools in their area are failing

3

their children. Parents and students have a right to expect that the government – and the political parties – will achieve this.

Mumsnet, Guest Blog, 21 September 2012

Clifford Allen

1889–1939; Independent Labour Party socialist

We as Socialists are concerned with the sanctity of human life. When we are concerned about improved wages and better facilities for education, it is not merely the material things with which we are concerned, but the spiritual things. Our object is to make life expensive and valuable; war makes it cheap and of no account. As Socialists we must apply to foreign and international affairs the same philosophy as guides us in our social legislation.

ILP Conference Report (1915)

Salvador Allende

1908–73; Chilean President 1970–73

Between 3 September and 4 November, Chile is going to feel like a football being kicked about by Pelé.

Campaign speech predicting the struggle after his victory, 1970

Joe Anderson

b. 1958; Labour Party politician, Mayor of Liverpool 2012–

I believe that community cohesion is being seriously threatened by the lack of funding to our City and others, I believe that the so-called summer of discontent will happen again if we do not address this issue.

Letter to Prime Minister, David Cameron, 12 December 2012

Anonymous

A bayonet is a weapon with a worker at each end.
  British pacifist slogan, 1940

Someone has described this country as having socialism for the
rich and capitalism for the poor.
  Archetypal political–economic aphorism

War will cease when men refuse to fight.
  Pacifist slogan, from 1936

If your heart is on the left, don't carry your portfolio on the right.
  Graffiti from the French student riots of May 1968

What is the difference between Capitalism and Communism?
Capitalism is the exploitation of man by man. Communism is
the reverse.
  Joke from Warsaw

Better red than dead.
  Slogan of nuclear disarmament campaigners, late 1950s

Power to the people.
  Slogan of the Black Panther movement, from 1968 onward

We shall not be moved.
  Title of labour and civil rights song (1931) adopted from an earlier
  gospel hymn

Socialism without liberty is the barracks.
  Graffiti from the French student riots of May 1968

Leave the fear of red to horned animals.
  Poster from the French student riots of May 1968

Susan B. Anthony

1820–1906; American reformer and feminist

Men their rights and nothing more; women their rights and
nothing less.
  Motto of The Revolution (1868)

There never will be complete equality until women themselves
help to make laws and elect lawmakers.
  In *The Arena* (1897)

Aristotle

384–322 BC; Greek philosopher

Poverty is the parent of revolution and crime.
  Politics (4th century BC)

Equality consists in the same treatment of similar persons.
  Politics (4th century BC)

Joe Ashton

b. 1933; Labour Party politician

Whips do twist their arms up the back literally – and sometimes
physically.
  BBC Radio, *Week in Westminster*, 1986

Clement Attlee

1883–1967; Labour Party leader, Prime Minister 1945–51

The people's flag is palest pink,
It is not red blood but only ink.
It is supported now by Douglas Cole,
Who plays each year a different role.

Now raise our Palace standard high,
Wash out each trace of purple dye,
Let Liberals join and Tories too,
And Socialists of every hue.

'On the Popular Front', published anonymously in the *Daily Herald*,
22 February 1939

There is nothing more misleading than to try to apply to all
countries a cast-iron theory of historical necessity and to argue
that Britain must go the Moscow road unless she follows the
examples of Berlin or Rome. The theorists at the end of the
eighteenth century might equally well have argued that Britain
must go the way of France unless she was prepared to align
herself with Austria and Prussia.

The Labour Party in Perspective (1937)

Trouble with Winston: nails his trousers to the mast. Can't
climb down.

On Winston Churchill

We are facing a new era. Labour can deliver the goods.

On becoming Prime Minister, 1945

I have no easy words for the nation. I cannot say when we shall
emerge into easier times.

Introducing emergency measures in 1947

As long as the workers have it in their power to achieve their
ends by the use of the ballot-box, they have no right to seek to
obtain them by other means.

The State in Theory and Practice (1935)

If a Capitalist Government is in power, the workers must resist
everything that the Government does. If a Socialist Government
is in power, the Capitalists will do the same. The result is that

the country ceases to count as a factor in world affairs. It is immobilised until the class struggle is resolved.

The Labour Party in Perspective (1937)

I could not consent to the introduction into our national life of a device so alien to all our traditions as the referendum, which has only too often been the instrument of Nazism and Fascism.

Letter to Winston Churchill, 21 May 1945

The voice was the voice of Churchill, but the mind was the mind of Beaverbrook.

In reply to Churchill's claim that Labour would establish a Gestapo, BBC Radio speech, 5 June 1945

You have no right whatever to speak on behalf of the Government. Foreign affairs are in the capable hands of Ernest Bevin ... a period of silence on your part would be welcome.

Letter to Harold Laski, 20 August 1945

I believe that the foundation of democratic liberty is a willingness to believe that other people may perhaps be wiser than oneself.

Speech to Labour Party Conference, 1948

I have none of the qualities which create publicity.

In conversation with Harold Nicolson, 14 January 1949

I think the British have the distinction above all other nations of being able to put new wine into old bottles without bursting them.

Time magazine, 6 November 1950

Just when we were beginning to win the match, our inside left has scored against his own side.

On Aneurin Bevan's resignation in Indo-China, cited in P. Williams, *Hugh Gaitskell* (1985)

Few thought he was even a starter
There were many who thought themselves smarter
But he ended PM
CH and OM
An earl and a knight of the garter.
    Attlee on himself, 8 April 1956

Democracy means government by discussion, but it is only effective if you can stop people talking.
    Cited in A. Sampson, *Anatomy of Britain* (1962)

He is a magnet to all young men. And I warn you if you talk to him no good will come of it. Beware of flattery.
    Warning against Lord Beaverbrook, 1945

If I must have foreign friends, I prefer them to be black or brown.
    Opposing membership to the EEC

Russian Communism is the illegitimate child of Karl Marx and Catherine the Great.
    Speech, 11 April 1956

[The new government was] resolved to carry out as rapidly and energetically as we can the distinctive side of Labour's programme: our socialist policy, our policy of nationalisation.
    Cited in S. Beer, *Modern British Politics* (1965)

I must remind the Rt Hon. Gentleman that a monologue is not a decision.
    To Winston Churchill, 1945

We have seen today a gallant, civilised and democratic people betrayed and handed over to a ruthless despotism.
    On the Munich Agreement, 1938

The idea that every nation ought to have an atomic bomb, like every woman of fashion ought to have a mink coat, is deplorable.

Cited in S. Beer, *Modern British Politics* (1965)

The House of Lords is like a glass of champagne that has stood for five days.

Cited in S. Beer, *Modern British Politics* (1965)

Fundamentally nationalisation had got to go ahead because it fell in with the planning, the essential planning of the country.

Cited in S. Beer, *Modern British Politics* (1965)

I am not prepared to abrogate to myself a superiority to the rest of the movement ... I am prepared to submit to their will even if I disagree.

The Labour Party in Perspective (1937)

The parliament of the party.

On the Labour Party Conference, popular attribution

One of the heaviest indictments against the Capitalist system is that it is destructive of beauty.

The Labour Party in Perspective (1937)

I joined the socialist movement because I did not like the kind of society we had and I wanted something better.

Cited in A. Crosland, *The Future of Socialism* (1956)

B

Walter Bagehot
1826–77; political theorist

Poverty is an anomaly to rich people. It is very difficult to make out why people who want dinner do not ring the bell.
Literary Studies

Mikhail Bakunin
1814–76; Russian anarchist

The urge for destruction is also a creative urge!
Jahrbuch für Wissenschaft und Kunst

The State ... is the most flagrant negation, the most cynical and complete negation of humanity.
Federalism, Socialism and Anti-Theologism (1868)

Where the State begins, individual liberty ceases, and vice versa.
Federalism, Socialism and Anti-Theologism (1868)

Every State must conquer to be conquered.
Federalism, Socialism and Anti-Theologism (1868)

It is impossible to arouse the people artificially. People's revolutions are born from the course of events.
Letter to Sergey Nechayev, 1870

To *exploit* and to *govern* mean the same thing ... Exploitation and government are two inseparable expressions of what is called politics.
The Knouto-Germanic Empire and the Social Revolution (1871)

Idealism is the despot of thought, just as politics is the despot of will.

A Circular Letter to My Friends in Italy (1871)

There are but three ways for the populace to escape its wretched lot. The first two are by the route of the wine shop or the church; the third is by that of social revolution.

God and the State (1882)

Throw theory into the fire. It only spoils life.

Letter to his sisters, 4 November 1842

I do not want to be I. I want to be We.

Letter, 7 February 1870

We wish, in a word, equality – equality in fact as corollary, or rather, as primordial condition of liberty. From each according to his faculties, as each according to his needs; that is what we wish sincerely and energetically.

Declaration signed by forty-seven anarchists on trial after the failure of their uprising at Lyons in 1870 in J. Morrison Davidson, *The Old Order and the New* (1890)

Intellectual slavery, of whatever nature it may be, will always have as a natural result both political and social slavery. At the present time Christianity, in its various forms, and along with it the doctrinaire and deistic metaphysics which sprang from Christianity and which essentially is nothing but theology in disguise, are without doubt the most formidable obstacles to the emancipation of society.

Federalism, Socialism and Anti-Theologism (1868)

A revolutionary idea is a revolutionary, vital, real and true because it expresses and only so far as it forms popular instincts which are the result of history.

Letter to Nechayev, 1870

Property is a god. This god already has its theology (called state politics and juridical right) and also its morality, the most adequate expression of which is summed up in the phrase: 'That man is worth so much!'

The Knouto-Germanic Empire and the Social Revolution (1871)

If there is a human being who is freer than I, then I shall necessarily become his slave. If I am freer than another, then he will become my slave. Therefore, equality is an absolutely necessary condition for freedom ... That is the entire programme of revolutionary socialism, of which equality is the first condition, the first word. It admits freedom only after equality, in equality and through equality, because freedom outside of equality can create only privilege.

Collected Works

The terms 'scientific socialist' and 'scientific socialism', which we meet incessantly in the works and speeches of the Lassallists and Marxists, are sufficient to prove that the so-called people's state will be nothing but a despotism over the masses, exercised by a new and quite small aristocracy of real or bogus 'scientists'. The people, being unlearned, will be completely exempted from the task of governing and will be forced into the herd of those who are governed. A fine sort of emancipation.

Cited in T. Wright, *Socialisms: Old and New* (1996)

Stanley Baldwin
1867–1947; Conservative Party politician, Prime Minister 1923–24, 1924–29 and 1935–37

Socialism and *laissez-faire* are like the north and south poles. They don't really exist.

Attributed

Ed Balls
b. 1967; Labour Party politician, shadow Chancellor of the Exchequer 2011–

Doing a wedding speech when you don't know either the bride or the groom.
> On responding to the Autumn Statement, interview, BBC Radio, *Today* programme, 6 December 2012

Sometimes my stammer gets the better of me.
> On responding to the Autumn Statement, interview, BBC Radio, *Today* programme, 6 December 2012

Just think of the people in whose footsteps we now follow. Working men and women who, in the years before, had seen a hardship many of us will never experience.
> Speech to Labour Party Conference, 1 October 2012

You either learn the lessons of history – or you repeat the mistakes of history – that is the choice the world faces today.
> Speech to Labour Party Conference, 26 September 2011

If Britain and the world are to avoid repeating the mistakes of that 1930s 'lost decade' and the 2008 global crisis, then we badly need political leadership in Britain, Europe and the world.
> Speech to the Fabian Society, 14 January 2012

We need now to win the argument for an alternative economic plan that is rooted in economic history and analysis, as well as our values and principles.
> Speech at Bloomberg, 'There is an alternative', 27 August 2010

I see the Hon. Gentleman's press releases regularly. They come across my desk two or three times a day. I want to give him some support. *[Interruption.]* I want to give him some support. The Hon. Gentleman has a campaign to reverse the cancellation of funding for a dilapidated school in his constituency following the cancellation of Building Schools for the Future. I am right behind him. He has called for a new pedestrian crossing and to unblock the money for it, which is being blocked by a Tory council. I am with him. He has campaigned to keep his local library open. I am right behind him on that one. He wants to keep Thetford Forest safe. Yes, I am with him on that one. He asks how we can deal with the pressures on the voluntary sector. I have to say, I think that he is in the wrong party.

    Responding to Matthew Hancock MP, debate on the Budget, 24 March 2011

For the first time I'm free to be myself.

    Interview, *Daily Telegraph*, 21 May 2010

I'm a very loyal person and I allowed myself to be defined as somebody who was doing Gordon's bidding. I should have fought back harder to define myself at an earlier stage.

    Interview with Mehdi Hasan, 'Ed Balls: Man In A Hurry', *New Statesman*, 31 March 2011

My mobile phone battery runs out all the time because all the messages come straight to me.

    Interview, *Daily Telegraph*, 21 May 2010

It was a mistake. On the information we had, we shouldn't have prosecuted the war. We shouldn't have changed our argument from international law to regime change in a non-transparent way. It was an error for which we as a country paid a heavy price, and for which many people paid with their lives.

    Interview, *Daily Telegraph*, 21 May 2010

I do my politics on the record.

    Opposition Day debate on the economy, House of Commons, 22 June 2011

As long as we don't allow ourselves to be caricatured as an anti-referendum party, which we're not – we've absolutely not ruled

out a referendum – I personally think that for now this is quite
a comfortable position for us. If we allow ourselves either to be
the 'status quo party' on Europe, or the 'anti-referendum party'
on Europe, then we've got a problem. But I think we would
be pretty stupid to allow ourselves to get into either of those
positions.

Quoted in *Daily Mirror*, 11 February 2013

People say New Labour is finished. New Labour is renewed
tonight – we will fight on.

Acceptance speech on being re-elected as Member of Parliament for
Morley and Outwood, 7 May 2010

I always want the Labour candidate to win, but I recognise
there's an issue in places like North Norfolk, where my family
live, where Norman Lamb (Lib Dem) is fighting the Tories, who
are in second place. And I want to keep the Tories out.

Interview, *New Statesman*, 4 May 2010

The nature of politics, Dermot, is that the first minute or two
really matters.

Interview with Dermot Murnaghan, Sky News, 9 December 2012

I said I didn't think a double-dip recession was the most likely
outcome and that turned out to be more optimistic than the
reality. I don't think a triple-dip recession is the most likely
outcome.

Quoted by Guido Fawkes, 25 January 2013

I want to escape the manipulated view of what I've done in the
past.

Interview with Steve Richards, *The Independent*, 8 September 2010

The truth about me, Ed and Yvette is that we've known each
other for twenty years. We've all come from the same part of
the party, intellectually. I did a Bevan lecture recently which
Ed might have done, or Yvette, because we're all from the ...

I'd call it 'visionary pragmatic tradition'. You want to be in
government but you also want to change the world.

Interview, *Total Politics*, December 2011

It doesn't take a genius such as Einstein to realise that when a
plan isn't working, you change the plan. So even our Chancellor
should now be seeing sense.

On George Osborne's insistence not to deviate from Plan A, 'It's still not
too late, Chancellor, to go for growth', *Evening Standard*, 13 March 2013

Thomas Balogh

1905–85; Labour policy adviser and peer

I doubt whether the moral or psychological handicaps could be
overcome without extending public ownership.

Unequal Partners (1963)

Tony Banks

1942–2006; Labour Party politician, Minister for Sport 1997–99

We have gone along with the Party shifting to the right in
desperation to win an election.

Interview with York University student magazine, quoted in *The Times*,
16 October 1997

Even a right-wing moron in a hurry would feel completely
unembarrassed to vote for us.

On the modernised Labour Party

One of mankind's greatest intellectual forces.

On Karl Marx, *Tribune*, 18 June 1983

The only real issue now facing the Labour Movement is to
ensure total victory of the miners.

During the miners' strike

I am glad that my Rt Hon. Friend the Leader of the Opposition [Neil Kinnock] made it clear earlier that he was not prepared to press the nuclear button.

Hansard, 14 January 1992

Is it not time to consider the possibility of legalising soft drugs, especially cannabis?

Hansard, 16 January 1992

Bringing the leadership to its knees occasionally is a good way of keeping it on its toes.

On the 1990 Conservative leadership battle

She is a half-mad old bag lady. The Finchley whinger. She said the poll tax was the government's flagship. Like a captain she went down with her flagship. Unfortunately for the Conservative Party she keeps bobbing up again. Her head keeps appearing above the waves.

On Mrs Thatcher

She is happier getting in and out of tanks than in and out of museums or theatre seats. She seems to derive more pleasure from admiring new missiles than great works of art. What else can we expect from an ex-spam hoarder from Grantham, presiding over the social and economic decline of the country?

On Mrs Thatcher

She is about as environmentally friendly as the bubonic plague. I would be happy to see Margaret Thatcher stuffed, mounted, put in a glass case and left in a museum.

On Mrs Thatcher

We are all New Labour now.

Evidence to the Select Committee on Culture, Media and Sport, Hansard, 14 May 1998

If a Prime Minister needs political advice, he or she should not be Prime Minister.

Hansard, 22 May 1984

Semi-fascist comics.

Describing *The Sun*, *Daily Express* and *Daily Mail*

I try to look a bit smart. It's as George Bernard Shaw said – if you're going to say unorthodox things, say them in unorthodox clothes.

Attributed

Those who hunt foxes are no better in the final analysis than those perverts who bait badgers, course hares, hunt steers, stage dog fights and inflict mindless suffering on domestic pets and wildlife.

Introducing a bill to ban fox hunting, Hansard, 27 April 1993

I don't believe we will ever be allowed to use Parliament to achieve socialism. The obvious alternative is some sort of violent overthrow of society, and that must remain a possibility. We are a long way from revolution, and it wouldn't give me any satisfaction, but I don't actually believe the ruling classes would allow a socialist government to change the whole basis and economic structure through parliamentary means. It could well be that a socialist government is elected and challenges the system and a crisis follows which then might end in some form of revolution.

House Magazine, 10 April 1989

Corrupt political systems inevitably produce corrupt economic systems. Honest business – if that is not an oxymoron – cannot long survive with a crooked government. It is just possible for crooked business to try to survive under an honest government, but if that government is honest they will, of course, move rapidly to deal with crooked businessmen.

House of Commons, 14 November 1996

I look forward to a socialist United States of Europe.

June 1990

Abolition [of the GLC] was an act of political malice, carried out by probably the most vindictive, dogmatic, bigoted, authoritarian Prime Minister that this country has had to suffer since the days of the Duke of Wellington – from the Iron Duke to the Iron Maiden, linked together through 150 years only by their own personal arrogance. It is not my intention to re-fight the old battle, because I cheer myself up with the old saying 'Don't get mad, get even'.

House of Commons, 21 February 1996

I got pretty pissed at university and I've never been pissed like that since. Over the years as an MP your tolerance builds up. I'm hardened. I'm no hair-shirt socialist. I like to relax and I like relaxing with a drink.

The Observer, 8 December 1996

He is undoubtedly living proof that a pig's bladder on a stick can be elected as a Member of Parliament.

On Conservative Party politician Terry Dicks

That this House is appalled, but barely surprised, at the revelations in MI5 files regarding the bizarre and inhumane proposals to use pigeons as flying bombs; recognises the important and life-saving role of carrier pigeons in two world wars and wonders at the lack of gratitude towards these gentle creatures; and believes that humans represent the most obscene, perverted, cruel, uncivilised and lethal species ever to inhabit the planet and looks forward to the day when the inevitable asteroid slams into the earth and wipes them out thus giving nature the opportunity to start again.

Early Day Motion 1255, 21 May 2004

A foetus.

> Description of then Conservative Party leader William Hague, on the
> fringe at Labour Party Conference, September 1997

To be honest, I found it intellectually numbing, and tedious
in the extreme. I most certainly won't miss the constituency
work. I've got to tell you that honestly. It's twenty-two years
of the same cases, but just the faces and the people changing.
It might sound a little disparaging to say this about people's
lives and their problems and we did deal with them … but I
got no satisfaction from this at all. I really didn't. And all you
were was a sort of high-powered social worker and perhaps
not even a good one at that. I will miss being chairman of the
works of art committee … because I was having so much
intellectual enjoyment, and indeed just straightforward fun, out
of reorganising our collection, and that kept me in touch with
history.

> Interview with Robin Oakley on BBC Radio 4, 26 November 2004 on
> his intention to stand down as Member of Parliament

A one-man food mountain.

> Describing Conservative Party MP, Nicholas Soames

Videogames are worse than child pornography.

> Interview on Channel 4, *Richard and Judy*, 8 December 2004

She behaves with all the sensitivity of a sex-starved boa
constrictor.

> On Mrs Thatcher, quoted in *The Independent*, 8 January 2006

… so unpopular, if he became a funeral director people would
stop dying.

> On John Major, 'The Wit and Wisdom of Tony Banks', BBC News, 8
> January 2006

He was a fairly competent chairman of Housing [on Lambeth
Council]. Every time he gets up now I keep thinking, 'What on

earth is Councillor Major doing?' I can't believe he's here and sometimes I think he can't either.

On John Major entering Parliament, 'The Right Hon. Wag', *The Guardian*, 10 January 2006

I have gone to a safe house, as they say, so I might as well have a different name.

On entering the House of Lords, 'Banks Changes Name For Lords Life', BBC News, 23 June 2005

At one point Portillo was polishing his jackboots and planning the next advance. And the next thing is he shows up as a TV presenter. It is rather like Pol Pot presenting the Teletubbies.

On former Conservative Minister Michael Portillo, *Tribune* rally, September 1997

I think my exact words were 'Fuck me!'

On being appointed a minister, *Daily Telegraph*, obituary, 9 January 2006

To be offered the Minister for Sport by the Prime Minister was rather like being offered a place in heaven without having to die first.

On being appointed a minister, *Daily Telegraph*, obituary, 9 January 2006

I've done as much to destroy my own self politically as anyone else. Probably more so. Being brutally frank has let me down. I should have tempered my words more. But when people ask me a question I like to give them an answer.

Daily Telegraph, obituary, 9 January 2006

If people wish to eat meat and run the risk of dying a horrible, lingering hormone-induced death after sprouting extra breasts and large amounts of hair, it is, of course, entirely up to them.

On meat-eating, *Daily Telegraph*, obituary, 9 January 2006

The only thing you can be certain about in politics is that you can't be certain about anything.

Total Politics, 10 April 1992

I am so clean you could eat your food off me.

Total Politics

I didn't actually find many facts, but I had a good time.

On a fact-finding mission to Japan, 2000

Joel Barnett

b. 1923; former Chief Secretary to the Treasury

When calm returns to the industrial scene, this week's agreement between the Government and the TUC will prove to be a major turning point, which will provide the basis for a great Labour victory at the general election.

On the ending of the winter of discontent; Labour lost the following election

To my mind, the only give and take in the social contract was that the government gave and the unions took.

Inside the Treasury (1982)

Michael Barratt Brown

b. 1918; political theorist, Labour Party member

The rivalry today is not so much between capitalist *states*, in which finance capital is integrated with the state machine, as between transnational *companies*.

From Labourism to Socialism (1972)

Socialism is not primarily about equality, as Crosland insisted, not even about liberty, important as reforms in these directions may be; it is about the eradication of class, about social control and production for use, instead of profit, for socially formulated needs in place of privately managed markets.

From Labourism to Socialism (1972)

The division emerging in the ruling class in the 1970s is between the giants of industry and finance with international connections and the pygmies in the national market.

From Labourism to Socialism (1972)

The transnational company has now reached a size where it can challenge the power of all but the largest nation states.

From Labourism to Socialism (1972)

Brian Barry

1936–2009; political theorist

Does the public health service have long waiting lists and inadequate facilities? Buy private health insurance. Has public transport broken down? Buy a car for each member of the family above driving age. Has the countryside been built over or the footpaths eradicated? Buy some elaborate exercise machinery and work out at home. Is air pollution intolerable? Buy an air-filtering unit and stay indoors. Is what comes out of the tap foul to the taste and chock-full of carcinogens? Buy bottled water. And so on. We know it can all happen because it has: I have been doing little more than describing Southern California.

The Continuing Relevance of Socialism (1996)

David Basnett

1924–89; former president of the General and Municipal Workers Union

Our job as trade unionists is not merely to haggle about slices of economic 'cake'. We are in politics. We are concerned about where the power lies, and concerned that that power is not abused.

Socialist commentary, 1973

Otto Bauer

1881–1938; Austrian socialist

We must construct socialist society gradually, by planned organised activity, proceeding step by step towards a clearly conceived goal. Each one of the successive measures which lead us to a socialist society needs to be carefully considered. It must not only achieve a more equitable distribution of goods, but also improve production; it should not work to destroy the capitalist system of production without establishing at the same time a socialist organisation which can produce goods at least as effectively.

What is Austro-Marxism? (1927)

Where the working class is divided, one workers' party embodies sober, day-to-day *Realpolitik*, while the other embodies the revolutionary will to attain the ultimate goal. Only where a split is avoided are sober *Realpolitik*, and revolutionary enthusiasm united in *one* spirit.

What is Austro-Marxism? (1927)

The result of this balance of forces, or rather the weakness of both classes, is the triumph of fascism, which serves the capitalists by crushing the working class, and yet, despite being in their pay, so far outgrows them that they cannot help making it the undisputed master over the whole people, themselves included.

Austrian Democracy Under Fire (1934)

It was impossible to govern the industrial district in opposition to the workers … it was equally impossible to govern the great agrarian districts in opposition to the peasants. The economic structure of the country therefore created a balance of power between the classes which could only have been abolished by force in a bloody civil war … Large sections of the proletariat did not realise these dangers, but it was the duty of Social Democracy to see them.

The Austrian Revolution (1924)

Lord Max Beaverbrook

1879–1964; Canadian newspaper magnate

Bevan done and lost and friends – one-quarter Bloody
Revolution one-quarter pacifist one-half same policy as the
Tories but with jobs.

   On Aneurin Bevan, cited in A. J. P. Taylor, *Beaverbrook* (1972)

August Bebel

1840–1913; German socialist politician

In time of war the loudest patriots are the greatest profiteers.

   Speech to the Reichstag, November 1870

The field of politics always presents the same struggle. There are
the Right and the Left, and in the middle is the Swamp.

   Speech to the annual congress of the SPD, 1906

Woman was the first human being that tasted bondage. Woman
was a slave before the slave existed.

   Die Frau und der Sozialismus (1879)

Anti-Semitism is the socialism of fools.

   Anti-Semitism and Social Democracy (1893)

Margaret Beckett

b. 1943; Labour Party politician, deputy leader 1992–94, leader May–
July 1994, Foreign Secretary 2006–07

Achieving climate security must be the core of foreign policy.

   Speech at the British Embassy, Berlin, on climate change and security,
   23 October 2006

We face a timetable that is driven by nature, science and by the predicted effect of climate change on our world, not by our own negotiating processes.

Speech to energy and environment ministers, 1 November 2005

One of the reasons I came into politics was because I thought I lacked the skills to be a social worker.

BBC TV, *Question Time*, 13 November 2008

Being effective is more important to me than being recognized.

Independent on Sunday, 2 January 2000

Pack it in!

Losing her temper with the presenter Edward Stourton when questioned about the situation in the Middle East, BBC Radio, *Today* programme, 31 July 2006

Daniel Bell

1919–2011; American political theorist

The irony ... for those who seek 'causes' is that the workers, whose grievances were once the driving energy for social change, are more satisfied with the society than the intellectuals. The workers have not achieved utopia, but their expectations were less than those of the intellectuals, and the gains correspondingly larger.

The End of Ideology (1960)

Tony Benn

b. 1925; Labour Party politician, Minister of Technology 1966–70, Secretary of State for Industry 1974–75

It was then that my political position changed, because the more I saw of this process [i.e. state coaxing of the private sector] the more I became convinced that it would not work, that it was corporatist, and that it was anti-trade union and undemocratic.

On his time in Wilson's Cabinets, *Parliament, People and Power* (1982)

When you get to No. 10, you've climbed there on a little ladder called 'the status quo'. And when you're there, the status quo looks very good.

1995

I'm supposed to be the Millbank representative in Chesterfield ... You can feel like an Avon lady calling, not a Labour MP.

Interview, *The Observer*, 4 July 1999

I am a public library.

Interview, *The Observer*, 4 July 1999

Mrs Thatcher will be remembered not as a great executive leader, because every Prime Minister is powerful, but because she is a teacher. The weakness of the Labour Party over a long period is that it hasn't done any teaching.

8 February 1992, cited in I. Dale (ed.), *As I Said To Denis* (1998)

We are saying at this conference that the crisis that we inherit when we come to power will be the occasion for fundamental change and not the excuse for postponing it.

Speech to Labour Party Conference, 1973

If you are accountable always to the person above you to promote you or marginalise you, then clearly there will be an enormous pressure to respond to that structure. If on the other hand you are accountable to the people who elected you then it's a different pressure. There is a corrective element in democracy which corrects that tendency to corruption.

Cited in J. Adams, *Tony Benn: A Biography* (1992)

If we've changed our mind to win, we could change our mind when we've won. What's wrong with that? We could not talk about nuclear disarmament because we might not win. But we've won, so we change back again ... I mean, you can change one way, you can change the other.

The Independent, 30 September 1991

She has fought resolutely for the class she represents and there are some lessons we might learn from that.

On Mrs Thatcher

She believes in something. It is an old-fashioned idea.

On Mrs Thatcher, cited in S. R. Letwin, *The Anatomy of Thatcherism* (1992)

I did not enter the Labour Party forty-seven years ago to have our manifesto written by Dr Mori, Dr Gallup and Mr Harris.

The Guardian, 13 June 1988

A Christian whose political commitment owes much more to the teachings of Jesus – without the mysteries within which they are presented – than to the writings of Marx, whose analysis seems to lack an understanding of the deeper needs of humanity.

On himself, *Arguments for Democracy* (1981)

Until there is a new constitutional settlement between capital and labour and the electorate, what will happen is that capital when it is strong will be deadlocked by labour and the economy will fail.

Capital and Class (1982)

We have waited too long for the transformation of the public corporation ... We should be talking about the transfer of power within industry, and we should not accept existing forms of nationalisation as a form of the future. We have had enough experience now to know that nationalisation plus Lord Robens does not add up to socialism.

Arguments for Socialism (1980)

I opposed the Suez war, I opposed the Falklands war, I opposed the Libyan bombing and I opposed the Gulf war and I never believed that any of those principled arguments lost a single vote – indeed, I think they gained support, though that was not why you did it. What has been lacking in Labour politics over a long period is a principled stand.

Cited in J. Adams, *Tony Benn: A Biography* (1992)

I can really see significant long-term opportunities for ordinary people in Britain and in the Six if we could persuade the British public to vote for entry.

On the Common Market, speech, Bristol, July 1971

Britain's continuing membership of the Community would mean the end of Britain as a completely self-governing nation.

Letter to constituents, December 1974

Political democracy wrested the control of Parliament from those who owned the lands and the factories. Industrial democracy is a logical and necessary development of it.

Arguments for Socialism (1980)

In developing our industrial strategy for the period ahead, we have the benefit of much experience. Almost everything has been tried at least once.

Hansard, 13 March 1974

It is as wholly wrong to blame Marx for what was done in his name, as it is to blame Jesus for what was done in his.

Cited in A. Freeman, *The Benn Heresy* (1982)

I think Mrs Thatcher did more damage to democracy, equality, internationalism, civil liberties, freedom in this country than any other Prime Minister this century. When the euphoria surrounding her departure subsides you will find that in a year or two's time there will not be a Tory who admits ever supporting her. People in the streets will say, thank God she's gone.

Channel 4, *The Thatcher Factor*, December 1990

The House of Lords is the British Outer Mongolia for retired politicians.

New York Times, 11 February 1962

I have planted quite a number of little acorns and they have grown into oak trees.

Declaring his intention to stand down as an MP, 27 June 1999

The flag of radicalism which has been hoisted in Wolverhampton is beginning to look like the one that fluttered twenty-five years ago over Dachau and Belsen.

On Enoch Powell's campaign, speech, 1970 general election

Virtually the whole British Establishment has been, at least until recently, educated without any real knowledge of Marxism, and is determined to see that these ideas do not reach the public … Anyone today who speaks of class in the context of politics runs the risk of excommunication and outlawry.

Marx Memorial Lecture, 1982

It would be as unthinkable to try to construct the Labour Party without Marx as it would to be to establish university faculties of astronomy, anthropology or psychology without permitting the study of Copernicus, Darwin or Freud, and still expect such faculties to be taken seriously.

Marx Memorial Lecture, 1982

I try to operate on two unconnected levels. One of the practical levels of action in which I am extremely cautious and conservative. The second is the realm of ideas where I try to very free.

1971

Very charming ... an agreeable and skilful politician, marvellous at getting his own way ... a shrewd political figure.

On Jim Callaghan, *Against the Tide* (1989)

If I rescued a child drowning, the press would no doubt headline the story 'Benn Grabs Child'.

The Observer, 2 March 1975

I am interested in technology spiritually because it liberates the mind.

1967

I have often thought of the parallel between Castro entering Havana and a new government entering power here ... and had thought that the two events should be as similar as possible.

1966

If we keep faith with those we represent and if we keep our nerve, there is nothing that can stop us from restoring our society to a new and fairer basis ... The greatest problem is that many people don't believe what we say and don't know whether we would do it if we were elected.

The Guardian, 5 September 1981

We are ... paying a heavy political price for twenty years in which, as a party, we have played down our criticism of capitalism and soft-peddled our advocacy of socialism.

Speech to Labour Party Conference, 1976

The trouble about a personal diary is that it is entirely subjective. It is not history, nor has it any value except such as it gets from the personal slant on events. But of course these events are the framework on which the thin personal story is woven. Every now and again one has to step back a little and assess the changes that are taking place outside.

Years of Hope (1994)

I think the truth is that the Labour Party isn't believed anymore because people suspect it will say anything to get votes. The rebuilding of some radical alternative to Thatcherism – and by that I mean all-party Thatcherism – will require us to do some very difficult things.

The End of an Era (1994)

The most radical and comprehensive programme ever produced by the Labour Party.

On the Alternative Economic Strategy in the Labour Party's Programme for Britain, cited in M. Hatfield, *The House the Left Built* (1978)

Every generation has to fight the same battles, again and again.

Interview, *Morning Star*, 28 March 2011

Socialism is about democracy, people taking control.

Interview, *Morning Star*, 28 March 2011

WikiLeaks is important because information is a source of power.

Interview, *Morning Star*, 28 March 2011

We won't accept a world dominated by wealth.

Interview, *Morning Star*, 28 March 2011

Being in my 80s is such fun – if only I'd known, I'd have done it years ago.

Quoted in *The Guardian*, 31 May 2007

The Labour party has never been a socialist party, although there have always been socialists in it.

Interview, BBC Radio, *Today* programme, 10 February 2006

Well I came across Marx rather late in life actually, and when I read him, two things: first of all I realised that he'd come to the conclusion about capitalism which I'd come to much later, and I was a bit angry he'd thought of it first; and secondly, I see Marx who was an old Jew, as the last of the Old Testament

Prophets, this old bearded man working in the British Library, studying capitalism, that's what *Das Kapital* was about, it was an explanation of British capitalism. And I thought to myself, 'Well anyone could write a book like that, but what infuses, what comes out of his writing, is the passionate hostility to the injustice of capitalism.' He was a Prophet, and so I put him in that category as an Old Testament Prophet.

Interview with John Cleary, ABC Radio, 23 February 2003

Ideas are more powerful than guns.

Wikinews interview, 8 August 2007

I think New Labour is probably over.

Quoted in *The Guardian*, 31 May 2007

Clement Attlee had as much charisma as a mouse. He was absolutely monosyllabic. People say conversation is supposed to be like a game of tennis, but with Attlee it was like tossing biscuits to a dog.

Quoted in *Iain Dale's Diary*, 1 June 2007

I want to leave plenty of time for discussion: I have heard myself speak before.

Quoted in *The Guardian*, 31 May 2007

Having served for nearly half a century in the House of Commons, I now want more time to devote to politics and more freedom to do so.

The Independent, 28 June 1999

Choice depends on the freedom to choose and if you are shackled with debt you don't have the freedom to choose.

When interviewed by Michael Moore on healthcare in the US, in *Sicko*, 2007

Alan Bennett

b. 1934; English actor and playwright

The real solvent of class distinction is a proper measure self-esteem – a kind of self consciousness. Some people are at ease with themselves, so the world is at ease with them. My parents thought this kind of ease was produced by education ... they didn't see that what disqualified them was temperament – just as, though educated to the hilt, it disqualifies me. What keeps us in our place is embarrassment.

BBC TV, *Dinner at Noon*, (1988)

We started off trying to set up a small anarchist community but people wouldn't obey the rules.

Getting On (1972)

You see it fading away.

On the importance of class, interview, BBC Radio, *Front Row*, 20 March 2013

Eduard Bernstein

1850–1932; German socialist politician

One avoids anxiously every concern with the future organisation of society, but one substitutes for it a sudden leap forward, from capitalism into socialism.

'General Observations on Utopianism and Eclecticism', *Die Neue Zeit*, 28 October 1896

I frankly admit that I have extraordinarily little feeling for, or interest in, what is usually termed 'the final goal of socialism'. This goal, whatever it may be, is nothing to me, the movement is everything. And by the movement I mean both the general movement of society i.e. social progress, and the political

and economic agitation and organisation to bring about this
progress.

Cited in H. Tudor and J.M. Tudor (eds.) *Marxism and Social Democracy*
(1988)

It is my firm conviction that the present generation will already
see realised a large part of socialism, if not in official form,
at least in content. The constant enlargement of social duties,
i.e. of the duties and corresponding rights of the individual
against society and of the duties of society to the individual, the
extension of the right of society, as organised in the nation
or the state, to supervise economic life, the construction of
democratic self-government at village, district and provincial
levels, and the extension of the tasks of these associations
– and that for me is development towards socialism.

Cited in T. Wright, *Socialisms: Old and New*, 1996

Annie Besant

1847–1933; socialist

The economic forces which replaced the workshop by the
factory will replace the private shop by the municipal store
and the private factory by the municipal one.

Industry under Socialism (1889)

Aneurin Bevan

1897–1960; Labour Party politician, Secretary of State for Health 1945–51

Whereas in Britain we are slaves to the past, in Russia they are
slaves to the future.

Remark, 1930

Honest politics and Tory politics are contradictions in terms.
Lying is a necessary part of a Tory's political equipment, for it is

essential for him to conceal his real intentions from the people. This is partly the reason for his success in keeping power.

Why Not Trust the Tories? (1944)

The Prime Minister wins debate after debate and loses battle after battle. The country is beginning to say that he fights debates like a war and a war like a debate.

House of Commons, 2 July 1942

It is among the solid artisan classes that you will find the most tolerance and the least bellicosity. Their attitude corresponds most closely with democratic socialism. Their lives are rounded by the consciousness of acquired skills and by the rhythm of daily labour.

In Place of Fear (1952)

It is not going to be possible to prevent those hundreds of millions of populations over-running Western civilisation or bringing it down unless we can bring to them assistance from our own resources, and that assistance cannot come from capitalism, because those areas are no longer possible areas of profitable investment. This is as I see it the central issue of the election.

Speech to Labour Party Conference, 1951

The advance from State ownership to full Socialism is in direct proportion to the extent that workers in the nationalised industry are made aware of a changed relationship between themselves and the management. The persistence of a sense of dualism in a publicly owned industry is evidence of an immature industrial democracy.

In Place of Fear (1952)

The Socialist dares not to invoke the authority of Parliament in meeting economic difficulties unless he is prepared to exhaust its possibilities. If he does not, if he acts nervously, without vigour, ingenuity and self-confidence, then it is upon him and his that the consequences will alight. He will have played his

last card and lost, and, in the loss, parliamentary institutions
themselves may be engulfed.

In Place of Fear (1952)

The social furniture of modern society is complicated and
fragile and it cannot support the jackboot. We cannot run the
processes of modern society by attempting to impose our will
upon nations by armed forces.

Speech, London, 5 December 1956

I need hardly to say that my adherence to the cause of Labour
and Socialism is stronger than ever and that I believe that
renewed efforts by all of us will result in another thrust towards
the goal of our hopes.

Following his resignation from the Cabinet in 1951, *The Times*, 23 April
1951

This island is made mainly of coal and surrounded by fish. Only
an organised genius could produce a shortage of coal and fish at
the same time.

Speech, 24 May 1945

No amount of cajolery, and no attempts at ethical and social
seduction, can eradicate from my heart a deep burning hatred of
the Tory party ... So far as I am concerned they are lower than
vermin.

Speech, Manchester, 4 July 1948

You cannot educate a man to be a trained technician inside
a factory and ask him to accept the status of a political robot
outside ... a totalitarian state or a one-party state is a persistent
contradiction with the needs of a thriving industrial community.

Tribune, 3 February 1950

The issue ... in a capitalist democracy resolves itself into
this: either poverty will use democracy to win the struggle

against property, or property, in fear of poverty, will destroy democracy.

In Place of Fear (1952)

How can wealth persuade poverty to use its political freedom to keep wealth in power? Here lies the whole art of Conservative politics in the twentieth century.

In Place of Fear (1952)

The function of parliamentary democracy, under universal suffrage, historically considered, is to expose wealth-privilege to the attack of the people. It is a sword pointed at the heart of property power.

In Place of Fear (1952)

I am as deeply concerned with maintaining the Socialist approach to this service as anyone on this side of the House.

On the National Health Service, cited in J. Campbell, *Nye Bevan: A Biography* (1987)

The language of priorities is the religion of Socialism.

Speech to Labour Party Conference, 1949

The people have not clothed the bones of political democracy with the flesh of economic power.

Why Not Trust the Tories? (1944)

We shall find people starving to death by the side of television sets if we are not careful.

Cited in M. Foot, *Aneurin Bevan* (1973)

Democratic parliaments under private property, under capitalism, are the professional public mourners for private economic crimes. So long as parliaments divest themselves of economic power, then democratic institutions are bound to be always the whipping-boys for private enterprise.

Socialist Values in a Changing Civilisation (1951)

The victory of socialism need not be universal to be decisive.
In Place of Fear (1952)

The purpose of power is to be able to give it away.
Cited in M. Foot, *Aneurin Bevan* (1973)

The argument is about power, because only by the possession of
power can you get the priorities right.
Labour Party Annual Conference Report (1959)

No one who is not a pacifist or a partisan of the Kremlin would
argue that military strength is not needed.
With H. Wilson and J. Freeman, *One Way Only* (1951)

In one sense the House of Commons is the most
unrepresentative of assemblies. It is an elaborate conspiracy
to prevent the real clash of opinion which exists outside from
finding an appropriate echo within its walls. It is a social shock
absorber placed between privilege and the pressure of popular
discontent.
In Place of Fear (1952)

The first function of a political leader is advocacy. It is he
who must make articulate the wants, the frustration, and the
aspiration of the masses.
In Place of Fear (1952)

I know that the right kind of political leader of the Labour Party
is a desiccated calculating machine.
Taken as meaning Hugh Gaitskell, *Tribune* rally, 29 September 1954

If the Labour Party is not going to be a Socialist Party, I don't
want to lead it ... When you join a team in the expectation
that you are going to play rugger, you can't be expected to be
enthusiastic if you are asked to play tiddly-winks.
Speech, 26 January 1956

A society in which the people's wants do not exceed their possessions is not a Socialist society.

Cited in M. Foot, *Aneurin Bevan* (1973)

Why read the crystal when he can read the book?

On Robert Boothby during a debate on Sterling's exchange rate, Hansard, 29 September 1949

Fascism is not in itself a new order of society. It is the future refusing to be born.

Cited in L. Harris, *The Fine Art of Political Wit* (1965)

[Winston Churchill] does not talk the language of the twentieth century but that of the eighteenth. He is still fighting Blenheim all over again. His only answer to a difficult situation is to send a gun-boat.

Speech to Labour Party Conference, 2 October 1951

Political toleration is a by-product of the complacency of the ruling class. When that complacency is disturbed, there never was a more bloody-minded set of thugs that the British ruling class.

Cited in M. Foot, *Aneurin Bevan* (1962)

I went to work when eleven years old for two and six a week, though I may not have been worth more.

Speech, House of Commons, 18 November 1952

This second-rate orator trails his tawdry wisps of mist over the parliamentary scene.

On Stanley Baldwin, 1937

The worst thing I can say about democracy is that it has tolerated the Rt Hon. Gentleman for four and half years.

On Neville Chamberlain, 1940

I welcome this opportunity of pricking the bloated bladder of lies with the poniard of truth.

Attacking Winston Churchill, speech, House of Commons, 29 September 1949

Righteous people terrify me ... Virtue is its own punishment.

Cited in M. Foot, *Aneurin Bevan* (1962)

In Germany democracy died by headsman's axe. In Britain it can be done by pernicious anaemia.

Attributed

Like an old man approaching a young bride – fascinated, sluggish and apprehensive.

On the Allies' advance into Italy, 1943

You call that statesmanship. I call it an emotional spasm.

Opposing unilateral disarmament, 1957

If you carry this resolution and follow out all the implications and do not run away from it you will send a British Foreign Secretary, whoever he may be, naked into the conference chamber.

Opposing unilateral nuclear disarmament, speech to Labour Party Conference, Brighton, 3 October 1957

This so-called affluent society is an ugly society still. It is a vulgar society. It is a meretricious society. It is a society in which priorities have gone all wrong.

Speech, Blackpool, 29 November 1959

Soviet Communism establishes a whole series of Trojan horses in every nation of the western economy.

Speech, London, 23 April 1951

There is only one hope for mankind – and that is democratic Socialism.

Speech, London, 23 April 1951

Democratic Socialism is not a middle way between capitalism and Communism. If it were merely that, it would be doomed to failure from the start. It cannot live by borrowed vitality. Its driving power must derive from its own principles and the energy released by them. It is based on the conviction that free men can use free institutions to solve the social and economic problems of the day, if they are given the chance to do so. [You cannot] inject the principles of ethical Socialism into an economy based upon private greed.

Speech, Blackpool, 29 November 1959

I read the newspaper avidly – it is my one form of continuous fiction.

1960

We know what happens to people who stay in the middle of the road – they get run over.

The Observer, 6 December 1953

I stuffed their mouths with gold.

On how he obtained the support of consultants when setting up the NHS, cited in B. Abel-Smith, *The Hospitals 1800–1948* (1964)

One of the central principles of socialism is the substitution of public for private ownership.

Tribune, 13 June 1952

Those who want the mainsprings of economic power transferred to the community and those who believe that private enterprise should still remain supreme but that its worst characteristics should be modified by liberal ideas of justice and equality.

On the battle over public ownership, cited in W. Greenleaf, *The British Political Tradition* (1983)

The absence of a written constitution gives British politics flexibility enjoyed by few nations.

In Place of Fear (1952)

Whenever the Labour Party has made a mistake, it has not been in consequence of pursuing its principles too roughly or too far, but by making too many concessions to conventional opinion.

In Place of Fear (1952)

The conversion of an industry to public ownership is only the first step towards Socialism. It is an all-important step, for without it the conditions of further progress are not established.

In Place of Fear (1952)

We have still to ensure that they [the boards of nationalised industries] are taking us towards democratic socialism, not towards the Managerial Society.

In Place of Fear (1952)

Audacity is the mood that should prevail among Socialists as they apply the full armament of democratic values to the problems of the times.

In Place of Fear (1952)

[There is] no way in which it is possible for anybody to carry out a plan in the modern state involving stability of employment, involving the proper dispersal of industry, involving all the things we mean by effective control over economic life, unless the power has passed from the hands of the oligarchs into the hands of the democrats.

Democratic Values (1950)

Are we seriously as Socialists going to be told that in 1952 we have discovered some royal road, some ingenious way of trying to achieve our socialist purposes which would not lead us through the old hard agony of public ownership? There is no royal road.

Speech to Labour Party Conference, 1952

Damn it all, you can't have the crown of thorns *and* the thirty pieces of silver.

Cited in M. Foot, *Aneurin Bevan* (1962)

In modern complex society it is impossible to get rational order by leaving things to private economic adventure. Therefore, I am a Socialist. I believe in public ownership.

Speech to Labour Party Conference, 1959

I do not believe in a monolithic society. I do not believe that public ownership should reach down into every piece of economic activity, because that would be asking for a monolithic society.

Speech to Labour Party Conference, 1959

We are living in the presence of a conspiracy.

On Gaitskell's plan to change Clause IV, cited by M. Foot, *Aneurin Bevan* (1973)

The fact of the matter is: modern capitalism has not succeeded; it has failed. We are asked in 1959 to believe that if we are only patient, if we only work hard, we will double the standard of living in twenty-five years. That is the same rate of progress as before the war. With all the techniques of modern production ... the capitalists of Great Britain can promise us exactly the same rate of progress as before the war.

Speech to Labour Party Conference, 1959

He seems determined to make a trumpet sound like a tin whistle ... He brings to the fierce struggle of politics the tepid enthusiasm of a lazy summer afternoon at a cricket match.

On Clement Attlee, *Tribune*, 1945

He has the lucidity which is the by-product of a fundamentally sterile mind ... Listening to a speech by Chamberlain is like paying a visit to Woolworth's: everything in its place and nothing above sixpence.

On Neville Chamberlain

The Prime Minister has got very many virtues, and when the time comes I hope to pay my tribute to them, but I am bound to say that political honesty and sagacity have never been among them.

On Winston Churchill, speech, House of Commons, 3 August 1943

He is a man suffering from petrified adolescence.

On Winston Churchill, cited in V. Brome, *Aneurin Bevan* (1953)

His ear is so sensitively attuned to the bugle note of history that he is often deaf to the more raucous clamour of modern life.

On Winston Churchill, 1940

Beneath the sophistication of his appearance and manner, he has all the un-plumb-able stupidities and unawareness of his class and type.

On Anthony Eden, cited in M. Foot, *Aneurin Bevan* (1962)

The juvenile lead.

On Anthony Eden

Why should I question the monkey when I can question the organ-grinder?

Ending his attack on Foreign Secretary Selwyn Lloyd over the Suez Crisis when Anthony Eden entered the House of Commons, 1956

William Beveridge

1879–1963; Liberal theorist

The object of government in peace and war is not the glory of rulers or of races, but the happiness of the common man.

Social Insurance and Allied Services (1942)

The plan for social security is put forward as part of a general programme of social policy. It is part only of an attack upon five giant evils: upon the physical Want with which it is directly concerned, upon Disease which often causes Want and brings many other troubles in its train, upon Ignorance which no democracy can afford among its citizens, upon Squalor which arises mainly through the haphazard distribution of industry and population, and upon Idleness which destroys wealth and corrupts men.

Social Insurance and Allied Services (1942)

Ernest Bevin

1881–1951; Labour Party politician, Foreign Secretary 1945–51

You have built the Soviet Union and you have a right to defend it. I have built the Transport Union and if you seek to break it I will fight you.

Labour Party Annual Conference Report (1946)

The mere transfer from private ownership to public ownership is the beginning of the business, it is not the end. An enormous amount of work needs to be done in adapting, consolidating, and, if need be, reforming and changing the organisation of socialist industries ... you must expect the new programme to be of a somewhat different character and a somewhat different tempo from the last, for we have to embody in it proposals for the consolidation of exiting achievements, proposals for laying still more firmly the economic foundations of society.

Labour Party Annual Conference Report (1948)

If you open that Pandora's box, you never know what Trojan 'orses will jump out.

On the setting up of the Council of Europe, 1949

Do not worry about what it costs ... You can easily rebuild wealth, but you cannot create liberty when it has gone. Once a nation is put under another, it takes years and generations of struggle to get liberty back.

Speech, Cardiff, November 1940

Civilisation cannot survive if it rests upon a property-less proletariat.

Speech, 18 August 1941

We must socialise the Bank of England, as other countries have socialised their Central Banks, in order to be free to pursue an expansionist monetary policy on the basis of a managed currency.

The Crisis (1931)

(George) Lansbury has been going about dressed in saint's clothing for years waiting for martyrdom. I set fire to the faggots.

Cited in R. T. McKenzie, *British Political Parties* (1963)

Not while I'm alive, he ain't.

On being told that Aneurin Bevan was his own worst enemy, cited in A. Bullock, *Ernest Bevin: Foreign Secretary* (1983)

My [foreign] policy is to be able to take a ticket at Victoria Station and go anywhere I damn well please.

The Spectator, 20 April 1951

The young man today is compelled by circumstances beyond his control to become a robot in a fatalistic scheme of things which must cause him to believe that he counts for very little.

1934

Foreign policy is a thing you have got to bring down to its essence as it applies to an individual. It is something that is great and big: it is common sense and humanity as it applies to my affairs and to yours, because it is somebody and somebody's kindred that are begin persecuted and punished and tortured, and they are defenceless. That is a fact.

1950

We are being congratulated on a balanced budget and the possibility of a surplus, but if we approach the question of balance correctly we must not do so in terms of money only, but in terms of life, health and opportunity.

The Britain I Want to See (1934)

We regard ourselves as one of the powers most vital to the peace of the world and we still have our historic role to play.

Cited in A. Shlaim, *Britain and The Origins of European Unity* (1978)

The most conservative man in the world is the British Trade Unionist when you want to change him.

Speech, 8 September 1927

You are placing ... the movement in an absolutely wrong position by hawking your conscience round from body to body asking to be told what you ought to do with it.

On George Lansbury, 1935

We've got to have this thing over here, whatever it costs ... We've got to have a bloody Union Jack flying on top of it.

On the desirability of a nuclear shield, cited in P. Hennessy, *Never Again* (1993)

Rodney Bickerstaffe

b. 1945; General Secretary of Unison 1995–2001

The question is not should we break the law, but which law shall we obey?

Speech to Labour Party Conference, 1984

Georges Bidault

1899–1983; French politician

The weak have one weapon: the errors of those who think they are strong.

The Observer, 15 July 1962

Steve Biko

1946–77; South African black nationalist leader

The most potent weapon in the hands of the oppressor is the mind of the oppressed.

Speech, 1971

Both black and white walk into a hastily organised integrated circle carrying with them the seeds of destruction of that circle – their inferiority and superiority complexes. The myth of integration as propounded under the banner of the liberal ideology must be cracked because it makes people believe that something is being achieved when in reality the artificially integrated circles are a soporific to the blacks while saving the consciences of the few guilt-stricken whites.

Speech, 1971

We are aware that the white man is sitting at our table. We know he has no right to be there; we want to remove him from our table, strip the table of all the trappings put on it by him, decorate it in true African style, settle down and then ask him to join us on our terms if he wishes.

Speech, 1971

Tony Blair

b. 1953; Labour Party leader, Prime Minister 1997–2007

There will be few politicians standing for election next time on a platform advocating free markets.

October 1987

Britain needs successful people in business who can become rich by their success, through the money they earn.

Speech to the CBI, 1995

The spirit of the time is community.

Speech to Labour Party Conference, 1998

It is, if you will, social-ism. It contains an ethical and subjective judgement that individuals owe a duty to one another and to a broader society – the left view of citizenship.

Socialism (1994)

One reason I changed the Labour Party is so that we can remain true to our principles.

General election campaign, April 1997

The children would love it if I had the Spice Girls around in the evening rather than John Prescott or Gordon Brown.

April 1997

Powers that are constitutionally there can be used ... it's like any Parish council ... sovereignty will rest with me as an English MP.

On the Scottish Parliament, April 1997

When Britain's interests are at stake, I am perfectly prepared to be isolated in Europe.

15 April 1997

[There is a need to] integrate the notion of constitutional changes and a more democratic structure for our society into our politics so that our constitution is not actually a fringe issue any more but is central to the whole of political life.

Is There Democratic Life after Maastricht? (1992)

Would the Prime Minister be in favour of persuading the country that it was right to join a single currency? I say yes to that.

House of Commons, March 1995

This is not a landslide country.

30 April 1997

I am a socialist not through reading a textbook that has caught my intellectual fancy, nor through unthinking tradition, but because I believe that, at its best, socialism corresponds most closely to an existence that is both rational and moral. It stands for co-operation, not confrontation; for fellowship, not fear. It stands for equality, not because it wants people to be the same but because only through equality in our economic circumstances can our individuality develop properly.

Maiden speech in the House of Commons, 6 July 1983

I am not about to start spraying around commitments as to what we are going to do when the government carries through its proposals.

Daily Telegraph, January 1995

We'll negotiate a withdrawal from the EEC which has drained our natural resources and destroyed jobs.

Election address, 1983

I voted for Britain to remain in the EEC in 1975. I fought to persuade my party to become a party of Europe.

Speech, 30 May 1995

Obviously some people will interpret this in a way which is harsh and unpleasant but I think the basic principle here is to say: yes it is right to be intolerant of people homeless on the streets.

Interview, *Big Issue*, January 1997

The mild tinkering with the economy proposed by the Social Democrats nowhere near measures up to the problem. A massive reconstruction of industry is needed ... the resources required to reconstruct manufacturing industry call for enormous state guidance and intervention.

Lecture to the Murdoch University, Australia, cited in K. Jefferys, *Leading Labour* (1999)

Having fought long and hard for [their freedoms, unions] will not give them up lightly. We shall oppose the Bill which is a scandalous and undemocratic measure against the trade union movement.

On the Trade Union Bill, 1983

If you look at Labour's policies, no one can conceivably say that's a cautious programme. It's a very radical programme.

New Statesman, 5 July 1996

A Labour government will encourage people to become wealthy if they do so by hard work, taking risks and above all creating jobs. There are a number of steps we can take – business schools could run entrepreneur courses for mature students with experience in manufacturing as they do in the United States.

Speech at Cranfield, 11 June 1996

Interviewer: Do you give money to beggars?
Tony Blair: I don't, no.

Interview, *Big Issue*, January 1997

I don't think that anyone actually wants that to be a priority of the Labour Party at the moment ... I don't think anyone is saying now ... that this is the sort of thing we should focus on.

Stating his position on Clause IV, June 1994; he scrapped it a year later

The goal of economic policy must be to raise the standard of living and provide a decent quality of life for all. This requires active government, ready to intervene for the common interest and create a partnership for economic success.

Change and National Renewal (Blair leadership manifesto), 23 June 1994

A large social security budget is not a sign of Socialist success but a necessary consequence of economic failure.

Speech in Southampton, 13 July 1994

Winning the next election for Labour requires not a delicate shift in tactics or strategy, but a project. It should start with the Labour Party's historic principles, the values that define its identity. It should then apply them, for the modern world, to both its policies and its organisation.

The Guardian, 30 June 1992

The Labour Party got into problems [in the early 1980s] when, like many left-of-centre parties, it ... started to confuse ... principles and values with particular means of implementation, which might be relevant for a particular time but which then have to change from generation to generation.

Financial Times, 11 June 1994

To be able to reach out and build new support – that is the purpose of New Labour. Because if you don't do, what you become yourself, as a political party, is a glorified pressure group – which is what the Labour Party was for much of the eighties.

Interview, *Big Issue*, January 1997

I can't hope to replace the trust and affection in which the country held John [Smith]. I'm too young for that. I have to something different. I have to be bold and exciting.

July 1994

The only way to rebuild social order and stability is through strong values, socially shared, inculcated through individuals, family, government and the institutions of civil society.

Speech, *The Spectator* Lecture, 22 March 1995

There are many good schools in Britain, but not enough; many good teachers, but not enough; many well educated children, but not enough.

The Times, 7 July 1997

Contrary to the Tory canard, constitutional reform is not an issue for the 'chattering classes', irrelevant to most people. Properly done, it will go to the heart of public concerns. It is important not only for its own sake, but because it makes possible the attainment of other vital goals: a stronger economy, better transport, good schools and crime prevention.

The Economist, 14 September 1996

The risk of community becoming merely a synonym for government is met by reinventing government. Co-operation, to secure desirable social and economic objectives, need not happen through central government, operating in old ways. Indeed, often it is better if it doesn't.

Speech, *The Spectator* Lecture, 22 March 1995

It is not, as some claim, a simple question of moving from an 'unfair' to a 'fair' voting system. An electoral system must meet two democratic tests: it needs to reflect opinion, but it must also aggregate opinion without giving disproportionate influence to splinter groups. Aggregation is particularly important for a Parliament whose job is to create and sustain a single, mainstream government.

The Economist, 14 September 1996

Parties that do not change die, and this party is a living movement not an historical monument. If the world changes and we don't, then we become of no use to the world. Our principles cease being principles and ossify into dogma.

Speech to Labour Party Conference, 1994

A party of the centre as well as the centre-left.

> On the Labour Party, speech to the British American Chamber of
> Commerce, New York, 11 April 1996

The new right had struck a chord. There was a perception that there was too much collective power, too much bureaucracy, too much state intervention and too many vested interests around it.

> Cited in J. Sopel, *Tony Blair* (1995)

How do we give our own people security and opportunity in this new age? Our answer is not to turn the clock back ... But we do have to move on from the 1980s. There were good times as well as bad. We seek not to dismantle but to build.

> *Daily Telegraph*, 11 January 1996

Our task today is not to fight old battles but to show that there is a third way, a way of marrying together an open, competitive and successful economy with a just, decent and humane society.

> Speech to the Party of European Socialist Congress, Malmö, 6 June
> 1997

It is the confident who can change and the doubters who hesitate. A changed Labour Party, with the vision and confidence to lead Britain in a changing world – that is our pledge to the people of this country.

> Acceptance speech on becoming leader of the Labour Party, 21 July
> 1994

We should stop saying what we don't mean and start saying what we do mean, what we stand by, what we stand for. It is time we had a clear, up-to-date statement of the objects and objectives of our party ... This is a modern party living in an age of change. It requires a modern constitution that says what we are in terms the public cannot misunderstand and the Tories cannot misrepresent.

> On Clause IV, speech to Labour Party Conference, 4 October 1994

Our values do not change. Our commitment to a different vision of society stands intact. But the ways of achieving that vision must change.

Speech, Faith in the City, 29 January 1996

The real objection to equality is not reason but prejudice.

Hansard, 21 February 1994

The great thing is to stick by what we think and believe.

Interview, *The Times*, 6 July 1994

Responsibility is a value shared. If it doesn't apply to everyone it ends up applying to no one.

Speech to Labour Party Conference, 4 October 1994

A young country that wants to be a strong country cannot be morally neutral about the family.

Speech to Labour Party Conference, 3 October 1995

My view of Christian values led me to oppose what I perceived to be a narrow view of self-interest that Conservatism — particularly in its modern, more right wing form — represents. Every human being is self-interested. But Tories, I think, have too selfish a definition of that self-interest. They fail to look beyond to the community and the individual's relationship with the community.

Sunday Telegraph, 7 April 1996

One Britain. That is the patriotism for the future. Where your child is my child; your parent ill and in pain is my parent; your friend unemployed or helpless, my friend; your neighbour, my neighbour.

Speech to Labour Party Conference, 3 October 1996

It is no good waving the fabric of our flag when you have spent the last sixteen years tearing apart the fabric of our nation, tearing apart the bonds which tie communities together and make us a United Kingdom.

Speech to Labour Party Conference, 3 October 1996

We have reached the limit of the public's willingness simply to fund an unreformed welfare system through ever higher taxation and spending.

Hansard, 15 May 1997

The solutions of neither the old left nor the new right will do. We need a new radical centre in modern politics that can answer this competitive challenge whilst enhancing social stability and cohesion.

Speech in New York, 11 February 1996

Labour does need a bold and radical identity. It does need to be clear as to what it stands for, as well as what it is against. It does require vision. No left of centre party has ever won a clear majority to govern without it.

Fabian Review, September/October 1993

New Labour does not believe it is the job of government to interfere in the running of business.

Speech to Nottingham Chamber of Commerce, January 1996

There is no going back on the Thatcherite trade union reforms.

Daily Telegraph, January 1996

New Labour moves beyond the solutions of old left and new right. We are a radical party.

Renewal, October 1995

We understand both the need for a new moral purpose in politics and have the individual, family and social values capable of sustaining it.

Speech to Newscorp, 17 July 1995

People accuse me of distancing the Labour Party from the unions. It's not distance I want but clarity.

Speech to the TUC Conference, 12 September 1995

The unions will get fairness but no favours from us and anyone who thinks we have created today's Labour Party only to hand it over to the unions or anyone else does not know me and has not been listening to a word I have said these past three years. This is a party that will govern for all the people, the whole country – and no single interest group within it.

Labour Election Press Conference, 25 March 1997

In a Stakeholder Economy, there will be a proper relationship of trust between business and Government ... The same relationship of trust and partnership applies within a firm. The successful companies are the ones who invest, treat their employees fairly and value them as a resource not merely of production but of creative innovation ... A shared responsibility for success, a sense of mutual purpose ... Close and long-term relationships are established with key suppliers ... In decision-making, managers keep a firm eye on the future development of the business, as well as this week's or this year's bottom line.

Speech to British Retail Consortium, 14 February 1996

The economics of the centre and centre-left today should be geared to the creation of the Stakeholder Economy which involves all our people. Not a privileged few or even a better-off 30 per cent or 40 per cent or 50 per cent. It is surely time to shift the emphasis in corporate ethos towards a vision of a company as a community of partnership in which each employee has a stake and where a company's responsibilities are more clearly delineated.

Speech in Singapore, 8 January 1996

Business leaders recognise that what New Labour is saying fits exactly with current thinking in industry. Some of our great companies are stakeholder firms – John Lewis, Rover, M&S,

BP. Business advisers like John Kay and Charles Handy say that competitiveness and success come from a stakeholder approach.

Speech in Derby, 18 January 1996

Empowering the individual in a strong and cohesive society is what the Stakeholder Economy is about.

Speech to Nottingham Chamber of Commerce, 19 January 1996

We must always be willing to help the vulnerable and disadvantaged ... Christianity is full of mercy and compassion.

7 April 1996

New Labour is pro-business, pro-enterprise, and we believe there is nothing inconsistent between that and a decent and just society.

Financial Times, 16 January 1997

A high spend economy is not a high success economy.

Speech in Swansea, 10 May 1996

There are no hidden spending increases, there are no spending commitments that are not made absolutely clear here, and where they are made they are entirely properly costed and funded.

Leading Britain into the Future, Press Conference, 8 January 1997

Serious change was required to improve competitiveness at the end of the 1970s. The emphasis on enterprise, on initiative and incentive and on tackling lack of responsiveness of the public sector was necessary.

Speech in New York, 11 February 1996

Progressive parties today are parties of fiscal responsibility and prudence. You do not do anything by making a wreckage of the economy.

29 May 1997

Penal rates of taxation do not make economic or political sense. They are gone for good.

Speech to CBI Conference, 13 November 1995

New Labour is not an old-style tax-and-spend party but wants a tax system that is fair, that rewards enterprise, at the bottom as well as the top income levels.

Speech to *Time* magazine dinner, 30 November 1995

Labour is the party of law and order in Britain today. Tough on crime and tough on the causes of crime.

Speech to Labour Party Conference, 30 September 1993

No one but a fool would excuse crime on the basis of social conditions.

Speech to Labour Party Conference, 30 September 1993

Ask me my main three priorities for government and I will tell you: education, education and education.

Speech to Labour Party Conference, 3 October 1996

The local party grows out of – and is part of – local life. That is its strength. That is why my constituents are singularly unimpressed when told that the Labour Party is extreme. They see extremism more as an import from outside that is destroying their livelihoods.

Maiden speech in the House of Commons, 6 July 1983

Our Party. New Labour. Our mission. New Britain. New Labour. New Britain. New Britain!

Speech to Labour Party Conference, 4 October 1994

Those who seriously believe we cannot improve on words written for the world of 1918 when we are now in 1995 are not learning from our history but living it.

On Clause IV, 11 January 1995

What modernisation to me is about is not dumping principle. It's the opposite. It's retrieving what the Labour Party is really about.

19 April 1995

What you have to remember is that those who are running the save Clause Four campaign – the Campaign Group and the NUM – those are the people who were in charge of the Labour Party in the early 1980s, when it nearly went out of existence.

Interview in *The Observer*, 1995

The solutions of neither the old Left nor the new Right will do. We need a radical centre in modern politics and today's Labour Party – New Labour – is a party of the centre as well as the centre-left.

Speech to the British American Chamber of Commerce, 11 April 1996

The reason we have been out of power for fifteen years is simple – that society changed and we refused to change with it.

New Statesman, 15 July 1994

I think one of the tragedies of the Left was that it allowed the term 'equality' to really become a term of abuse about levelling down.

BBC Radio, 14 December 1995

There are three clear tasks in the creation of New Labour. One is the clear reconstruction of a modern ideology. The second is to produce an organisation that is fighting fit with a political culture that is open and welcoming ... The third is to take the new aims and values and describe them, in terms of the ideas underpinning them and in the development of policy.

The Spectator, 22 March 1995

By re-establishing its core identity, the Labour Party and the left can regain the intellectual self-confidence to take on and win the battle of ideas. For too long, the left has thought it has had a choice: to be radical but unacceptable; or to be cautious and electable.

18 June 1994

A new dawn has broken. Isn't it wonderful? We always said that if we had the courage to change we could do it and we did it. The British people have put their trust in us. It is a moving and humbling experience.

The size of our majority places a special responsibility on us. We have been elected as New Labour and we will govern as New Labour. We were elected because as a party today we represent the whole of this nation, every single day.

Speech to Labour supporters on election night at the Royal Festival Hall, 5.30am, 2 May 1997

Individuals prosper best within a strong and cohesive society.

Speech, *The Spectator* Lecture, 22 March 1995

[The] key to survival in the modern world is access to knowledge and information.

Education is the best economic policy there is.

Speech to Labour Party Conference, 1995

We need a new settlement on welfare for a new age, where opportunity and responsibility go together.

Let Us Face the Future (1995)

To strengthen the rights and obligations of citizens; to take decision-making closer to the people; and to improve the democratic credentials of Westminster.

On the Labour Party's constitutional programme, *The Economist*, 14 September 1996

Our ambition is to create a young Britain with a new politics which treats people as full citizens, gives them greater power over government.

Speech, The John Smith Memorial Lecture, 7 February 1996

I want to enable local communities to decide more things for themselves through local councils.

Speech, The John Smith Memorial Lecture, 7 February 1996

I want the twenty-first century to be the century of radicals.

Speech to Labour Party Conference, 1997

The socialism of Marx, of centralised state control of industry and production, is dead.

Socialism (1994)

The Thatcherite project of the 1980s is over.

Socialism (1994)

I didn't join a party of protest, I joined a party of government.

Daily Telegraph, 13 September 1995

There is still too great a fear of the unknown as far as the Labour Party is concerned.

In conversation with Peter Mandelson, cited in J. Sopel, *Tony Blair* (1995)

You can measure how well you're doing by the number of invitations you get to address businessmen.

The Guardian, 19 June 1991

Our project is to redefine radical left-of-centre politics for the new millennium.

Speech, Clause IV Conference, 29 April 1995

I don't like cliques. They are dangerous, insular, exclusive and politically unhelpful.

Interview, *Sunday Times*, 17 July 1994

Unreconstructed wankers.

On the Scottish media, 1996

There is never any point in willing the ends without a commitment to the means to achieve them.

Speech, 2 June 1999

Fairness and social justice. Liberty and equality of opportunity. Solidarity and responsibility to others. We will never sacrifice those principles.

Speech, 8 June 1999

People in the public sector are more rooted in the concept that 'if it's always been done this way, it must always be done this way' than any other group of people I've ever come across. You try getting change in the public sector and public services – I bear the scars on my back after two years in government.

The Guardian, 8 July 1999

While I am leader of my party and Prime Minister of this country, I will never again have Britain forced to choose between a Labour Party that ignored the importance of business and ambition and a right-wing Conservative Party that ignored the need for justice and compassion.

Daily Telegraph, 23 June 1999

Everything makes sense after 14 pints. John Redwood looks sane. Michael Portillo looks loyal … even William Hague looks like a Prime Minister.

Twisting William Hague's boast of being able to drink '14 pints a night', speech to Labour Party Conference, 26 September 2000

The art of leadership is saying no, not yes. It is very easy to say yes.

Mail on Sunday, 2 October 1994

Any parent wants the best for their children. I am not going to make a choice for my child on the basis of what is the politically correct thing to do.

On the decision to send his son to an 'opted-out' school, quoted in *The Guardian*, 2 December 1994 from an interview with ITV's *Good Morning* programme, 1 December 1994

I didn't come into politics to change the Labour Party. I came into politics to change the country.

Speech to Labour Party Conference, 3 October 1995

I can't stand politicians who wear God on their sleeves.

Sunday Telegraph, 7 April 1996

Isn't it extraordinary that the Prime Minister of our country can't even urge his Party to back his own position. Weak! Weak! Weak!

House of Commons, Prime Minister's Question Time questioning then Prime Minister John Major on Europe, 30 January 1997

My message to Sinn Fein is clear. The settlement train is leaving. I want you on that train. But it is leaving anyway and I will not allow it to wait for you.

Speech at the Royal Ulster Agricultural Show, 16 May 1997

I was born in 1953, a child of the Cold War era, raised amid the constant fear of a conflict with the potential to destroy humanity. Whatever other dangers may exist, no such fear exists today. Mine is the first generation able to contemplate the possibility that we may live our entire lives without going to war or sending our children to war. That is a prize beyond value.

Speech at a summit in Paris between NATO and Russia, 27 May 1997

She was the people's princess and that is how she will stay, how she will remain in our hearts and our memories for ever.

Statement on the death of Diana, Princess of Wales, 31 August 1997

I would never do anything to harm the country or anything improper. I think most people who have dealt with me think I'm a pretty straight sort of guy, and I am.

Interview, BBC TV's *On the Record*, commenting on the Bernie Ecclestone donation affair, 16 November 1997

A day like today is not a day for, sort of, sound bites, really – we can leave those at home – but I feel the hand of history upon our shoulders, I really do.

Statement on arriving at Hillsborough Castle for the Northern Ireland talks, 8 April 1998

A New Britain where the extraordinary talent of the British people is liberated from the forces of conservatism that so long have held them back, to create a model 21st-century nation, based not on privilege, class or background, but on the equal worth of all.

Speech to Labour Party Conference, 28 September 1999

There have been the most terrible, shocking events taking place in the United States of America within the last hour or so, including two hi-jacked planes being flown deliberately into the World Trade Center. I am afraid we can only imagine the terror and the carnage there and the many, many innocent people who will have lost their lives. I know that you would want to join with me in sending the deepest condolences to President Bush and to the American people on behalf of the British people at these terrible events. This mass terrorism is the new evil in our world today. It is perpetrated by fanatics who are utterly indifferent to the sanctity of human life and we, the democracies of this world, are going to have to come together to fight it together and eradicate this evil completely from our world.

Speech to the Trades Union Congress. 11 September 2001

For the moment, let me say this: Saddam Hussein's regime is despicable, he is developing weapons of mass destruction, and we cannot leave him doing so unchecked. He is a threat to his own people and to the region and, if allowed to develop these weapons, a threat to us also.

Statement, House of Commons, 10 April 2002

I don't like it, to be honest, when politicians make a big thing of their religious beliefs, so I don't make a big thing of it.

Interview, BBC TV, *Newsnight*, 16 May 2002

I make no apology for saying I'm a moderniser for the Labour Party.

Interview, BBC TV, *Newsnight*, 16 May 2002

[The Joint Intelligence Committee] concludes that Iraq has chemical and biological weapons, that Saddam has continued to produce them, that he has existing and active military plans for the use of chemical and biological weapons, which could be activated within 45 minutes, including against his own Shia population, and that he is actively trying to acquire nuclear weapons capability.

Statement, House of Commons, on publication of the dossier concerning Iraq and Weapons of Mass Destruction (sometimes referred to as the 'dodgy dossier'), 24 September 2002

Sometimes, and in particular dealing with a dictator, the only chance of peace is a readiness for war.

Speech to Labour Party Conference, 1 October 2002

We've been at our best when we've been at our boldest.

Speech to Labour Party Conference, 1 October 2002

We are asked now seriously to accept that in the last few years – contrary to all history, contrary to all intelligence – Saddam decided unilaterally to destroy those weapons. I say that such a claim is palpably absurd.

House of Commons debate on Iraq, 18 March 2003

I thought that it was the most predictable speech that we could have heard from the Rt Hon. and learned Gentleman. He may want to pose as the nice Dr Jekyll, but we know that, deep down, he is still the same old Mr Howard.

Speech, House of Commons, 26 November 2003

The prospect of Britain actually exiting the European Union … would be a disaster for the country.

Interview, BBC Radio, *The World At One*, 23 January 2013

I fear my own conscience on Africa. I fear the judgement of future generations, where history properly calculates the gravity of the suffering. I fear them asking: but how could wealthy people, so aware of such suffering, so capable of acting, simply turn away to busy themselves with other things? What greater call to action could there be? Did they really know and yet do nothing? I feel that judgement of the future alongside the now. It gives me urgency. It fills me with determination.

Speech on the launch of the Commission for Africa Report, 11 March 2005

It's important, however, that those engaged in terrorism realise that our determination to defend our values and our way of life is greater than their determination to cause death and destruction to innocent people in a desire to impose extremism on the world.
Whatever they do, it is our determination that they will never succeed in destroying what we hold dear in this country and in other civilised nations throughout the world.

Statement in response to the terrorist attack on the London Underground, 7 July 2005

Sometimes it is better to lose and do the right thing than to win and do the wrong thing.

Speech, House of Commons, 9 November 2005

He wants a Bill of Rights for Britain drafted by a committee of lawyers. Have you ever tried drafting anything with a committee of lawyers?

Attacking David Cameron's plans, speech to Labour Party Conference, 26 September 2006

I couldn't live with myself if I thought that these big strategic choices for my generation were there, and I wasn't even making them – or I was making them according to what was expedient rather than what I actually thought was right.

Interview, *Newsweek International*, 25 February 2007

So, of course, the visions are painted in the colours of the rainbow, and the reality is sketched in duller tones of black and white and grey. But I ask you to accept one thing. Hand on heart, I did what I thought was right. I may have been wrong. That is your call. But believe one thing, if nothing else. I did what I thought was right for our country.

Resignation speech, Trimdon Labour Club, 10 May 2007

The British are special. The world knows it. In our innermost thoughts we know it. This is the greatest nation on earth. So it has been an honour to serve it. I give my thanks to you, the British people, for the times that I have succeeded, and my apologies to you for the times I have fallen short. But good luck.

Resignation speech, Trimdon Labour Club, 10 May 2007

The fear of missing out means today's media, more than ever before, hunts in a pack. In these modes it is like a feral beast, just tearing people and reputations to bits. But no one dares miss out.

Speech, Reuters, 12 June 2007

Some may be little politics but we who are engaged in it know that it is where people stand tall. Although I know that it has many harsh contentions, it is still the arena that sets the heart beating a little faster. If it is, on occasions, the place of low

skulduggery, it is more often the place for the pursuit of noble causes. I wish everyone, friend or foe, well. That is that. The end.
Last Prime Minister's Question Time, 27 June 2007

Whatever the dangers of the action we take, the dangers of inaction are far, far greater.
Speech to Labour Party Conference, 2 October 2001

It's not an arrogant government that chooses priorities, it's an irresponsible government that fails to choose.
Speech to Labour Party Conference, 26 September 2000

We therefore here in Britain stand shoulder to shoulder with our American friends in this hour of tragedy and we, like them, will not rest until this evil is driven from our world.
Statement, Downing Street, 11 September 2001

I cannot think of a set of circumstances in which a government can go to war without the support of Parliament.
Evidence to the Liaison Select Committee, 21 January 2003

I think the journey for a politician goes from wanting to please all the people all the time, to a political leader that realises in the end his responsibility is to decide. And when he decides, he divides. I think what I'd say to Tony Blair in 1997 is: 'It's not possible for a political leader, especially in a world of such fundamentally difficult decisions, to keep all the people on-side all of the time.
Interview, 'Tony Blair Versus ShortList', *ShortList*, September 2010

In Downing Street they called me 'Boss'. Civil servants would always call me 'Prime Minister'.
Interview, 'Tony Blair Versus ShortList', *ShortList*, September 2010

Power without principle is barren, but principle without power is futile. This is a party of government, and I will lead it as a party of government.

Speech to Special Conference on Clause IV, 29 April 1995

What people should understand is that I adore the Labour party.

Interview, *The Guardian*, 1 September 2010

Whatever you do, I'm always with you. Head and heart. You've given me all I have ever achieved, and all that we've achieved, together, for the country. Next year I won't be making this speech. But, in the years to come, wherever I am, whatever I do. I'm with you. Wishing you well. Wanting you to win. You're the future now. Make the most of it.

Final speech to Labour Party Conference, 26 September 2006

I did not join the Labour Party to protest. I joined it as a party of government and I will make sure that it is a party of government.

Speech to TUC conference, 12 September 1995

My project will be complete when the Labour Party learns to love Peter Mandelson.

Daily Telegraph, 2 March 1996

At the time of the election, there will just be 1,000 days to the new millennium – 1,000 days to prepare for 1,000 years, a moment of destiny for us.

Speech to Labour Party Conference, 1 October 1996

Seventeen years of hurt. Never stopped us dreaming. Labour's coming home.

Speech to Labour Party Conference, 1 October 1996

I know exactly what the British people feel when they see the Queen's head on a £10 note. I feel it too.

The Sun, 17 April 1997

It will be a government that seeks to restore trust in politics in this country.

First speech in Downing Street, 2 May 1997

We are not the master now. The people are the masters. We are the servants of the people. We will never forget that.

Speech to Labour MPs at Church House, 7 May 1997

I don't ever stop being Prime Minister.

On his decision not to take paternity leave, 9 April 2000

John is John and I'm lucky to have him as my deputy.

On John Prescott following his altercation with a protestor, 16 May 2001

It's not a burning ambition for me to make sure that David Beckham earns less money.

Interview, BBC TV, *Newsnight*, 4 June 2001

It has been a remarkable and historic victory for my party but I am in no doubt at all as to what it means. It is a mandate for reform and for investment in the future and it is also very clearly an instruction to deliver.

Speech on election victory, 8 June 2001

I take full responsibility for decisions. I stand by them. I believe they were the right decisions.

Speaking at the Hutton inquiry, 28 August 2003

I can only go one way, I've not got a reverse gear.

Speech to Labour Party Conference, 30 September 2003

My health is absolutely fine – I'm feeling great.

After a heart scare, 2 December 2003

It does not mean forgetting the pain of the past but it does mean recognising it's time to move on.

After talks with Libya's Colonel Gaddafi, 25 March 2004

If I am elected, I would serve a full third term. I do not want to serve a fourth term – I don't think the British people would want a Prime Minister to go on that long. But I think it's sensible to make plain my intention now.

Interview with BBC's Andrew Marr, 1 October 2004

Every time I've ever introduced a reform in government, I wish in retrospect I had gone further.

Speech to Labour Party Conference, 27 September 2005

In no relationship at the top of any walk of life is it always easy, least of all in politics, which matters so much and which is conducted in such a piercing spotlight. But I know New Labour would never have happened, and three election victories would never have been secured, without Gordon Brown. He is a remarkable man. A remarkable servant to this country. And that is the truth.

Speech to Labour Party Conference, 26 September 2006

At least I don't have to worry about her running off with the bloke next door.

Speech to Labour Party Conference, on Cherie's alleged criticism of Gordon Brown, 26 September 2006

They say I hate the party, and its traditions. I don't. I love this party. There's only one tradition I hated: losing.

Speech to Labour Party Conference, 26 September 2006

This was not a win. It was a landslide. After about two hours for a time I actually became worried. The moving line at the bottom of the TV screen was showing over a hundred Labour seats.

The Tories had just six. I began to think I had done something unconstitutional.

On the 1997 election win, *Tony Blair: A Journey*, 2010

The curse of Gordon was to make these people co-conspirators, not free-range thinkers. He and Ed Balls and others were like I had been back in the 1980s, until slowly the scales fell from my eyes and I realised it was more like a cult than a kirk.

Tony Blair: A Journey, 2010

If I did seem to be enjoying it, then it was a supreme instance of acting. I hated it.

On Prime Minister's Question Time, *Tony Blair: A Journey*, 2010

Have you any conception of how despairing it is for me when the two people that have been closest to me for more than a decade, and who in their different ways are the most brilliant minds of their generation will not lay aside personal animosity and help me win?

In letter to Peter Mandelson after he had stormed out of a meeting with Gordon Brown, May 1996

Psychological flaws.

On Gordon Brown, a comment that first appeared in *The Observer*, 18 January 1998 but whose likely source was Alastair Campbell

The Alastair Campbell I know is an immensely able, fearless, loyal servant of the cause he believes in, who was dedicated not only to that cause but to his country. He is a strong character who can make enemies but those who know him best, like him best.

Quoted in *The Guardian*, 29 August 2003

Louis Blanc

1811–82; French socialist politician

From each according to his abilities, to each according to his needs.

The Organisation of Work (1840)

What the proletarian lacks is capital, and the duty of the state is to see that he gets it. Were I to define the state, I should prefer to think of it as the poor man's bank.

The Organisation of Work (1840)

Robert Blatchford

1851–1943; editor of *Clarion*

John Smith, do you know what Socialism is? You have heard it denounced many times, and it is said that you do not believe in it, but you know what it is? Good or bad, wise or foolish, it is all I have to offer as a remedy.

Merrie England (1894)

I never was a Collectivist myself; I was always a Communist of the Morris School.

The Clarion, February 1913

Socialism is only a method of extending State management.

Britain for the British (1906)

Léon Blum

1872–1950; French socialist politician, three times Prime Minister

A revolution is legality on holiday.

Attributed

No government can remain stable in an unstable world.
1945

Socialist assumptions and axioms have been taken over by
men and parties who have waged the most ferocious of wars
against socialist organisations. It is on the foundation of socialist
principles that societies, whether consciously or not, are
everywhere being reconstituted.

Speaking at the end of the Second World War on socialism reaching its
'triumphant period', cited in T. Wright, *Socialisms: Old and New* (1996)

David Blunkett

b. 1947; Labour Party politician, Home Secretary 2001–04

Democracy is best built up from local roots and activities.
With B. Crick, *The Labour Party's Aims and Values: An Unofficial Statement*
(1988)

I wouldn't be seen dead saying it [that the Conservatives would
win the next election].

Speaking to Sir Robin Day on *The World At One*, BBC Radio 4, 1987

Often traumatic … dramas … with Kinnock employing
persuasion, cajoling, bullying and arm-twisting to get his way.
On NEC meetings, interview, ITV, 26 July 1993

Labour must back those who show enterprise, and whose self-
reliance is not founded on indifference to the plight of others,
but on self-respect and a desire for something better. People
want quality public services and sensitivity to the needs of the
individual and family. They don't want bureaucratic indifference
or the mollycoddling of those who think the world owes them a
living.

New Statesman and Society, 26 June 1992

I want to see schools and education authorities taking responsibility for raising education standards and clearly demonstrating that everything that can be done is being done.

The Times, 21 May 1997

I was the first person from our family to go to university and almost certainly the first person within a two-mile radius of our home.

On A Clear Day (1995)

I am not prejudiced against gays and lesbians but there is no point trying to delude myself that I feel anything but revulsion at the idea of touching another male.

Tribune, 5 December 1986

We could live in a world which is airy fairy, libertarian, where everybody does precisely what they like and we believe the best of everybody and then they destroy us.

Speaking on LWT's *Dimbleby* programme, 11 November 2001

I have always been honest about my recollection of events.

On resigning as Home Secretary, quoted in BBC online, 15 December 2004

It would be dangerous territory if I wasn't practising what I preach which is to always accept responsibility, always accept the consequences of your actions.

On revelations about his private life, BBC interview, 6 December 2004

I don't think anyone can say I have said one thing in public and done another in private.

On revelations about his private life, BBC interview, 6 December 2004

I have built my reputation on honesty, I have sometimes been too honest.

On resigning as Home Secretary, quoted in BBC online, 15 December 2004

I have never tried to fiddle my role as leader of the city of Sheffield, as an MP or as a minister.

> On resigning as Home Secretary, quoted in BBC online, 15 December 2004

You wake up and you receive a phone call – Shipman's topped himself. You have just got to think for a minute: is it too early to open a bottle?

> Remark made at a press lunch about hearing of the death of serial killer, Dr Harold Shipman, 15 January 2004

Any deal with Labour would be 'a coalition of the defeated'.

> Comment made to the BBC on the possibility of a coalition, 11 May 2010

Norberto Bobbio

1909–2004; Italian political scientist

No left-winger can deny that the left today is not what it used to be.

> *Left and Right* (1996)

Lady Violet Bonham Carter

1887–1969; Liberal Party politician

Sir Stafford has a brilliant mind until it is made up.

> On Stafford Cripps, cited in M. Asquith, *Autobiography* (1936)

Tom Bottomore

1920–92; socialist

Socialism is only a possible future.

> *Sociology and Socialism* (1984)

Bessie Braddock

1889–1970; Labour Party politician

He is a man of many opinions, most of them of short duration.
> On Richard Crossman, *The Braddocks* (1963)

Ben Bradshaw

b. 1960; Labour Party politician, Secretary of State for Culture, Media and Sport 2009–10

Labour has been gifted something rare for an opposition – a position that is both in the national interest and the right politics.
> Following David Cameron's decision to promise a referendum on Europe, *Progress*, February 2013

H. N. Brailsford

1873–1958; ILP socialist

The fundamental fact is the rapid accumulation of surplus capital. It grows in the hands of trust magnates, bankers and ground landlords more rapidly than the demand for it at home.
> *The War of Steel and Gold* (1915)

Had a little more of the profits of a trade 'boom' gone to labour, and a little less to capital, it is manifest that labour would have had more money to spend, and the new surplus capital … might have been employed in meeting this new demand.
> *The War of Steel and Gold* (1915)

Willy Brandt

1913–92; Social Democratic Chancellor of Germany, 1969–74

Threat and extortion can make an impression for a limited period, but one cannot make friends that way.
  1973

[I came to] know and respect him as a man who not only acted on Bismarck's dictum that politics is the art of the possible, but did so with vigorous pragmatism and a well-developed feeling for the art of the opportune. This facility enabled him to represent the Labour Party to the British people as the 'natural' party of government – in itself no mean feat.
  On Harold Wilson, *People and Politics* (1978)

Leonid Brezhnev

1906–82; Soviet leader

When the internal and external forces that are hostile to Socialism try to turn the development of some Socialist country towards the restoration of a capitalist regime ... it becomes not only a problem of the people of the country concerned, but a common problem and concern of all socialist countries.
  Speech to the Congress of the Polish Communist Party, 12 November 1968

George Brown

1914–85; Labour Party politician, First Secretary of State 1964–66

The House of Commons ... is a Palace of Illogicalities.
  In My Way (1971)

I could never be shouted down in the other place and I'm not going to be shouted down here.
  After his entry into the House of Lords

He's just a little man who has been stupid.
  On Harold Wilson, 1976

Gordon Brown
b. 1951; Labour Party politician, Chancellor of the Exchequer 1997–
2007, Prime Minister 2007–10

[Old Labour] tried to counter the injustices and failing of free
market forces by substituting government for market.
  Speech, 24 September 1994

People do not live in isolation. People do not live in markets.
People live in communities. I think of Britain as a community
of citizens with common needs, mutual interests, shared
objectives, related goals and most of all linked destinies.
  Constitutional Change and the Future of Britain (1992)

We will ensure that the undeserving rich, the real beneficiaries
of the something-for-nothing society, put something back into
society.
  Labour Party press release, September 1994

A strong and flourishing economy demands a strong and socially
just society.
  Fair Is Efficient (1994)

At the heart of our analysis is the enduring socialist message
that it only by using the power of the community to spread
opportunities to all that can we ensure that all our citizens are
not only free from the threat of poverty, unemployment, disease
and discrimination, but have the education, the skills and the
opportunities to fulfil their potential to the full.
  Fair Is Efficient (1994)

We reject equality of outcome not because it is too radical but because it is neither desirable nor feasible.

Speech, The Anthony Crosland Memorial Lecture, 13 February 1997

Equality of opportunity should not be a one-off, pass-fail, life-defining event but a continuing opportunity for everyone to have the chance to realise their potential to the full.

Speech, Second John Smith Memorial Lecture, 1996

This is not workfare in the sense that it is understood – as the penalising of the unemployed for being unemployed, and asking people to work in return for their benefit.

The Guardian, 10 November 1995

With these new opportunities for young people come new responsibilities. There will be no fifth option – to stay at home on full benefit. So when they sign on for benefit they will be signing up for work.

Budget speech, as reprinted in *The Times*, 3 July 1997

I think people would now accept that the state has got to be both active and accountable in the way it ensures that individuals have access to health care, to education, to affordable housing, to childcare; particularly at points in the life-cycle where things are difficult for individuals and for families.

Marxism Today, January 1991

The next Labour government will not tax for its own sake. Labour is not against wealth, nor we will seek to penalise it … We only tax if it increases the opportunities for individuals or for the community as a whole. If we cut taxes – and I hope that we will be able to do this – we will ensure that everyone benefits and not just an elite few as has happened under the Tories.

Speech, Labour Finance and Industry Group, 17 August 1993

Labour will be committed to meeting the golden rule of borrowing – over the economic cycle, government will only borrow to finance public investment and not to fund public consumption.

Speech, Labour Finance and Industry Group, 17 August 1993

I believe in socialist values ... liberty, equality, democracy and internationalism.

Interview, *The Guardian*, 24 April 1999

The welfare state must be about supporting people as they respond to these challenges – extending their choices and opportunities; acting as a trampoline rather than as a safety net.

Fair Is Efficient (1994)

Socialists must neither place their faith in an Armageddon of capitalist collapse nor in nationalisation alone.

The Red Paper on Scotland (1975)

A Scottish Parliament and an Assembly for Wales go hand in hand with the offer of greater regional democracy throughout Britain.

Speech, Westminster, 12 January 1995

There is and always has been more to Scottish politics than identity politics. Solidarity – and working together – offers Scotland more than separation – and splitting ourselves apart. That is why a politics based on the expansive vision of social justice will defeat the narrow divisiveness of Nationalism.

With D. Alexander, *New Scotland, New Britain* (1999)

I'm a father; that's what matters most. Nothing matters more.

On the birth on his son, John, quoted in *The Observer*, 19 October 2003

Serious people for serious times.

> On his appointment of Peter Mandelson to the Cabinet, '"Proud" Mandelson Back In The Cabinet', *The Guardian*, 3 October 2008

I'm not perfect.

> Speech widely viewed as kickstarting the general election campaign, 20 February 2010

Peter asked me for 10p to phone a friend the other day. I said: 'Here, take 20p and ring them all.' When people ask me if I have a close relationship with Mandelson, I answer: 'How would I know? I haven't spoken to him for eighteen months.

> Speech to *Tribune* rally speaking about Peter Mandelson, Labour Party Conference, 1996

If I get angry, I get angry with myself.

> Interview, *Channel Four News*, 20 February 2010

I have been accused of being too serious, too focused on policy and sometimes too impatient.

> Speech to Labour Party activists, Adam Smith College, Kirkcaldy, 9 April 2010

There is one thing you can be sure of. I will fight and fight and fight. Fight on, for you and your family, and I will not let you down.

> Speech to Labour Party activists, Adam Smith College, Kirkcaldy, 9 April 2010

I realise I am not slick and the honest truth is I don't really want to be.

> Speech to Labour Party activists, Adam Smith College, Kirkcaldy, 9 April 2010

Those suffering from injustice or disadvantage have
lost a powerful voice. A strong European, a committed
internationalist, and a distinguished foreign secretary with
friends in every country, he will be mourned greatly not only
by his family, friends, colleagues and constituents, but in every
continent of the world.

> On the death of Robin Cook, quoted in *The Scotsman*, 7 August 2005

There is nothing that you could say to me now that I could ever
believe.

> To Tony Blair after he appeared to reverse a decision not to fight a
> third term in government, comments from Robert Peston's 'Brown's
> Britain' quoted in the *Daily Telegraph*, 10 January 2005

Our new economic approach is rooted in ideas which stress the
importance of macro-economics, post neo-classical endogenous
growth theory and the symbiotic relationships between growth
and investment, and people and infrastructure.

> Speech to the conference on 'New Policies for The Global Economy',
> 26 September 1994

My first rule – the golden rule – ensures that over the economic
cycle the Government will borrow only to invest, and that
current spending will be met from taxation.

> First Budget speech, 2 July 1997

Prudence for a purpose.

> Budget speech, 17 March 1998

Under this Government, Britain will not return to the boom
and bust of the past.

> Pre-Budget Report statement, 9 November 1999 and often repeated
> thereafter

It is an absolute scandal … I say it is time to end the old Britain where what mattered was the privilege you were born to not the potential you were born with. Remove the old barriers, open up our universities and let everyone move ahead.

Speech at a Trades Union Congress (TUC) reception on thirty years of equal legislation, on Oxford University's refusal to offer a place to high-flying state school pupil Laura Spence, 25 May 2000

I want to lead a government humble enough to know its place – where I will always strive to be – and that is on people's side.

Speech at the launch of his leadership campaign at the Imagination Gallery, London, 11 May 2007

In the weeks and months ahead, my task is to show I have the new ideas, the vision and the experience to earn the trust of the British people.

Speech at the launch of his leadership campaign at the Imagination Gallery, London, 11 May 2007

On this day I remember words that have stayed with me since my childhood and which matter a great deal to me today, my school motto: 'I will try my utmost'. This is my promise to all of the people of Britain and now let the work of change begin.

Statement at Downing Street on becoming Prime Minister, 27 June 2007

I am a conviction politician like her, and I think many people will see Mrs Thatcher as not only a person who saw the need for change in our country and took big decisions to achieve that, but also is, and remains, a conviction politician, true to the beliefs that she holds.

Monthly Downing Street press conference, 4 September 2007

Everyone knows that I'm all in favour of apprenticeships, but let me tell you this is no time for a novice.

Speech at Labour Party Conference, 23 September 2008

I agree with Nick.

> First leaders' television debate, on his consistency of approach with
> Liberal Democrat leader Nick Clegg, 15 April 2010

That was a disaster. Should never have put me with that woman.
Whose idea was that? It was Sue I think. Just ridiculous. [The
media] will use it. [She said] everything, she was just a sort of
bigoted woman who said she used to be Labour. I mean it's
ridiculous.

> Comments caught on microphone following a confrontation with
> Rochdale pensioner Gillian Duffy, who asked about Brown's stance on
> immigration, 28 April 2010

Above all, I want to thank Sarah for her unwavering support as
well as her love, and for her own service to our country. I thank
my sons John and Fraser for the love and joy they bring to our
lives. And as I leave the second most important job I could ever
hold, I cherish even more the first – as a husband and father.
Thank you and goodbye.

> Resignation speech, 11 May 2010

I did maths for a year at university. I don't think I was very good
at it. And some people would say it shows.

> April 2007

There is nothing worse than a precious baby taken from you.
You never come to terms with it. Two weeks ago she would have
been going to school for the first time.

> Interview with Kay Burley, Sky News, about the death of his daughter
> Jennifer Jane in 2002, 14 September 2006

The Arctic Monkeys really wake you up in the morning.

> Interview in *New Woman* magazine, May 2006

I don't see politics as one or two people just making or
delivering announcements – it's also about winning public

support and the public enthusiasm. You've got to win
public support.

Interview, *Time* magazine, 10 May 2007

So another challenge for our generation is to create global
institutions that reflect our ideas of fairness and responsibility,
not the ideas that were the basis of the last stage of financial
development over these recent years.

TED Talk, July 2009

I do not roll over.

Interview, BBC TV, *The Andrew Marr Show*, 27 September 2009

Tony Blair is the best friend I've had in politics.

Interview, *The Times*, 22 November 2001

We had lost the art of communication – but not, alas, the gift of
speech.

On Labour's 1983 election campaign, cited in *Total Politics*, 1997

I want us to do even more to encourage the risk takers.

Mansion House speech, 17 June 2004

No newspaper has done as much for me in the last two years.

First leaders' television debate, thanking David Cameron for a poster
campaign which showed him smiling, 15 April 2010

Step outside Posh Boy.

Labour poster campaign during the 2010 general election designed to
play on a 'hard man'/Dirty Harry image

When the record of my time as Prime Minister is looked at –
and all the papers will be there for people to see – they will
show that we stood up to News International, that we refused
to support their commercial ambitions when we thought they
were against the public interest.

Evidence to the Leveson inquiry into phone hacking, 12 July 2012

We need to fight; not bow out, not walk away, not give in, not give up, but fight. Fight to win for Britain

Speech to Labour Party Conference, 29 September 2009

We are the Labour Party and our abiding duty is to stand. And fight. And win. And serve.

Speech to Labour Party Conference, 29 September 2009

I'll not be calling an election. I have a vision for change in Britain and I want to show people how in government we're implementing it.

Interview with Andrew Marr, BBC, 6 October 2007

Andy Burnham
b. 1970; Labour Party politician, Secretary of State for Health 2009–10

Labour – the best hope of the NHS. Its only hope.

Speech to Labour Party Conference, 3 October 2012

It's brilliant to see the London media set coming here and having all their preconceptions about our city smashed to bits.

'Andy Burnham on the Hillsborough disaster, holding the Labour Party Conference in Liverpool – and his stag do', *Liverpool Echo*, 26 September 2011

We are here tonight because 139,815 people have asked this House to revisit events twenty-two years old. They are right, because those events concern one of the biggest injustices of the twentieth century. For twenty-two years, the Hillsborough families faced insults and had obstacles placed in their way at every step as they pursued their dignified campaign for truth and justice.

Speech, House of Commons, 17 October 2011

Cameron's Great NHS Carve-Up is coming to your community.

Speech to Labour Party Conference 3 October 2012

Sir Fred Burrows

1887–1973; President of the National Union of Railwaymen, 1942–44

Unlike my predecessors I have devoted more of my time to shunting and hoofing than to hunting and shooting.

Daily Telegraph, 24 April 1973

Stephen Byers

b. 1953; Labour Party politician, Secretary of State for Transport, Local Government and the Regions 2001–02

I know the political obituaries will be full of talk of spin doctors, emails and who said what to whom. In today's political world that is inevitable.

Resignation statement outside 10 Downing Street, 28 May 2002

Our action today will see the end of Railtrack. In my judgement, time had come to take back the track and put the interests of the travelling public first.

On the decision to put Railtrack into administration, 7 October 2001; comment carried on BBC online, 'Railtrack in administration', 8 October 2001

I'm a bit like a sort of cab for hire.

On offering his lobbying services to an undercover investigative reporter, Channel 4, *Dispatches*, 'Politicians For Hire' with the *Sunday Times*, first broadcast 22 March 2010

Liam Byrne

b. 1970; Labour Party politician, Chief Secretary to the Treasury 2009–10

Dear Chief Secretary, I'm afraid there is no money. Kind regards – and good luck! Liam.

Note left for incoming Chief Secretary, David Laws MP, after the 2010 general election but apparently written on 6 April 2012

C

James (Jim) Callaghan
1912–2005; Labour Party politician, Prime Minister 1976–79

You can never reach the promised land. You can march towards it.
  1978

I am not proposing to seek your votes because there is a blue sky ahead today.
  When announcing his intention not to hold a general election,
  September 1978

It demonstrated how much steady understanding and support existed for what we had been trying to do.
  Recalling the 1979 general election defeat

The rule of law should be upheld by all political parties. They should neither advise others to break the law, nor encourage others to do so even when they strongly disagree with the legislation put forward by the government of the day.
  1972

CRISIS? WHAT CRISIS?
  Headline in *The Sun*, summarising the remark of 10 January 1979
  on the winter of discontent: 'I don't think other people in the world
  would share the view [that] there is mounting chaos.'

If the law is a bad law, there is always the contingent right to take action that you would not otherwise take.
  On proposed action by the TUC, 1982

You know there are times, perhaps once every thirty years, when there is a sea change in politics. It then does not matter what you say or what you do. There is a shift in what the public wants and what it approves of. I suspect there is now such a sea change and it is for Mrs Thatcher.

Just prior to Mrs Thatcher's election victory, May 1979

There is not a single injustice in Northern Ireland that is worth the loss of a single British soldier or a single Irish citizen either.

1970

I've never been one to say that Britain was joining a happy band of brothers.

On entry to the EEC, 1976

This is like 1945 – but in space.

Describing the Labour Party's 1997 general election victory

There is an extraordinary difference between campaigns then and now. I was not conscious of any interference from Transport House. We fought our own election. We were isolated. There weren't all these quantities of leaflets or instructions or things you ought to concentrate on.

On the 1945 election, cited in A. Mitchell, *Election '45: Reflections on the Revolution in Britain* (1995)

I sum up the prospects for 1967 in three short sentences. We are back on course. The ship is picking up speed. The economy is moving. Every seaman knows the command at such a moment, 'Steady as she goes'.

Budget speech 1967, shortly before the devaluation of the pound

Society today is so organised that every individual group has the power to disrupt it. How is their power to be channelled into constructive channels?

1978

I do not think that this would be the right moment to cut people's standard of life in terms of private consumption any further.

House of Commons, July 1976

Your strike will not win. You cannot be allowed to succeed.

To the Fire Brigades Union at the beginning of the winter of discontent, cited in K. O. Morgan, *Callaghan: A Life* (1997)

I stand or fall that no one will beat the ten per cent this year.

On the government's incomes policy, cited in K. O. Morgan, *Callaghan: A Life* (1997)

Let me say that of course there has been a fall in people's standard of life. And it has fallen this year and will fall again next year.

BBC TV, October 1976

I have promised nobody that I shall be at the altar in October, nobody at all.

On the prospect of an election in 1978, speech, Brighton, 5 September 1978

On his way out, [Maudling] put his head round the door carrying a pile of suits over his arm. His comment was typical: 'Sorry, old cock, to leave it in this shape...' And with that he ambled off down the garden path...

The outgoing Chancellor to the new Chancellor in 1974, *Time and Chance* (1987)

In all the offices I have held I have never experienced anything more frustrating than sitting at the Chancellor's desk watching our currency reserves gurgling down the plughole day by day and knowing that the drain could not be stopped.

Time and Chance (1987)

The serious and widespread industrial dislocation caused by the strikes of January 1979, short-lived though they were, sent the Government's fortunes cascading downhill, our loss of authority in one field leading to misfortune in others just as an avalanche, gathering speed, sweeps all before it.

Time and Chance (1987)

During the 1960s the pound sterling sign had been turned into a symbol of national pride.

Time and Chance (1987)

The Government's moral authority was undermined.

On the TUC's rejection of government pay proposals, *Time and Chance* (1987)

I have [as] little authority in the PLP as I have in the NEC.

Cited in P. Jenkins, *Mrs Thatcher's Revolution* (1987)

We used to think that you could spend your way out of a recession and increase employment by cutting taxes and boosting government spending. I tell you in all candour that that option no longer exists, and in so far as it ever did exist, it only worked on each occasion since the war by injecting a bigger dose of inflation into the economy, followed by a higher level of unemployment as the next step.

Speech to Labour Party Conference, 1976

Dom Hélder Câmara

1909–99; Archbishop of Recife, Brazil

When I feed the poor, they call me a saint. When I ask why the poor have no food, they call me a Communist.

Attributed

Alastair Campbell

b. 1957; spin doctor, Director of Communications and Strategy for Prime Minister Tony Blair 2000–2003

We don't do God.

Interrupting an interview with Tony Blair by David Margolick, *Vanity Fair*, 2003

It is time to move on and do other things, and let others support the prime minister in the next phase of the government's programme of change.

On his resignation as Director of Communications and Strategy, quoted in *The Guardian*, 29 August 2003

People say, 'Well, it's a problem because you have become the story,' and they keep talking about you and writing about you and there's not much you can do about it.

Interview with then BBC Political Editor Andrew Marr on the reasons behind his resignation, 29 August 2003

Don't accept that you are in crisis just because everyone says you are.

From 2008, quoted in *The Observer*, 29 March 2009

I think I'm highly lovable.

BBC TV, *Cracking Up*, 12 October 2008

My public caricature – that of a self-confident alpha male – is only partly accurate.

Daily Telegraph, 27 July 2012

The media are obsessed with spin doctors and with portraying them as a bad thing, yet seem addicted to our medicine.

Quoted by BBC News online, 29 August 2003

What we don't do is sit around wallowing and navel-gazing.
What you do is come out fighting and make your case.

After Tony Blair was jeered and heckled at the Women's Institute
conference, 8 June 2000

Some twat with a Trot poster came up to me on the way in and
yelled 'Butcher!' 'Traitor!' at me. I stopped and mustered as
much visual contempt as I could, then assured him that if we
win the general election then don't worry, thanks to wankers
like him, there will always be another Tory government along
afterwards. These people make me vomit.

The Blair Years: The Alastair Campbell Diaries (2007)

For all its faults, our political process is a good one, and the
means by which much meaningful change is made. That is not a
very fashionable view to hold, but as someone who has operated
at senior levels in journalism and politics, around a decade in
each, it is my respect for the media that has shrunk, and my
respect for politics that has grown.

The Blair Years: The Alastair Campbell Diaries (2007)

When I finally cracked, Neil [Kinnock] was making a speech and
my head literally exploded.

On his breakdown in the 1980s, quoted in *The Observer*, 29 March 2009

The junk food of political journalism ... all reshuffle stories are
crap.

Quoted on TotalPolitics.com, 1998

New Labour, Old Bag.

On Barbara Castle after her protest over pensions, quoted on
TotalPolitics.com, October 1997

The day of the 'bog standard' comprehensive is over.

Signalling the start of the Labour government's efforts to improve
secondary schools, 12 February 2001

I think that there's not a leader in the world that can't learn from Lincoln.

On Abraham Lincoln, BBC TV, *Culture Show*, 12 February 2013

Albert Camus
1913–60; French novelist

As to the famous Marxist optimism, it just makes me laugh. Few men have mistrusted their fellows more completely. Marxists do not believe in persuasion or dialogue. A bourgeois cannot be made into a worker, and in their world economic conditions represent a more terrible form of fatality than the whims of God.

Notebooks (1937–51)

Communism is the logical consequence of Christianity. It is a Christian kind of business.

Notebooks (1937–51)

All modern revolutions have ended in a reinforcement of the State.

L'Homme révolté (1951)

Every revolutionary ends as an oppressor or a heretic.

L'Homme révolté (1951)

The smallest and most inoffensive State is still criminal in its dreams.

L'Homme révolté (1951)

Thomas Carlyle
1795–1881; Chartist

A man willing to work, and unable to find work is perhaps the saddest sight that fortune's inequality exhibits under this sun.

Chartism (1839)

Edward Carpenter

1844–1929; early British socialist

We should be able to say to private owners of industries that if
they managed their own concerns in the public interest, with
fair consideration for the health and welfare of their employees,
the day for taking over those structures might be indefinitely
postponed.

Cited in C. Tsuzuki, *Edward Carpenter 1844–1929* (1980)

Barbara Castle

1910–2002; Labour Party politician, Minister of Transport 1965–68,
Secretary of State for Employment 1968–70

She is so clearly the best man among them.

On Mrs Thatcher, *The Castle Diaries, 1964–1976* (1990)

The papers are full of Margaret Thatcher. She has lent herself
with grace and charm to every piece of photographer's
gimmickry, and don't we all when the prize is big enough? What
interests me now is how blooming she looks. She has never been
prettier. I am interested because I understand this phenomenon.
She may have been up late on the Finance Bill Committee, she's
beset by enemies but she sails through it looking her best. I
understand why – she's in love – in love with power, success and
herself.

The Castle Diaries, 1964–1976 (1990)

Economic might has become social right and the Devil has taken
the communal interest.

Labour Party Annual Conference Report (1959)

Men never feel at ease with a woman politician who looks as if
her hair has just been permed.

The Castle Diaries, 1964–1976 (1990)

In politics, guts is all.

> *The Castle Diaries, 1964–1976* (1990)

Curious movement with its curious contradictions.

> On the Labour Party, *The Castle Diaries, 1964–1976* (1990)

I'm taking a terrific gamble and there is absolutely no certainty that it will pay off. My only comfort is that I am proposing something I believe in. I see no objection in principle to asking the trade union movement to adapt itself to changing circumstances and my one aim is to strengthen it. One doesn't do that by clinging to things as they are.

> On her 'In Place of Strife' proposals, *The Castle Diaries, 1964–1976* (1990)

This treachery caused immense bitterness.

> On pro-European Labour MPs supporting the Heath government on EEC membership, *Fighting All The Way* (1993)

It is always dangerous for a political party to repudiate its past.

> *Tribune*, 28 April 1995

[I am] not interested in the state acquiring a few shares here and there in order to share the capitalist swag.

> *Tribune*, 13 September 1957

We have watched New Labour jettison the achievements of the past years as ideological baggage which must be dumped in the name of modernisation.

> *The Independent*, 23 June 1999

Let me make it clear, I was never Harold's mistress. These rumours prevent Harold getting the credit he deserves. Harold believed in women. He believed in their importance in society. He was always looking for ways of promoting women. In a way that still hasn't been properly recognised, Harold was a true progressive.

Interview, *New Statesman*, 28 February 2000

Let us just say that the jury's out.

On the Blair government, interview, *New Statesman*, 28 February 2000

Ted Castle

1907–79; British journalist

In place of strife.

Title of a Labour government White Paper, 17 January 1969, suggested to his wife Barbara Castle, then Secretary of State for Employment

Fidel Castro

b. 1926; Cuban revolutionary leader

So there exists an enemy who can be called universal, and if there ever was in the history of humanity an enemy who was truly universal, an enemy whose acts and moves trouble the entire world, threaten the entire world, attack the entire world in one way or another, that real and really universal enemy is precisely Yankee imperialism.

Speech, 12 January 1968

Look at how machismo works in Latin America. There are many countries where it is a good idea for the candidate in order to be elected to have a lot of girlfriends, where being a womaniser is a virtue.

Saying that inquiries into Bill Clinton's personal life were a violation of his human rights, 1994

You Americans keep saying that Cuba is ninety miles from the United States. I say that the United States is ninety miles from Cuba and for us, that is worse.

In conversation with Herbert Matthews

The duty of every revolutionary is to make a revolution.

In conversation with Herbert Matthews

Whoever hesitates while waiting for ideas to triumph among the masses before initiating revolutionary action will never be a revolutionary. Humanity will, of course, change. Human society will, of course, continue to develop – in spite of men and the errors of men. But that is not a revolutionary attitude.

1967

Power ... is the simple and indestructible will of the people.

Speech, 1970

History will absolve me.

Speech, 16 October 1953

There are times when political documents, called Marxist, give the impression that someone has gone to an archive and asked for a form: form 14, form 13, form 12; they are all alike, with the same empty words, in language incapable of expressing real situations. Very often, these documents are divorced from real life. And then many people are told that this is Marxism ... and in what way is this different from a catechism, and in what way is it different from a litany, from a rosary?

Speech to the OLAS conference, in Havana's Chaplin Theater, 10 August 1967

Warfare is a means and not an end. Warfare is the tool of revolutionaries. The important thing is the revolution, the revolutionary ideas, the revolutionary cause, revolutionary objectives, revolutionary sentiments and revolutionary virtues.

Eulogy to Che Guevara, 1967

Hugo Chávez

1954–2013; socialist President of Venezuela 1999–2013

Every day I become more convinced, there is no doubt in my mind, as many intellectuals have said, that it is necessary to transcend capitalism. But capitalism cannot be transcended through capitalism itself; it must be done through socialism, true socialism, with equality and justice. I'm also convinced that it is possible to do it under democracy, but not in the type of democracy being imposed by Washington.

> Closing speech at the World Social Forum in Porto Alegre, Brazil,
> 31 January 2005

We have to reinvent socialism. It can't be the kind of socialism that we saw in the Soviet Union, but it will emerge as we develop new systems that are built on co-operation, not competition.

> Closing speech at the World Social Forum in Porto Alegre, Brazil,
> 31 January 2005

I nationalise strategic companies and get criticised, but when Bush does it, it's OK … Bush is turning socialist. How are you, comrade Bush?

> Statement, 21 September 2008, quoted in 'Credit Crisis Fools Latin
> America's Leaders: Alexandre Marinis', Bloomberg.com, 21 October
> 2008

It seems we will have to become accustomed to live with these rumours, because it is part of the laboratories of psychological war, of dirty war.

> Dismissing rumours of his death, quoted by ITV News online, 23 April
> 2012

It's coming to the place it never should have left.

> On his decision to repatriate foreign bullion reserves from western
> bank vaults, quoted in *The Guardian*, 26 November 2011

Winston Churchill

1874–1965; British statesman, Prime Minister 1940–45, 1951–55

No socialist system can be established without a political police
... They would have to fall back on some form of Gestapo.
  On the outcome of a Labour government, election broadcast, BBC
  Radio, 4 June 1945

The inherent vice of capitalism is the unequal sharing of
blessings; the inherent virtue of socialism is the equal sharing of
miseries.
  Speech, House of Commons, 22 October 1945

Government of the duds, by the duds and for the duds.
  On socialist governments, following the 1927 Budget

Socialism is the philosophy of failure, the creed of ignorance and
the gospel of envy.
  Speech, Scottish Unionist Conference, 28 May 1948

Labour is not fit to govern.
  Election speech, 1920

He is a modest man who has a great deal to be modest about.
  On Clement Attlee, *Chicago Sunday Tribune Magazine of Books*, June 1954

They are not fit to manage a whelk stall.
  On the Labour Party

He will be as great a curse to this country in peace as he was a
squalid nuisance in time of war.
  On Aneurin Bevan

He is a sheep in sheep's clothing.
  On Clement Attlee, cited in M. Foot, *Aneurin Bevan* (1962)

An empty taxi arrived at 10 Downing Street, and when the door was opened Attlee got out.

On Clement Attlee, cited in K. Harris, *Attlee* (1982)

There but for the grace of God, goes God.

On Stafford Cripps

He has all of the virtues I dislike and none of the vices I admire.

On Stafford Cripps

Their worst misfortune was his birth, their next worst, his death.

On Lenin, *The World Crisis 1911–1918* (2007)

We know that he has, more than any man, the gift of compressing the largest amount of words into the smallest amount of thought.

On Ramsay MacDonald, speech, House of Commons, 1933

He is the greatest living master of falling without hurting himself.

On Ramsay MacDonald

I remember, when I was a child, being taken to the celebrated Barnum's Circus, which contained an exhibition of freaks and monstrosities. But the exhibit on the programme that I most desired to see was the one described as 'The Boneless Wonder'. My parents judged that the spectacle would be too revolting and too demoralising for my youthful eyes, and I waited fifty years to see the Boneless Wonder sitting on the Treasury Bench.

On Ramsay MacDonald, speech, House of Commons, 28 January 1931

Charles Clarke

b. 1950; Labour Party politician, Home Secretary 2004–06

I don't think Gordon (Brown) will lead Labour into the next election.

Interview, *Evening Standard*, 23 September 2009

Are we just going to stand by and watch the whole Labour ship crash on to the rocks of May 2010?

Interview, *Evening Standard*, 23 September 2009

Ivor Clemitson

1931–97; Labour Party politician

It was easier for a camel to go through the eye of a needle than for a rich man to get into the Kingdom of Heaven, so if the rich are taxed more heavily at least it would be partially for their own good.

1975

Bill Clinton

b. 1946; US President 1993–2001

I end tonight where it all began for me: I still believe in a place called Hope.

Speech to the Democratic National Convention, 16 July 1992

When I was in England I experimented with marijuana a time or two, and didn't like it, and didn't inhale and never tried inhaling again.

Interview, quoted in the *New York Times*, 31 March 1992

Our democracy must be not only the envy of the world but the engine of our own renewal. There is nothing wrong with America that cannot be cured by what is right with America.

Inaugural address, 20 January 1993

The road to tyranny, we must never forget, begins with the destruction of the truth.

Speech, Dedication of the Thomas J. Dodd Archives and Research Center in Storrs, Connecticut, 15 October 1995

Our rich texture of racial, religious and political diversity will be a Godsend in the twenty-first century. Great rewards will come to those who can live together, learn together, work together, forge new ties that bind together.

Inaugural address, 20 January 1997

I did not have sexual relations with that woman, Miss Lewinsky. I never told anybody to lie, not a single time, never. These allegations are false, and I need to go back to work for the American people.

National television address, 26 January 1998

Indeed, I did have a relationship with Miss Lewinsky that was not appropriate. In fact, it was wrong. It constituted a critical lapse in judgment and a personal failure on my part for which I am solely and completely responsible. But I told the grand jury today and I say to you now that at no time did I ask anyone to lie, to hide or destroy evidence or to take any other unlawful action.

Televised address to the nation, 17 August 1998

Whether our ancestors came here on the Mayflower, on slave ships, whether they came to Ellis Island or LAX in Los Angeles, whether they came yesterday or walked this land a thousand years ago our great challenge for the twenty-first century is to find a way to be One America. We can meet all the other challenges if we can go forward as One America.

State of the Union Address, 19 January 1999

Yesterday is yesterday. If we try to recapture it, we will only lose tomorrow.

Speech, University of North Carolina, 12 October 1993

Today's possibilities are not tomorrow's guarantees.

State of the Union Address, 27 January 1998

A lot of presidential memoirs, they say, are dull and self-serving. I hope mine is interesting and self-serving.

On the release of his autobiography, June 2004

Because primarily of the power of the Internet, people of modest means can band together and amass vast sums of money that can change the world for some public good if they all agree.

TED Talk, March 2007

History has shown us, that you can't allow the mass extermination of people, and just sit by and watch it happen.

On the war in Bosnia, rally held inside the East St. Louis High gymnasium, quoted in the *LA Times*, 6 August 1992

Strength and wisdom are not opposing values.

Supporting John Kerry, Democratic National Convention, 26 July 2004

The problem with ideology is, if you've got an ideology, you've already got your mind made up. You know all the answers and that makes evidence irrelevant and arguments a waste of time. You tend to govern by assertion and attacks.

Speech, Georgetown University with the Center for American Progress, 18 October 2006

If a politician doesn't wanna get beat up, he shouldn't run for office. If a football player doesn't want to get tackled or want the risk of an occasional clip he shouldn't put the pads on.

Quoted in the *New York Times*, 26 March 2008

The world has always been more impressed by the power of our [America's] example than by the example of our power.

Speech, Democratic National Convention, 27 August 2008

It's the economy, stupid.

Campaign message for party workers during the 1992 presidential campaign, coined by strategist James Carville as 'The economy, stupid'

Brian Clough

1935–2004; manager of Nottingham Forest Football Club 1975–93

For me, socialism comes from the heart. I've been lucky, I've made a few bob, got a nice car and house, but I think as many as possible should have the same. There are a few who've got on and made a few bob who don't think that way. Every bairn should have books, a nice classroom and the same opportunity to get on. I brought up my kids not to be greedy, to be generous with their time and their smiles. It's not all about money.

Cited in P. Murphy, *His Way: The Brian Clough Story* (2004)

I don't see why certain sections of the community should have the franchise on champagne and big houses.

Quoted in P. Rostron, *We Are The Damned United* (2004)

Of course I'm a Champagne Socialist. The difference between me and a good Tory is that he keeps his money while I share mine.

Cited in P. Murphy, *His Way: The Brian Clough Story* (2004)

John Clynes
1869–1949; Labour Party politician

A Communist is no more a left-wing member of the Labour Party than an atheist is a left-wing member of the Christian Church.

Cited in I. Gilmour, *Inside Right*

Ken Coates
1930–2010; former Labour Party Member of the European Parliament 1989–99

Whatever the British socialists may be doing, whatever experiments they feel meet to conduct, either in community or trade union agitation, the one thing they should *not* do is to turn their backs on the official Labour movement.

Socialist Register (1973)

Public relations is all today. Understanding the 'Blair revolution' demands recognition of the role of the public relations people not only in the presentation, but now in the development of politics.

With M. Barratt Brown, *The Blair Revolution* (1996)

He is, quite simply, a Liberal ... This young man has not the faintest idea of how socialists think and does not begin to understand the mentality of the party he has been elected to lead.

On Tony Blair, *Daily Telegraph*, 13 January 1995

G. D. H. Cole
1889–1959; economist and historian

Poverty is the symptom; slavery the disease.

Self-Government in Industry (1917)

The ideal society that matters is not the Utopia of our dreams, but the best sort of society we can hope to build out of the materials that lie ready to our hands.

The Next Ten Years (1929)

What, I want to ask, is the fundamental evil in our modern society which we should set out to abolish? There are two possible answers to that question, and I am sure that very many well-meaning people would make the wrong one. They would answer POVERTY, when they ought to answer SLAVERY.

Self-Government in Industry (1917)

The solution must surely lie in a rational division of functions, allowing both producer and consumer a say in the control of what is, after all, supremely important to both.

The World of Labour (1928)

That sad failure of Socialism, endeavouring, by a trick, to seem stronger than it really is.

The World of Labour (1928)

Fascism is *nonsense*; and that is perhaps the gravest indictment of all. It not merely is nonsense; it spews nonsense out of its mouth. It believes in nonsense, believes that the ordinary man is moved by nonsense, and *ought to be so moved*. It not merely deems men fools and irrational, but wants to keep them so.

The People's Front (1937)

In the State of today, in which democratic control through Parliament is little better than a farce, the Collectivist State would be the Earthly Paradise of bureaucracy.

Self-Government in Industry (1917)

Hitherto most socialists had contended that the disease of unemployment was incurable except by socialisation ... But now it appeared, if Keynes was right, that full employment could be maintained without socialisation, merely by manipulating the correct levers at the centre in the money and investment markets. There might be a case for socialising this or that industry on other grounds ... but not in order to cure unemployment.

Socialist Economics (1950)

The finest thing that can be accomplished by Labour Unrest is a heightening sense of being alive, an awakening that will lead men from mere discontent to the positive striving for a better life.

The World of Labour (1928)

The class structure is established in our social institutions, and it is only by means of the class struggle that we can escape from it.

The World of Labour (1928)

They believe that working class ideals begin and end with higher wages, with the securing of a slightly better standard of material comfort. They do not realise that the foundation of inefficiency in industry lies in the divorce of the mass of the workers from power and responsibility.

The World of Labour (1928)

Men will rightly work far better if their task is made as light as possible, and if they are clearly conscious that it is worth performing. This was the truth behind Guild Socialism, the valuable truth which has outlived its cant.

The Next Ten Years in British Social and Economic Policy (1930)

Regarded merely as the instruments of collective wage bargaining, the Unions are the most powerful weapons in the hands of labour; if they are in addition the germs of the future organisation of industry as a whole, their importance becomes at once immeasurable greater.

The World of Labour (1928)

The control of industry may be the future existing destiny of the trade unions; the direct control of the whole national life is most emphatically not for them.

The World of Labour (1928)

They cannot logically take advantage of the economic situation for an attack on capitalism, if in so doing they hamper the country in the conduct of the war.

Labour in Wartime (1915)

The class struggle is suspended, or largely suspended, in terms of external strife, not because the State is greater than the Trade Union, but because the individuals in such times transcend the groups through which they ordinarily act.

Labour in the Commonwealth (1919)

The State, as it exists today, is a mere parody of the true expression of the national unity; Labour, in giving it allegiance, is offering it service in virtue of what it might be.

Labour in Wartime (1915)

In politics democracy can nibble, but it may not bite; and it will not be able to bite until the balance of economic power has been so changed as to threaten the economic dominance of capital.

Self-Government in Industry (1917)

Even if strikes can succeed in raising real wages and in bettering conditions, it does not follow that they can ever by themselves bring about the expropriation of the capitalist.

The World of Labour (1928)

Under either system [State Capitalism or State Socialism], the power of the State is arrayed on side of the wage system; but the chance of developing the Guild idea and the Guild demand among the workers seems to me very much greater under national ownership than under State capitalism.

Self-Government in Industry (1917)

In politics we do not call democratic a system in which the proletariat has the right to organise and exercise what pressure it can on an irresponsible body of rulers; we call it modified aristocracy; and the same name adequately describes a similar industrial structure.

Guild Socialism Re-stated (1920)

In the Society of today, the State is a coercive power, existing for the protection of private property, and merely reflecting, in its subservience to Capitalism, the economic class structure of the modern world.

Self-Government in Industry (1917)

It is in warring Capitalism that they [the unions] will learn to do without Capitalism; but they must realise their freedom in partnership with, and not in opposition to, the State.

The World of Labour (1928)

The best way of effecting a peaceful change to Socialism by the organisation of the workers politically to capture the power of the State, and industrially to take over the control and management of the industrial machine.

ILP Conference Report (1921)

The workers must be prepared, if necessary to assume, through their trade unions, a half share in the ownership of capital, as a step in the direction of National Guilds. They must not, however, accept any joint responsibility with capitalism in return for less than a half-share in ownership.

Self-Government in Industry (1917)

Voting is merely a handy device; it is not to be identified with democracy, which is a mental and moral relation of man to man.

Essays In Social Theory (1950)

To my mind, there have always been two fundamental cleavages in socialist thought – the cleavage between revolutionaries and reformists, and the cleavage between centralisers and federalists.

Cited in T. Wright, *Socialisms: Old and New* (1996)

A quite unpractical Socialist who was so little in the swim he refused to join the Fabian Society.

On William Morris, *Self-Government in Industry* (1917)

Some sort of Socialist faith was the necessary basis for the consolidation of the Labour Party into an effective national force.

A History of the Labour Party from 1914 (1948)

The most important book on economics since Marx's *Das Kapital*.

On Keynes' *The General Theory of Employment, Interest and Money*, cited in the *New Statesman*

Maureen Colquhoun

b. 1928; Labour Party politician

Although we were not displeased in the Labour lady members' room when Margaret Thatcher got the Opposition leadership, we knew that she was what the American feminists irreverently call 'a man with tits' and would do little if nothing either for women in the House (of Commons) or women outside it.

Commission on Social Justice

The best indicator of the capacity of our economy tomorrow is the quality of our children today.

Report (1994)

Markets need to be shaped and regulated in the common interest, not abolished.

Report (1994)

Social cohesion has economic value, social division has economic cost.

Report (1994)

Companies and countries which lead the way in raising environmental standards, gain a competitive advantage in increasingly environmentally aware markets.

Report (1994)

The welfare state needs actively to facilitate change and reduce rigidity by promoting opportunities and life chances across the life-cycle for all citizens.

Report (1994)

James M. Connell
1852–1929; Irish socialist songwriter

The people's flag is deepest red;
It shrouded oft by martyred dead,
And ere their limbs grew stiff and cold,
Their heart's blood dyed its every fold.
Then raise the scarlet standard high,
Within its shade we'll live or die.
Tho' cowards flinch and traitors sneer,
We'll keep the red flag flying here.

'The Red Flag' (1899)

James Connolly
1870–1916; Irish Labour leader

Social democracy must proceed from the bottom upward, whereas capitalist political society is organised from above downward.

Cited in Owen Dudley Edwards and Bernard Ransom (eds.), *James Connolly, Selected Political Writings* (1973)

The workers will be industrially organised on the economic field and, until that organisation is perfected ... the Socialist Party will carry on an independent campaign of education and attack upon the political field.

Cited in Owen Dudley Edwards and Bernard Ransom (eds.), *James Connolly, Selected Political Writings* (1973)

The worker is the slave of capitalist society, the female is the slave of that slave.

The Re-conquest of Ireland (1915)

It is not Socialism but capitalism that is opposed to religion ... Religion, I hope, is not bound up with a system founded on buying human labour in the cheapest market, and selling its product in the dearest; when the organised Socialist working class tramples upon the capitalist class it will not be trampling upon a pillar of God's Church but upon a blasphemous defiler of the Sanctuary, it will be rescuing the Faith from the impious vermin who made it noisome to the really religious men and women.

The Harp, January 1909

Arthur Cook

1883–1931; British trade unionist

Not a penny off the pay, not a second on the day.

Slogan of the 1926 miners' strike

Robin Cook

1946–2005; Labour Party politician, Foreign Secretary 1997–2001

It is our commitment that we will draw a line under the sterile, negative and fruitless confrontation which was the policy of the previous British government.

On the Labour government's relations with Europe, speech, Paris, May 1997

The Tories are now conscious that they have lost the fight for
public support.

Labour Herald, October 1981

The commitment of this movement to nuclear disarmament is
clearly established and it is not up for change.

Speech to Labour Party Conference, 1983

Papua New Guinea is the only other country with a poll tax. The
time has come for the Tory Party to conclude that Mrs Thatcher
could serve Great Britain best as our ambassador there.

March 1990

I come to this rostrum to beg conference, to ask conference,
to plead with conference to vote for unilateral nuclear
disarmament.

Speech to Labour Party Conference, 29 September 1982

Nonsense on stilts.

On Britain pretending to be a nuclear power, cited in A. Roth,
Parliamentary Profiles

Europe has to be competitive. It's got to focus on the basic
issues of job creation and employability. The way to do that is
not by letting in more and more and more regulations. The way
to do that is to make sure people in the labour market have got
the skills they require.

The Scotsman, 24 May 1997

This is not just a government which does not know how to
accept blame; it is a Government which knows no shame.

The arms to Iraq debate, House of Commons, 26 February 1996

Bin Laden was, though, a product of a monumental
miscalculation by Western security agencies. Throughout the 80s
he was armed by the CIA and funded by the Saudis to wage jihad
against the Russian occupation of Afghanistan. Al-Qaida, literally

'the database', was originally the computer file of the thousands of Mujahideen who were recruited and trained with help from the CIA to defeat the Russians.

'The struggle against terrorism cannot be won by military means', *The Guardian*, 8 July 2005

I can't accept collective responsibility for the decision to commit Britain now to military action in Iraq without international agreement or domestic support.

Statement on resigning from the Cabinet, 'Cook quits over Iraq crisis', BBC online, 17 March 2003

What is happening in the killing fields of Kosovo is unforgivable.

CNN, 20 April 1999

The intelligence was wildly wrong.

CNN, 30 January 2004

This is a government more united on points of policy than any previous government that I can actually recall and we're going to keep it that way.

Interview, BBC TV, *Frost on Sunday*, 26 November 2000

As a contribution to George Bush's war on terrorism, Iraq has been a spectacular own goal.

Quoted by BBC online, 'In Quotes: Robin Cook', 7 August 2005

We should not accept the implicit assumption of Bush's muscular foreign policy that freedom can be delivered from 38,000ft through the bomb doors.

Independent on Sunday, 23 January 2005

I find it difficult to reconcile what I knew, and what I am sure the PM knew, with what he said.

On Iraq's alleged weapons of mass destruction. Quoted by BBC online, 'In Quotes: Robin Cook', 7 August 2005

I've never met one that wants to talk politics.

> On his love of racehorses, *The Times*, Quotes of the Day, 30 September 2004

It is revealing that Britain now has a prime minister who uses 'liberal' as a term of abuse, in the way that a North American politician would.

> *The Independent*, 23 July 2004

The tricky thing about a quagmire is you never know you have walked into one until it is too late.

> *The Independent*, 14 May 2004

Tony Blair is a man of immense, attractive charm, which he maintains by shrinking from disagreeable exchanges.

> *The Independent*, 16 April 2004

I can just about forgive him Iraq. But dropping a Scottie on his head, that's really stupid.

> Complaining about George Bush dropping his dog, *Daily Record*, 6 February 2000

I'm a Commons man.

> Appearing to make himself available to leading rebels, speaking on BBC TV, *Breakfast with Frost*, 23 March 2003

Chicken tikka masala is now Britain's true national dish, not only because it is the most popular, but because it is a perfect illustration of the way Britain absorbs and adapts external influences.

> Speech on British identity, 19 April 2001

The tragic paradox of the last century was that those who murdered one person were more likely to be brought to justice than those who plotted the genocide of millions.

> 'Tyrants Beware', *The Guardian*, 3 April 2001

Our foreign policy must have an ethical dimension and must support the demands of other peoples for the democratic rights on which we insist for ourselves. The Labour Government will put human rights at the heart of our foreign policy.

Speech launching New Labour's ethical foreign policy, 12 May 1997

Calvin Coolidge

1872–1933; US President 1923–29

The government of the past could be fairly characterised as devices for maintaining in perpetuity the place and position of certain privileged classes ... The Government of the United States is a device for maintaining in perpetuity the rights of the people, with the ultimate extinction of all privileged classes.

Speech, 1924

Yvette Cooper

b. 1969; Labour Party politician, Secretary of State for Work and Pensions 2009–2010

Weak on crime, weak on the causes of crime – that is David Cameron's Conservative Party.

Speech to Labour Party Conference, 3 October 2012

Sexism in politics is nothing new when you're standing for election. But don't stand for election and it's almost as bad. Shockingly, David Cameron thought it acceptable to claim this week that my decision not to run for the Labour leadership was because my husband, Ed Balls, 'stopped [me] from standing'.

'Why I'm not standing for Labour leader – this time', *The Guardian*, 28 May 2010

Jeremy Corbyn
b. 1949; Labour Party politician

There must be a total defence of ANY socialist threatened with expulsion from the [Labour] Party.

Cited in A. Roth, *Parliamentary Profiles*

To hold nuclear weapons is immoral.

Hansard, 19 November 1991

The [CND] campaign is here to stay.

Hansard, 22 November 1991

Nuclear weapons are not a deterrent.

Hansard, 14 January 1992

In one hilarious meeting, the Greenham [Common] Women addressed us, They were trying to buy bolt-cutters to cut the fences at Greenham Common, but anytime they turned up at a shop anywhere near, they were denied the right to buy them. So, each Campaign Group member agreed to buy one set of bolt-cutters and donate to the Greenham Women. Which we duly did!

Interview, *Total Politics*, 28 June 2011

Frank Cousins
1904–86; Trade Union leader, Labour Party politician, Minister of Technology 1964–66

We cannot have socialism without nationalisation.

Labour Party Annual Conference Report (1959)

Bernard Crick

1929–2008; political scientist

The short-term is relatively easy: for all leaders and activists to live by egalitarian values and talk them up. The middle term is to persuade the electorate that good public services and support for all our people have to be paid for. In the long run there is no democratic socialism (or say a socially just society) on the cheap. But if we only achieve our aims gradually, we can live by our values now and every day.

In G. Marsden (ed.), *Low Cost Socialism* (1997)

Put in the simplest and most basic terms, socialism has both an empirical theory and a moral doctrine.

In Defence of Politics (1962)

Stafford Cripps

1889–1952; Labour Party politician, Chancellor of the Exchequer 1947–50

From my experience there is not yet a very large body of workers in Britain capable of taking over large enterprise … until there has been more experience of the managerial side of industry, I think it would be almost impossible to have worker-controlled industry, even if it were on the whole desirable.

Cited in K. Coates and A. Topham, *Industrial Democracy in Great Britain* (1968)

The ruling classes will go to almost any length to defeat parliamentary action.

On the 1931 crisis, cited in D. Marquand, *The Progressive Dilemma* (1991)

It seems absolutely necessary to throw off once and for all the attitude of compromise which was impressed upon us by reason of the minority position in which the Labour Government found itself ... We must, I feel, completely divorce ourselves from the past.

The Life of Richard Stafford Cripps (1957)

The clearest demonstration of the power of capitalism to overthrow a popularly elected government by extra-parliamentary means.

On the 1931 crisis, *Can Socialism Come by Constitutional Methods?* (1933)

To me, the central factor in our decision must turn not so much upon what we as a country should or should not do, but upon who is in control of our actions.

Labour Party Annual Conference Report (1935)

It is impossible for us to serve two masters – our own selfish interests as British imperialists and our desire for peace as world citizens. The interests of the British Empire and the world are not identical.

The Struggle for Peace (1936)

Stella Creasy

b. 1977; Labour Party politician, shadow Minister for Crime Prevention 2011–

One of the challenges for politics in future is that it's not about 650 people (in Parliament) all acting individually. It's about trying to do things together.

The Observer, 25 November 2012

There is no more central rite of passage than learning to live with the disappointment of love unrequited.

Sleeve notes to reissue of the Wedding Present album *Seamonsters*, 2012

Credit should not be lent in a way that is detrimental to consumers without those that profit from exploiting them being made liable for the consequences.

On her campaign against 'legal loan sharks', 'Private debt is this government's public injustice', Labour Uncut, 15 April 2011

Anthony (Tony) Crosland

1918–77; Labour Party politician, Secretary of State for Education and Science 1965–67, Foreign Secretary 1976–77

It is now clear that capitalism is undergoing a metamorphosis into a quite different system, and that this is rendering academic most of the traditional socialist analysis.

New Fabian Essays (1952)

The new managers (like the capitalists before them) pursue the goals of growth, profits and personal wealth. But such broad statements are true of any industrial system; as true, for example, of managers in Kharkov as of managers in Birmingham or Detroit.

The Conservative Enemy (1962)

[The] more serious question of socially imposed restrictions on the individual's private life and liberty. They come to mind at once the divorce laws, licensing laws, prehistoric (and fragrantly unfair) abortion laws, obsolete penalties for sexual abnormality, the illiterate censorship of books and plays and the remaining restrictions on the equal rights of women. Most of these are intolerable and should be highly offensive to socialists, in whose blood there should always run a trace of the anarchist and the libertarian, and not too much of the prig and the prude.

The Future of Socialism (1956)

[There are] clear political implications here for the Labour Party, which would be ill-advised to continue making a largely proletarian class appeal when a majority of the population is gradually attaining a middle-class standard of life, and distinct symptoms even of a middle-class psychology.

The Future of Socialism (1956)

Keir Hardie cannot provide, any more than can Gracchi, the right focus with which to capture the reality of the mid-twentieth century world.

The Future of Socialism (1956)

State ownership of all industrial capital is not now a condition of creating a socialist society ... What is unjust in our present arrangements is the distribution of private wealth; and that can as well be cured in a pluralist as in a wholly state-owned economy, with much better results for social contentment and the fragmentation of power.

The Future of Socialism (1956)

The relief of this distress and the elimination of this squalor is the main object of social expenditure, and a socialist is identified as one who wishes to give this an exceptional priority over other claims on resources.

The Future of Socialism (1956)

If the inequality of rewards is excessively great, the creation of equality of opportunities may give rise to too intense a competition, with a real danger of increased frustration and discontent.

The Future of Socialism (1956)

Much could be done to make Britain a more colourful and civilised country to live in. We need not only higher exports and old-age pensions, but more open-air cafés, brighter and gayer streets at night, later closing hours for public houses, more local repertory theatres, better and more hospitable hoteliers and restaurants, brighter and cleaner eating-houses, more riverside cafés ... better design for furniture and pottery and women's clothes, statues in the centre of new housing estates,

better-designed street-lamps and telephone kiosks, and so on ad
infinitum.

The Future of Socialism (1956)

Class, in the sense of class consciousness and the existence
of clearly identified classes, is an exceptionally marker
phenomenon in British life. The hierarchies of education,
occupational prestige, and style of life all show pronounced
breaks; and these breaks broadly coincide.

The Future of Socialism (1956)

No one supposes that the Conservatives will now suddenly
dismantle the welfare state or utterly neglect the claims of the
socially underprivileged.

The Conservative Enemy (1962)

I feel clear that we need large egalitarian changes in our
education system, the distribution of poverty, the distribution
of resources in periods of need, social manners and style of life,
and the location of power within industry; and perhaps some,
but certainly a smaller, change in respect of incomes from work.
I think that these changes, taken together, will amount to a
considerable social revolution.

The Future of Socialism (1956)

[It simply means that] the ownership of the means of production
... is no longer the essential determinant of the distribution of
incomes; private ownership is compatible with a high degree
of equality, while state ownership, as the Russian experience
has demonstrated, may be used to support a high degree of
inequality.

The Future of Socialism (1956)

Whatever the modes of economic production, economic power
will, in fact, belong to the owners of political power.

The Future of Socialism (1956)

[Socialism] ... came to be applied to policies for the economic and institutional transformation of society, instead of the ultimate social purposes which that transformation was intended to achieve.

The Future of Socialism (1956)

The Labour Party owes its whole existence and historic growth to the working class; one cannot think of one without the other. Yet, today, ironically, this unique identification is a clear political liability, for the simple reason that the working class is shrinking in size.

The Conservative Enemy (1962)

A move to the left is needed, not in the traditional sense of a move towards old-fashioned Clause IV Marxism but in the sense of a sharper delineation of fundamental objectives, a greater clarity about egalitarian priorities, and a stronger determination to achieve them.

Socialism Now, and Other Essays (1974)

[The Labour Party was] not founded on any body of doctrine at all, and has always preserved a marked anti-doctrinal and anti-theoretical bias.

The Future of Socialism (1956)

Traditional socialism was largely concerned with the evils of traditional capitalism, and with the need for its overthrow. But today traditional capitalism has been reformed and modified almost out of existence, and it is with a quite different form of society that socialists must now concern themselves.

The Future of Socialism (1956)

If socialists want bolder planning they must choose bolder Ministers.

The Future of Socialism (1956)

For many years past the Labour Party has not fought elections primarily on the issue of nationalisation. It has fought them rather on housing, education, social services, planning, the distribution of income and foreign and colonial policy and it has found no difficulty whatsoever in differentiating itself from the Conservatives.

The Conservative Enemy (1962)

The higher the average level of real income, whatever the distribution, the greater the subjective sense of social equality.

The Future of Socialism (1956)

We want a more equal distribution of wealth, not because redistribution today will make all the workers rich, but to help create a more just, united and humane community.

The Conservative Enemy (1962)

Economic issues are the main determinants of political attitudes.

The Future of Socialism (1956)

Extreme class inequalities remain, poverty is far from eliminated, the economy is in a state of semi-permanent crisis and inflation is rampant. All this undoubtedly belies the relative optimism of *The future of socialism*.

Socialism Now (1974)

[Equality of opportunity should] be combined with measures, above all in the educational field, to equalise the distribution of rewards and privileges so as to diminish the degree of class stratification, the injustice of large inequalities, and the collective discontents which come from too great a dispersion of rewards.

The Future of Socialism (1956)

The present of distribution of wealth in Britain is flagrantly unjust.

The Future of Socialism (1956)

The pre-war reasons for a largely economic orientation [for 'socialism'] are therefore steadily losing their relevance; and we can increasingly divert our energies into more fruitful and idealistic channels, and to fulfilling earlier and more fundamental socialist aspirations.

The Future of Socialism (1956)

We interpret socialism not as an arid economic dogma, but in terms of freedom, equality, social justice and world co-operation. We believe that the British people, who rightly mistrust doctrinaire utopianism, will always respond to an idealistic appeal to remedy real evils by practical and radical reform.

Manifesto of the Campaign for Democratic Socialism (1960)

The price mechanism is now a reasonably satisfactory method of distributing the great bulk of consumer goods and industrial capital goods.

The Future of Socialism (1956)

So long as we maintain a substantial private sector ... socialists must logically applaud the accumulation of private profit.

The Future of Socialism (1956)

A socialist is identified as one who wishes to give this [social welfare] an exceptional priority over other claims on resources.

The Future of Socialism (1956)

Unemployment, even if politically more wearable equals grave loss of welfare, security, choice.

Cited in D. Marquand, *The Progressive Dilemma* (1991)

The older party stalwart, brought up in the inter-war years to equate Socialism with the nationalisation of the means of production, feels lost and bewildered if deprived of this familiar mental sheet anchor. The dogma of nationalisation informed and symbolised his early years of struggle; if he is asked to give it up, he feels that he is being asked to say that his whole political life, to which he sacrificed so much, was pointless and wasted.

'The Future of the Left', *Encounter*, March 1960

Nothing the matter with him except he's a bit cracked.

On Tony Benn

Our policy now must be under no circumstances to re-open Clause IV but to be completely silent on nationalisation and let it gradually become a forgotten issue, like the Swedish Socialists' commitment to republicanism. Then we must see what we can get away with when we come to the final Election Manifesto.

Cited in T. Jones, *Remaking the Labour Party* (1996)

Governments do not always see the public interest so much more clearly than private firms.

Socialism Now (1974)

I'm going to destroy every fucking grammar school in England. And Wales. And Northern Ireland.

Cited in S. Crosland, *Tony Crosland* (1982)

The school system in Britain remains the most divisive, unjust and wasteful of all aspects of social inequality.

The Future of Socialism (1956)

Richard Crossman

1907–74; Labour Party politician, Secretary of State for Housing and Local Government 1964–66, Secretary of State for Health and Social Services 1968–70

The planned economy and the centralisation of power are no longer socialist objectives ... The main task of socialism today is to prevent the concentration of power in the hands of *either* industrial management *or* the state bureaucracy – in brief to dismantle responsibility and so to enlarge freedom of choice.

Towards a Philosophy of Socialism

Labour's real dynamic has always been a moral protest against social injustice, not an intellectual demonstration that capitalism is bound to collapse; a challenge to capitalist privilege, not a proof that these privileges must inevitably be replaced by a classless society.

Planning for Freedom (1965)

Plans for Nationalisation which do not satisfy the aspirations towards workers' control are the technocrats' perversion of our socialist ideal.

Planning for Freedom (1965)

The Civil Service is profoundly deferential – 'Yes, Minister! No, Minister! If you wish it, Minister!'

The Diaries of a Cabinet Minister, Volume I (1975)

When the Tories are in trouble, they bunch together and cogger up. When we [the Labour Party] get into trouble, we start blaming each other and rushing to the press to tell them all the terrible things that somebody else has done.

The Diaries of a Cabinet Minister, Volume I (1975)

The two most important emotions of the Labour Party are a doctrinaire faith in nationalisation, without knowing what it means, and a doctrinaire faith in pacifism, without facing the consequences.

The Diaries of a Cabinet Minister, Volume I (1975)

I have led an interesting and varied life.

Cited in A. Howard, *Crossman: The Pursuit of Power* (1990)

The definition of the Left is a group of people who will never be happy unless they can convince themselves that they are about to be betrayed by their leaders.

The Diaries of a Cabinet Minister, Volume I (1975)

Whenever I am lectured on the virtues of moderation in Labour politics I feel as Hermann Goering did about culture and reach for my revolver. Westminster is a place where moderation thrives and vigour is readily sapped.

The Times, 15 November 1972

A revolutionary party is a contradiction in terms.

The Charm of Politics (1958)

Politicians are ambitious not to *make* important decisions but to *say* important things.

The Charm of Politics (1958)

The distinction between a statesman and a politician is that the former imposes his will and his ideas on his environment while the latter adapts himself to it.

The Charm of Politics (1958)

In a secret department the greatest temptation in the world is to use secrecy not in the national interest, but in the departmental interest – to cover up.

Speech, House of Commons, 7 November 1955

Philosophically he is not second-rate but non-existent. An intellectually negligible whizz-kid.

On Tony Benn

Building up his position as a plain-style man of the people who will have no nonsense … easily the most accomplished politician in the Labour Party.

On Jim Callaghan, cited in A. Howard (ed.), *The Crossman Diaries* (1991)

Social morality, freedom and equality do not grow by any law of economics.

Socialist Values in a Changing Civilisation (1950)

A tough politician who jumps from position to position, always brilliantly energetic and opportunist, always moving in zigzags, darting with no sense of direction but making the best of each position he adopts.

On Harold Wilson, *The Diaries of a Cabinet Minister*, Volume III (1977)

I don't feel part of a Government pledged to fundamental change, with any idea of where it is going.

The Diaries of a Cabinet Minister, Volume III (1977)

One of the difficulties of politics is that politicians are shocked by those who are really prepared to let their thinking reach any conclusion. Political thinking consists in deciding on the conclusion first and then finding good arguments for it. An open mind is considered irresponsible – and perhaps it really is.

The Diaries of a Cabinet Minister, Volume I (1975)

In our traditional cricket match the parties are strong and the best team wins; in the strip poker of American politics, the parties are weak and the best man wins.

The Charm of Politics (1958)

In terms of military power, of industrial development, of technological advance, of mass literacy and eventually, of mass consumption too, the planned socialist economy as exemplified in the Communist states, is proving its capacity to outpace and overtake the wealthy and comfortable western economies.

Labour in the Affluent Society (1960)

A socialist programme ... will involve transferring gigantic powers, which are now dispersed amongst the oligopolists, to the central Government and the planning authorities which it would have to establish.

Labour in the Affluent Society (1960)

Since 1964 nothing has really changed. We're still working from hand to mouth trying to overcome the immediate short-term problems.

The Diaries of a Cabinet Minister, Volume III (1977)

Dr Jack Cunningham

b. 1939; Labour Party politician, minister for the Cabinet Office 1998–99

Our agenda is in line with what the people of Britain want. They are looking for change, and for improvement. They do want to see a better Britain – for themselves, for their families and for their communities.

Fabian Review, Autumn 1998

The damage that Labour did to its reputation and its credibility way back in the early 1980s; surprisingly perhaps, it is still a major problem for us.

Interview, ITV, 31 May 1992, cited in A. McSmith, *John Smith: A Life* (1994)

D

Lord Ralf Dahrendorf

1929–2009; political theorist, Liberal Democrat peer

The point has to be made unequivocally that socialism is dead, and that none of its variants can be revived for a world awakening from the double nightmare of Stalinism and Brezhnevism.

Reflections on the Revolution in Europe (1990)

He is a dangerous fellow with every intention of tearing down the pillars of society if he can. He can hardly enter a railway train because there is no Fourth Class.

On Aneurin Bevan, *Sunday Express*, 1932

Hugh Dalton

1887–1962; Labour Party politician, Chancellor of the Exchequer 1945–47

Though politics is, of necessity, a highly competitive profession, not least in the Labour Party, we have a strong sense of social security near the top. To do a man out of his job, at that eminence, is against good fellowship.

Call Back Yesterday (1953)

The first sensation, tingling and triumphant, was of a new society to be built, and we had the power to build it. We felt exalted, dedicated, walking on air, walking with destiny …

High Tide and After (1962)

We had no attractive programme. People were content with the Tories. They had stolen the Socialists' clothes (full employment; welfare state, etc.).

Cited in B. Pimlott (ed.), *The Political Diary of Hugh Dalton* (1986)

A looming shadow of catastrophe.

On sterling prospects in 1947, cited in A. Cairncross, *Years of Recovery* (1985)

One of the most effective instruments of Socialist planning and national development.

On the National Investment Board, *Practical Socialism for Britain* (1935)

In a period when productive power is increasing you must be increasing purchasing power equally with productive capacity, and therefore ... more purchasing power is distributed to our people.

Labour Party Annual Conference Report (1932)

Their policy [the Keynesians], in order to be effective, needs to be pushed a good deal further than most of them seem willing to push it. I believe that freedom from the plague of recurrent booms and slumps can only be found in a planned economy.

Unbalanced Budgets (1934)

Tam Dalyell

b. 1932; Labour Party politician, Father of the House 2001–05

To be a good campaigner you have to be prepared to be a bore and to be labelled a bore. I have never flinched at boring people.

Interview, *The House*, November 2000

She is a bounder, a liar, a deceiver, a cheat, a crook and a disgrace to the House of Commons.

On Margaret Thatcher, 22 February 1987

The truth of the matter is that we Scots have always been more divided amongst ourselves than pitted against the English. Scottish history before the Union of the Parliaments is a gloomy, violent tale of murders, feuds and tribal revenge. Only after the Act of Union did Highlanders and Lowlanders, Picts and Celts, begin to recognise one another as fellow citizens.

Quoted in *The Scotsman* online, 30 August 2012

He should be branded as a war criminal and sent to The Hague.

On Tony Blair, *The Guardian*, 'Blair, the war criminal', 27 March 2003

This is garbage from right-wing think-tanks stuffed with chicken-hawks – men who have never seen the horror of war but are in love with the idea of war. Men like Cheney, who were draft-dodgers in the Vietnam war. This is a blueprint for US world domination – a New World Order of their making. These are the thought processes of fantasist Americans who want to control the world. I am appalled that a British Labour Prime Minister should have got into bed with a crew which has this moral standing.

Sunday Herald, 15 September 2002

The Importance of Being Awkward.

Title of autobiography, 2001

Alistair Darling
b. 1953; Labour Party politician, Chancellor of the Exchequer 2007–10

We should be concerned first and foremost about the consumers.

Cited in S. Driver and L. Martell, *New Labour* (1998)

We look back to the courage of the pioneers of the 1945 Labour Government.

Speech to Labour Party Conference, 1998

Support local authorities that declare nuclear-free zones.
  Speech to Labour Party Conference, 30 September 1981

[The Labour leadership has lost] the will to live.
  Interview, *The Observer*, 27 September 2009

Our goal is to make finance the servant, not the master, of the real economy.
  The Observer, 'After Lehman Brothers' fall, we must look beyond the banks', 13 September 2009

We were at the stage where in a very short period of time, one of the world's biggest banks would have to shut the door and switch off the electricity.
  On the Royal Bank of Scotland, interview, *The Independent*, 18 March 2011

Most Chancellors and Prime Ministers fall out from time to time.
  Interview, *The Independent*, 18 March 2011

Better Together is not just a slogan to me. It is something I passionately believe in. We are better and stronger together.
  John P. Mackintoch lecture, 10 November 2012

He will move Heaven and Earth not to have to confront the fact that a majority of people in Scotland don't want independence. He will muddy the waters, he will play fast and loose.
  On Alex Salmond and the vote for Scottish independence, cited in *New Statesman*, 31 July 2012

At the end of the day the biggest issue is the safeguarding of taxpayers' money. If nationalisation saves that money, that has to be the correct step in the long term.
  On the decision to nationalise the Northern Rock bank, quoted in *The Guardian*, 18 February 2008

Today's Budget will take Britain through the most serious global economic turmoil for over sixty years. The impact is being felt in every continent, country and community. When the world economy was plunged into deep crisis in the 1930s, the response, both nationally and internationally, was too little and too late. This failure to act turned a serious downturn into a prolonged depression. We will not repeat those mistakes again.

Budget speech, 22 April 2009

Denzil Davies

b. 1938; Labour Party politician, Minister of State at the Treasury 1975–79

We [the Labour Party] will send cruise missiles back to whence they came. They provide no additional security for Britain, and they make it more likely that the superpowers will fight a nuclear war over the soil of our country.

Speech to Labour Party Conference, 3 October 1984

Ernest Davies

1902–91; Labour Party politician, Parliamentary Private Secretary to Ernest Bevin

Maintenance of the welfare state and a planned economy to ensure maximum production, full employment and a fairer distribution of the national income are among the chief aims of Labour economic policy. There must therefore be complete freedom to plan, and power to control production, investment, prices and distribution of goods in short supply, all of which means that the preservation of Socialist democracy necessitates a closed economy.

Cited in M. Newman, *Socialism and European Unity* (1983)

Arthur Deakin

1890–1955; General Secretary of the Transport and General Workers'
Union 1945–55

Get rid of their whips, dismiss their business managers and
conform to the party Constitution.

On the Bevanites, speech to Labour Party Conference, 1952

Simone De Beauvoir

1908–86; French novelist and feminist

It is not in giving life but in risking life that man is raised
above the animal; that is why superiority has been accorded in
humanity not to the sex that brings forth but to that which kills.

Le deuxième sexe (1949)

Society cares for the individual only so far as he is profitable.

The Coming of Age (1970)

All oppression creates a state of war.

Le deuxième sexe (1949)

One is not born a woman: one becomes one.

Le deuxième sexe (1949)

Miguel De Cervantes Saavedra

1547–1616; novelist

There are only two families in the world; the Haves and the
Have-Nots.

Don Quixote (1605–15)

Marquis De Condorcet

1743–94; French President of the Legislative Assembly 1792

Either none of mankind possesses genuine rights, or everyone shares them equally; whoever votes against other's rights, whatever his religion, colour or sex, forswears his own.

Cited in P. Vansittart (ed.), *Voices of the Revolution* (1989)

Charles De Gaulle

1890–1970; French General, President of France 1959–69

Politics are too serious a matter to be left to politicians.

Replying to Clement Attlee's remark that 'De Gaulle is a very good soldier and a very bad politician' in C. Attlee, *A Prime Minister Remembers* (1961)

Eugene Debs

1855–1926; founder of the Socialist Party of the United States

While there is a lower class, I am in it; while there is a criminal element, I am of it; and while there is a soul in prison, I am not free.

Speech from the dock, 16 June 1913

The working class alone – and by the working class I mean all useful workers, all who by the labour of their hands or the effort of their brains, or both in alliance, as they ought universally to be, increase the knowledge and add to the wealth of society – the working class alone is the essential to society and therefore the only class that can survive in the worldwide struggle for freedom.

Unionism and Socialism (1907)

I would rather a thousand times be a free soul in jail than to be a sycophant and coward in the streets... If it had not been for the men and women who, in the past, have had the moral courage to go to jail, we would still be in the jungles.

Speech, Cleveland, Ohio, 16 June 1918

I'd rather vote for something I want and not get it than vote for something I don't want, and get it.

Comment made during 1912 presidential election campaign in which Debs secured nearly one million votes

The rights of one are as sacred as the rights of a million.

Speech, Girard, Kansas, 23 May 1908

When the great changes occur in history, when great principles are involved, as a rule the majority are wrong.

Speech from the dock, 12 September 1918

It is the government that should ask me for a pardon.

After being pardoned by President Harding

When I rise it will be with the ranks and not from the ranks. Full opportunity for full development is the unalienable right of all. He who denies it is a tyrant; he who does not demand it is a coward; he who is indifferent to it is a slave; he who does not desire it is dead. The earth for all the people! That is the demand.

Speech, 1904, 'American Appeal', 15 October 1927, the Debs Memorial Edition

Shaw Desmond

1877–1960; Independent Labour Party orator

We had but to blow our trumpets seven times outside the walls of the capitalist Jericho, and lo! The walls would fall and it would be transformed into the New Jerusalem with streets of shining gold.

Labour: The Giant with Feet of Clay (1921)

Donald Dewar
1937–2000; Labour Party politician, First Minister of Scotland 1999–2000

Feudalism has existed in Scotland since medieval times. In the new Parliament Scottish Labour will abolish it.
>   Speech, 12 April 1999, in Aberdeen, launching the Labour Party's Holyrood manifesto

He could start a party in an empty room and he often did.
>   On the late Labour leader, John Smith, quoted in *The Guardian*, 11 October 2000

I would never knowingly flaunt my legs in public.
>   On a claim that he was on his last legs politically, quoted in *The Guardian*, 11 October 2000

Cynicism, together with unrealistic expectation, are the two great bugbears of politics
>   To critics of the Scottish Parliament, quoted in *The Guardian*, 11 October 2000

Being on the catwalk at Butlin's.
>   On personality politics, quoted in *The Guardian*, 11 October 2000

I prefer to stay home with fish fingers and a book.
>   Elspeth Campbell, the wife of Menzies Campbell, recalling his response to being invited for Christmas dinner, quoted in *The Guardian*, 11 October 2000

Sloth is a great companion; lying on the floor with a novel.
>   On coping with a bachelor lifestyle

Events, dear boy, events pose the biggest headaches for politicians.
>   Reflecting on the first year of the Scottish government, *Daily Mirror*, 5 May 2000

There shall be a Scottish Parliament. I like that.

Speech, 18 December 1997, in Glasgow launching the Scotland Bill

There Shall Be A Scottish Parliament.

Inscription of the opening words of the Scotland Act on the base of a statue of Dewar in Glasgow

There has been much doubt, doom and gloom. Indeed, many Hon. Members present are privately fearful; others are openly dismissive. I would contend that the sceptics have been confounded.

House of Commons, Second Reading, Scotland Bill, 12 January 1998

This is a symbol of the great democratic tradition from which we draw our inspiration and our strength. At its head are inscribed the opening words of our founding statute: 'There shall be a Scottish Parliament'.

Speech made on the opening of the new Scottish Parliament, 1 July 1999

In well under 300 days we have set in train the biggest change in 300 years of Scottish history.

Speech, 18 December 1997 in Glasgow, launching the Scotland Bill

E. J. Dionne

b. 1952; American journalist, columnist for the *Washington Post*

Pressed by economic change and worries that the country is experiencing a moral and social breakdown. Angry at government, uneasy over the workings of the economic system. They [the Anxious Middle] crave self-reliance – and honor this virtue in others – but fear that both the government and the economy are blocking their own paths to sufficiency.

On the changing nature of the class structure in America, *They Only Look Dead: Why Progressives Will Dominate the Next Political Era* (1996)

Frank Dobson

b. 1940; Labour Party politician, Secretary of State for Health 1997–99

Some say Mrs Thatcher has a soft spot for the Nottinghamshire miners. But she is like one of those insects that consumes its mate after it has done the business.

Cited in I. Dale (ed.), *As I Said To Denis* (1998)

Yes, it's the politics of envy. We're envious of their wealth. These people are stinking lousy thieving incompetent scum.

On company directors, September 1992

Derek Draper

b. 1967; former lobbyist and Labour political adviser

I regret ever receiving the infamous email and I regret my stupid, hasty reply. I should have said straight away that the idea was wrong.

On having to resign as editor of LabourList after planning an 'attack blog', Red Rag, with No. 10 adviser Damian McBride, where rumours about leading Conservative politicians would be aired. *Daily Mail*, 'Derek Draper quits LabourList website in wake of Tory smear email scandal', 7 May 2009

Absolutely totally brilliant.

Discussion about launching an 'attack blog', Red Rag, with No. 10 adviser Damian McBride, where rumours about leading Conservative politicians would be aired. *Daily Mail*, 'Derek Draper quits LabourList website in wake of Tory smear email scandal', 7 May 2009

There are seventeen people that count (in the new Labour Government). To say that I am intimate with every one of them is the understatement of the century.

For the full story of LobbyGate see GregPalast.com, 5 July 1998

Tom Driberg
1905–1976; Labour Party politician, chairman of the Labour Party
1957–1958

Some of us do not accept the Establishment myth that bad laws
must be obeyed.

Speech, House of Commons, 24 July 1972

Alexander Dubček
1921–92; Czechoslovak politician; first secretary of the Czechoslovak
Communist Party, 1968–69

Give socialism back its human face.

Slogan used in 1968

We wish to meet people's longing for a society in which they
can feel human among human beings. This active, humane,
integrating quality of socialism, a society without antagonism, is
what we want to realise systematically and gradually.

Speech, 1 April 1968

Terence Duffy
President of the Amalgamated Engineering and Electrical Union 1978

I am no intellectual but just an ordinary, simple, working-class
lad from the shop floor with simple tastes. I am president today
because I can feel the pulse of the shop floor.

Attributed

John Dunn
b. 1940; political theorist

The best of socialist governments is, in the end, only a government.

The Politics of Socialism (1984)

The most serious political doubt about socialist policies in the advanced capitalist societies, a doubt now massively grounded in the experience of the populations of those societies wherever socialist policies have had any real success, is whether socialist governments do or can know what they are doing.

The Listener, Volume 114, 1985

Evan Durbin
1906–48; Labour Party politician, Parliamentary Private Secretary to Hugh Dalton

[Labour's economic policy] must be based upon the necessity of making a large quantity of *private* industry expand its demand for labour, at the existing level of wages, and upon the demand of the Trade Unions for the maintenance of money wage rates.

Socialist Credit Policy (1934)

Men will die like flies for theories and exterminate each other with every instrument of destruction for abstractions.

The Politics of Democratic Socialism (1940)

In so far as we are democratic we are already, in some degree, socialist, and to betray democracy is to betray socialism.

The Politics of Democratic Socialism (1940)

We are living in a society whose class composition is shifting steadily against Marx's proletariat.

The Politics of Democratic Socialism (1940)

Socialist thinkers and economists have been too ready to ignore
the overriding necessity of maintaining production and life
in the transition period – a period likely to be long – during
which the transfer of economic power to the state is being
effected.

The Politics of Democratic Socialism (1940)

[A socialist society is] fundamentally a demand for social justice
... for economic freedom and social equality.

Socialist Credit Policy (1934)

It would almost be true to say that we are all planners now.

Cited in R. Samuel, *The Cult of Planning* (1986)

E

John Edmonds

b. 1944; General Secretary of the GMB trade union 1986–2003

Life will not always be as good as these first triumphant weeks
… Our first instinct will always be to support the Labour
government. We did not vote Labour to see Labour fail. But our
loyalty cannot be unthinking. We will be a friend, but from time
to time we will also be candid. We have our own priorities set
by this congress, and they will not always be the priorities of the
government.

Speech to GMB Conference, 1997

Friedrich Engels

1820–95; German political economist

Naturally, the workers are perfectly free; the manufacturer does
not force them to take his materials and his cards, but he says to
them … 'If you don't like to be frizzled in my frying pan, you
can take a walk into the fire.'

The Condition of the Working Class in England in 1844 (1892)

The earth is the first condition of our existence. To make it
an object of trade was the last step towards making human
beings an object of trade. To buy and sell land is an immorality
surpassed only by the immorality of selling oneself into slavery.

Outlines of a Critique of Political Economy (1844)

If trade unionists failed to register their protest by striking,
their silence would regard as an admission that they acquiesced
in the pre-eminence of economic forces over human welfare.
Such acquiescence would be recognition of the right of the

middle classes to exploit the workers when business was flourishing and to let the workers go hungry when business was slack. The Condition of the Working Class in England in 1844 (1892) 'The removal of all social and political inequalities' is a very dubious phrase with which to replace 'the removal of all class distinctions'. There will always be *certain* inequalities in the standard of life in different countries, provinces and places. They can be reduced to a minimum, but they can never be removed ... The notion that a socialist society is a society of *equals* is a biased French idea inherited from the old revolutionary slogan: 'Liberty, equality, fraternity' ... the idea of equality should now be regarded as out of date since it leads only to confusion and hampers a precise examination of the problem.

Letter to August Bebel, 28 March 1875

The first act in which the state really comes forward as the representative of society as a whole – the taking possession of the means of production in the name of society – is at the same time its last independent act as a state ... The state is not 'abolished', it withers away.

Anti-Dühring (1878)

Force ... in the words of Marx ... is the midwife of every old society which is pregnant with the new.

Anti-Dühring (1878)

In England a real democratic party is impossible unless it be a working men's party.

Labour Standard, 23 July 1881

According to the materialist conception of history, the production and reproduction of real life constitutes in the *last instance* the determining factor of history. Neither Marx nor I ever maintained more. Now, when someone comes along and distorts this to mean that the economic factor is the *sole* determining factor he is converting the former proposition into a meaningless, abstract, and absurd phrase. The economic system is the basis, but the various factors of the superstructure, the political forms of the class struggles and their results – constitutions, etc., established by victorious classes after hard-won battles, legal reforms, and even the reflexes of all these real struggles in the brain of the participants, political, judicial, philosophical theories, religious conceptions which have been developed into systematic dogmas – all these exercise an influence upon the course of historical struggles and in many cases determine for the most part their form.

Letter to J. Bloch, 21 September 1890

The state is nothing but an instrument of oppression of one class by another – no less so in a democratic republic than in a monarchy.

Preface to the 1891 edition of Marx's *The Civil War in France*

Dictatorship of the Proletariat. Well and good, gentlemen, do you want to know what this dictatorship looks like? Look at the Paris Commune. That was the Dictatorship of the Proletariat.

Socialism, Utopian and Scientific (1892)

An ounce of action is worth a ton of theory.

Cited in R. Groves, *The Strange Case of Victor Grayson*

Its growth proceeds as spontaneously, as steadily, as irresistibly, and at the same time as tranquilly as a natural process. All government interventions have proved powerless against it. We can count even today on two and half million votes. If it continues in this fashion, by the end of the century we shall conquer the greater part of the middle section of society, petty bourgeois and small peasants, and grow into the decisive power in the land, before which all other powers will have to bow, whether they liked it or not. To keep this growth going without interruption until of itself it gets beyond the control of the ruling government system, not to fritter away this daily increasing shock force in advance guard fighting, but to keep it intact until the day of the decision, that is our main task ...

The irony of world history turns everything upside down. We, the 'revolutionaries', the 'rebels'– we are thriving far better on legal methods than on illegal methods and revolt. The parties of order, as they call themselves, are perishing under the legal conditions created by themselves.

On German social democracy, introduction to Karl Marx's *The Class Struggles in France* (1895)

Just as Darwin discovered the law of development of organic nature, so Marx discovered the law of development of human history.

At Marx's graveside, 1883

Amitai Etzioni

b. 1929; Israeli-American sociologist

Only if the family cannot cope should the local community become involved. Only if the problem is too big for it should the state become involved.

The Spirit of Community (1993)

Communitarians call to restore civic virtues, for people to live up to their responsibilities and not merely focus on their entitlements, and to shore up the moral foundations of society.

The Spirit of Community (1993)

Moss Evans

1925–2002; General Secretary of the Transport and General Workers' Union 1978–85

Money is not everything, but it does make poverty tolerable.

Following his unions' contributions to the NUM strike funds, 1984–85

F

Vic Feather
1908–76; TUC General Secretary 1969–73

The price of oil is not determined by the British Parliament. It is determined by some lads riding camels who do not even know how to spell national sovereignty.

1975

Sir Alex Ferguson
b. 1941; football manager, Manchester United Football Club 1986–2013

The true friend is the one who walks through the door when others are putting on their coats to leave.

Mirror Football, 'Opinion: Alastair Campbell on his friend Fergie', 23 May 2008

Frank Field
b. 1942; Labour Party politician, Minister of State Department of Social Security 1997–98

The universalisation of private pension provision offers a true partnership between public and private sector, puts self-improvement at the centre of the drive to reshape welfare, and also provides for the poor.

The Guardian, 25 October 1994

There is no general groundswell amongst middle-class groups for the redistribution of wealth to the poor, particularly in the aftermath of the Thatcher years. Politicians who maintain otherwise are a public menace distracting from the real task.

Making Welfare Work (1995)

Means tests penalise all those human attributes – such as hard work, work being adequately rewarded, savings, and honesty – which underpin a free, let alone a civilised, society. The present welfare system, therefore, reinforces this shift in morality, further eroding the fundamental law-abiding principles and wealth of the country.

Making Welfare Work (1995)

Democracy no longer works for the poor if politicians treat them as a separate race.

Quoted in *Third Way*, December 1994

Michael Foot

1913–2010; Labour Party politician, leader 1980–83

No rising hope on the political scene who offered his service to Labour when I happened to be its leader can be dismissed as an opportunist.

On Tony Blair, *The Independent*, 19 February 1995

A speech from Ernest Bevin on a major occasion had all the horrific fascination of a public execution. If the mind was left immune, eyes and ears and emotions were riveted.

Aneurin Bevan (1962)

Democratic socialism traces its origin to a moral revolt against the inhuman dictatorship which nineteenth-century capitalism imposed upon our people, and it has rejected with no less vigour in this century another form of inhuman dictatorship into which Marxism was tragically distorted.

G. Kaufman (ed.), *Renewal: Labour's Britain in the 1980s* (1983)

It is not necessary that every time he rises he should give his famous imitation of a semi-house-trained polecat.

On Norman Tebbit, Hansard, 2 March 1978

Men of power have no time to read; yet the men who do not read are unfit for power.

Debts of Honour (1980)

Think of it, a second chamber selected by the Whips – a seraglio of eunuchs.

On the House of Lords

I have no objections to politicians being interested in personal power – I think they should be.

1966

She [Mrs Thatcher] worships the profit motive, the money test. Nothing else, no other value in life, is allowed to count. She extols Victorian values without even a passing comprehension of the human suffering and indignity which the mass of our people had to endure ... [The Labour Party] came into being to vanquish the hard, pinched values of Victorian Britain.

Foreword to *New Hope for Britain*, cited in M. Jones, *Michael Foot* (1994)

We have got to sit down and rebuild the Labour Party.

After the 1983 election defeat, cited in R. Harris, *The Making of Neil Kinnock* (1984)

The members of our Secret Service have apparently spent so much time looking under the bed for Communists, that they haven't had time to look in the bed.

On the Profumo Affair, 1963

Rowdy, convulsive, vulgar, splenetic; threatening at moments to collapse into an irretrievable brawl.

On the 1952 party conference, *Aneurin Bevan* (1975)

I am asking this movement to exert itself as it has never done before, to show the qualities which we have, the Socialist imagination that exists in our movement, the readiness to re-forge the alliance, stronger than ever, between the Government and the trade unions, and above all to show the supreme quality in politics, the red flame of Socialist courage.

Speech, Blackpool, 29 September 1976

Only eagles could foul their own nests on a scale so alarming.

On Gaitskell's Clause IV plans, 'The Future of the Left', *Encounter*, July 1960

The finest Socialist Programme I have seen in my lifetime.

On Labour's Programme 1973, *The Guardian*, 3 October 1973

The storm has blown as hard as it did in the 1930s, but this time the weak have been shielded ... Individual men and women have been able to turn in their hour of need to a community which shows some compassion. That is what I call Socialism, or rather the beginnings of Socialism.

1979 election address to his Ebbw Vale constituency, cited in M. Jones, *Michael Foot* (1994)

Isabella Ford

1885–1924; ILP feminist

Moral evils which are eating at the heart of the nation, pressing the most heavily, as do all such evils, on the lives of the very poorest and most helpless women, and long experience has shown that they will never be remedied till women have full political power, and can themselves deal with them.

Women and Socialism (1904)

The sex problem is, at bottom, the Labour problem.

From Serfdom to Socialism (1907)

Michel Foucault

1926–84; French philosopher

Marxism exists in the nineteenth century though in the same way as a fish in water; that is, it stops breathing elsewhere.

Cited in D. Eribon, *Michel Foucault* (1989)

Charles Fourier

1772–1837; French social theorist

The extension of women's rights is the basic principle of all social progress.

Théorie des Quatre Mouvements (1808)

G

Hugh Gaitskell
1906–63; Labour Party politician, leader 1955–63

We, as middle-class socialists, have got to have a profound humility. Though it's a funny way of putting it, we've got to know that we lead them because they can't do it without us, with our abilities, and yet we must feel humble to working people. Now that's all right for us upper middle class, but Tony [Crosland] and Roy [Jenkins] are not upper, and I sometimes feel they don't have proper humility to working people.

Conversation with Richard Crossman, August 1959

We have long ago come to accept, we know very well, ... a mixed economy, in which case, if this is our view – as I believe it to be of 90 per cent of the Labour Party – had we better not say so instead of going out of our way to court misrepresentation.

On Clause IV, Labour Party Annual Conference Report (1959)

A certain basis of consent, a willingness to compromise, to accept the rules of the game is absolutely essential.

In Defence of Politics (1954)

I do not believe that Mr Khrushchev has any intention of deliberately starting an aggressive war in present circumstances ... but I do believe that if you give them the opportunity of advancing the cause they believe in without cost or risk to themselves, they will not reject the opportunity. I ask you, bearing in mind all these things, and reflecting on the events of recent years – what they did in Hungary ... to say that it would not be wise for us to take the risk.

On nuclear weapons, Labour Party Annual Conference Report (1960)

I have always looked upon the Trades Union Congress and the Labour Party as part of the same great Labour movement, and our close integration as one of our great strengths. I see no reason to change my mind.

Speech to Labour Party Conference, 1959

It is not in dispute that the vast majority of Labour Members of Parliament are utterly opposed to unilateralism and neutralism. So what do you expect them to do? Change their minds overnight? ... There are other people too, not in Parliament, in the Party, who share our convictions. What sort of people do you think they are? What sort of people do you think we are? Do you think we can simply accept a decision of this kind? Do you think that we can become overnight the pacifists, unilateralists and fellow travellers that other people are? ... There are some of us, Mr Chairman, who will fight and fight again to save the Party we love. We will fight and fight and fight again to bring back sanity and honesty and dignity, so that our Party with its great past may retain its glory and its greatness.

Speech to Labour Party Conference against the resolution passed in favour of unilateral nuclear disarmament, 5 October 1960

The 'sick man of Europe' today, we shall become the poor relation tomorrow.

Speech to Labour Party Conference, October 1961

We must be clear about this: it does mean, if this is the idea, the end of Britain as an independent European state. I make no apology for repeating it. It means the end of a thousand years of history. You may say 'Let it end', but, my goodness, it is a decision that needs a little care and thought. And it does mean the end of the Commonwealth. How can one really seriously suppose that if the mother country, the centre of the Commonwealth is a province of Europe (which is what federation means) it could continue to exist as the mother country of a series of independent nations? It is sheer nonsense.

Speech to Labour Party Conference, 3 October 1962

We regard as unjust a class structure in which a person's income, way of living, education, status, and opportunities in life depend upon the class into which he is born.

Socialism and Nationalisation (1956)

I am not prepared to lose another election for the sake of nationalisation.

Cited in T. Benn, *Years of Hope* (1994)

The recent improvements in living standards have been of a special kind. There has been a particularly notable increase in comforts, pleasures and conveniences in the home. Television, whether we like it or not, has transformed the leisure hours of the vast majority of our fellow-citizens. Washing machines, refrigerators, modern cookers, have made women's lives a good deal easier. And incidentally, I fancy that our failure this time was largely a failure to win support from the women ... It is no use dismissing the problem, as some do, by saying that women are too snobbish or too politically apathetic. They are voters and count just as much as men...

Speech to Labour Party Conference, 1959

I disagree equally with the other extreme view that nationalisation or even public ownership is the be all and end all, the ultimate first principle and aim of socialism. I believe that this view arises from a complete confusion about the fundamental meaning of socialism and, in particular, a misunderstanding about ends and means.

Speech to Labour Party Conference, 1959

The only official document which embodies such an attempt [to define the fundamental issues] is the Party Constitution, written over forty years ago. It seems to me that this needs to be brought up to date. For instance, can we really be satisfied today with a statement of fundamentals which makes no mention at all of colonial freedom, race relations, disarmament, full employment or planning?

Speech to Labour Party Conference, 1959

The democratic socialist *par excellence*.

On R.H. Tawney, memorial service, 8 February 1962

A clever fool.

On Tony Benn

I am sure that the Webbs and Arthur Henderson who largely drafted the Constitution would have been amazed and horrified had they thought that their words were to be treated as sacrosanct forty years later in utterly changed conditions.

On Clause IV, speech to Labour Party Conference, 1959

It became obvious that there were throughout the Party and the movement very strong feelings about the 1918 constitution. It might be misleading to call them sentimental, and if I used a term of that kind it would not be in any derogatory sense; but there was an attachment to that constitution.

Speech to Labour Party Conference, 1960

The extension of public ownership ... it seems to me ... is almost certainly necessary if we are to have a much more equal distribution of wealth.

Socialism and Nationalisation (1956)

J. K. Galbraith

1908–2006; Canadian-born economist

People are the common denominator of progress.

Campaign remarks, 20 October 1960

Political action is the highest responsibility of a citizen.

Campaign remarks, 20 October 1960

The decisive power in modern industrial society is exercised not by capital but by organisation, not by the capitalist but by the individual bureaucrat. This is true in the Western industrial systems. It is true also of the socialist societies.

The New Industrial State (1967)

In an atmosphere of private opulence and public squalor, the private goods have full sway.

The Affluent Society (1958)

Clearly the most unfortunate people are those who must do the same thing over and over again, every minute, or perhaps twenty to the minute. They deserve the shortest hours and the highest pay.

Made To Last (1964)

Anyone who says he isn't going to resign, four times, definitely will.

Quoted in the *New York Times*, 7 November 1973

Nothing is so admirable in politics as a short memory.

1968

There are times in politics when you must be on the right side and lose

The Observer, 'Sayings of the Week', 11 February 1968

It is a far, far better thing to have a firm anchor in nonsense than to put out on the troubled seas of thought.

The Affluent Society (1958)

The greater the wealth, the thicker will be the dirt.

The Affluent Society (1958)

Politics is not the art of the possible. Is consists in choosing between the disastrous and the unpalatable.

Letter to President Kennedy, 2 March 1962

Dear Mr Vice-President, It was very nice, indeed, of Senator John Chafee to nominate me for membership in the 'Republican Senatorial Inner Circle'. I make haste to accept ... You mention that there will be 'closed door' briefings of the members of the Republican Inner Circle ... I wonder if some of those so selected may be paying money for this privilege, even though you have no intention of offering it? Doesn't this put you in a no-win situation? Either you are offering information for money-making purposes that is not available to the public at large or you are guilty of a certain fraud in giving the impression that there will be such advantage. I do hasten to assure you that this does not trouble me in a personal way. I am not in business and will, of course, avoid making a contribution...

During an exchange of letters with Vice-President Dan Quayle

In the usual (though certainly not in every) public decision on economic policy, the choice is between courses that are almost equally good or equally bad. It is the narrowest decisions that are most ardently debated. If the world is lucky enough to enjoy peace, it may even one day make the discovery, to the horror of doctrinaire free-marketeers and doctrinaire planners alike, that what is called capitalism and what is called socialism are both capable of working quite well.

The American Economy: Its Substance and Myth (1949)

An occasional strike is an indication that countervailing power is being employed in a sound context where the costs of any wage increase cannot readily be passed along to someone else. It should be an occasion for mild rejoicing in the conservative press. The *Daily Worker*, eagerly contemplating the downfall of capitalism, should regret this manifestation of the continued health of the system.

American Capitalism (1957)

George Galloway

b. 1954; former Labour Party politician

Wanted 'the admission of Communists to the Labour Party'.

Cited in A. Roth, *Parliamentary Profiles*

Sir, I salute your courage, your strength, your indefatigability.

To Saddam Hussein, 19 January 1994

Some believe that those aeroplanes on September 11 came out of a clear blue sky. I believe they came out of a swamp of hatred created by us.

Debate with Christopher Hitchens, 14 September 2005

Mahatma Gandhi

1869–1948; Indian nationalist leader

So long as a minority conforms to the majority, it is not even a minority. They must throw in their whole weight in the opposite direction.

Indian Opinion, 14 September 1917

What difference does it make to the *dewa*, the orphans and the homeless, whether the mad destruction is wrought under the name of totalitarianism or the holy name of liberty or democracy?

Non-Violence in Peace and War (1942)

The moment the slave resolves that he will no longer be a slave, his fetters fall. He frees himself and shows the way to others. Freedom and slavery are mental states.

Non-Violence in Peace and War (1942)

I think it would be a good idea.

Responding to a reporter's question, 'Mr Gandhi, What do you think of Western civilisation?'

Victory attained by violence is tantamount to defeat, for it is momentary.

Satyagraha Leaflet No. 13, 3 May 1919

Non-violence is the first article of my faith. It is also the last article of my creed.

Speech at Shahi Bay, 18 March 1922

Anthony Giddens
b. 1938; sociologist

We should, and we can, look to achieve greater control over our runaway world. We shan't be able to do so if we shirk the challenges, or pretend that all can go on as before. For globalisation is not incidental to our lives today. It is a shift in our very life circumstances. It is the way we now live.

The Observer, 11 April 1999

The egalitarianism of the old left was noble in intent, but as its rightist critics say has sometimes led to perverse consequences – visible, for example, in the social engineering which has left a legacy of decaying, crime ridden housing estates. The welfare state, seen by most as the core of social democratic politics, today creates almost as many problems as it resolves.

The Third Way (1998)

I shall take it 'third way' refers to a framework of thinking and policy-making that seeks to adapt social democracy to a world which has changed fundamentally over the past two or three decades. It is a third way in the sense that it is an attempt to transcend both old-style social democracy and neoliberalism.

The Third Way (1998)

The overall aim of third way politics should be to help citizens pilot their way through the major revolutions of our time: *globalisation*, *transformations in personal life* and our *relationship to nature*.

The Third Way (1998)

Reports of the death of New Labour are, as Mark Twain might put it, greatly exaggerated. Most of the themes the party pioneered in its long march away from traditional leftism remain intact.

The Guardian, 1 December 2008

What matters now is where we go from here.

The Guardian, 1 December 2008

It was a fundamental mistake to try to make ideological changes while deferring policy debate to a later date.

On David Cameron's Conservative Party, *The Guardian*, 31 July 2007

The renewed polarisation of politics on the left and right is plainly threatening to political stability. However, the cause of the modernising left is by no means lost. It remains the only feasible way forward for European social democrats.

The Guardian, 3 May 2002

Julia Gillard

b. 1961; Australian Labor Party politician, Prime Minister 2010–13

I was offended by those things. Misogyny, sexism, every day from this leader of the opposition.

Speech in Parliament, in reply to a motion by Leader of the Opposition Tony Abbott, 9 October 2012

I will not be lectured about sexism and misogyny by this man. I will not. And the Government will not be lectured about sexism and misogyny by this man. Not now, not ever.

Speech in Parliament, in reply to a motion by Leader of the Opposition Tony Abbott, 9 October 2012

If he [the Leader of the Opposition] wants to know what
misogyny looks like in modern Australia, he doesn't need a
motion in the House of Representatives, he needs a mirror.
That's what he needs.

Speech in Parliament, in reply to a motion by Leader of the
Opposition Tony Abbott, 9 October 2012

Oliver Goldsmith

1730–74, novelist

One man is born with a silver spoon in his mouth, and another
with a wooden ladle.

The Citizen of the World

Laws grind the poor and rich men rule the law.

The Traveller (1764)

Mikhail Gorbachev

b. 1931; General Secretary of the Communist Party of the Soviet Union
1985–91

You may not know my work, but I've seen all your movies.

Introducing himself to Paul Newman

The Communist Party has no God-given right to rule.

Address to the Central Committee of the Communist Party,
11 January 1989

I am a Communist, a convinced Communist! For some that may
be a fantasy. But to me it is my main goal.

Speech, December 1989

Patrick Gordon Walker

1907–80; Labour Party politician, Foreign Secretary 1964–65

Whatever the originally intended meaning of Clause IV, it had in time lost its meaning. Partly because of the misrepresentation of our opponents, but mainly because of the gloss put on the Clause within our own ranks, 'common ownership' came to be identified with 'nationalisation'; and the word 'all' came to be assumed before the means of production, distribution and exchange.

'The Future of the Left', *Encounter*, July 1960

Maxim Gorky

1868–1936; Russian writer

Communism will pass away from Russia, but it will have lighted a torch for the world of workers not readily to be extinguished.

Interview cited in the *Milwaukee Sentinel*, 3 October 1921

Joe Gormley

1917–93; leader of the National Union of Mineworkers 1971–81

I am a Socialist. I was born a Socialist and I shall die a Socialist.

Battered Cherub (1982)

André Gorz

1923–2007; socialist theorist

The crisis of socialism is above all a reflection of the crisis of the proletariat.

Farewell to the Working Class (1982)

The source of the theoretical superiority of socialism over capitalism is thus the source of its practical inferiority. To argue that society should be the controlled, programmed result of its members' activity is to demand that everyone should make their conduct functional to the overall social result in view. Thus, there can be no room for any form of conduct which, if generalised, would not lead to the programmed social outcome. Classical socialist doctrine finds it difficult to come to terms with political and social pluralism, understood not simply as a plurality of parties and trade unions but as the coexistence of various ways of working, producing and living, various and distinct cultural areas and levels of social existence.

Farewell to the Working Class (1982)

Marx described the process of proletarianisation in such a way as to show that it would produce a proletariat conscious of its being, that is to say, forced by vital necessity to become what it is to be. The historical analysis was so weak, however, that it was incapable of factually supporting the thesis it was designed to underpin. At his conclusion, Marx had returned to his point of departure and had failed to develop an analysis which substantially enriched his initial intuition.

Farewell to the Working Class (1982)

Bryan Gould

b. 1939; former Labour Party politician; vice-chancellor of Waikato University, New Zealand

The purpose of retaining a deterrent is not to use it, or even to threaten to use it. We have no intention of keeping a nuclear deterrent, either to use it or to deter.

Daily Telegraph, 9 May 1989

We cannot just sit on our hands. We cannot stand terrified, rooted to the spot.

1987

The attempt to gain the confidence of the financial
Establishment is not only futile but not even desirable. The only
condition on which it can ever be attempted is the abandonment
of our programme.

Industrial Strategy Group Report (1989)

As more and more people have operated successfully in a
capitalist or at best a mixed economy, they have become
partisans of private property and of taking one's chances in the
market.

Socialism and Freedom (1985)

The problem for the Conservatives is that they were damned
with Mrs Thatcher but are also damned without her.

8 January 1991

A constant climate of suspicion and grievance ... which makes
it difficult for the Labour Party to maintain the unity and
discipline rightly expected of a party seeking office.

On the 'betrayal' that dominated the party in the 1980s, *The Guardian*,
14 June 1988

Socialism is a constant struggle against the forces in society
which naturally tend towards concentration of power.

Socialism and Freedom (1986)

Mrs Thatcher has succeeded to a considerable extent in changing
the terms and meaning of the debate so that the emphasis is
more on freedom than equality than it was in the 1960s and
1970s.

Socialism and Freedom (1986)

We must ensure that we are not lumbered with policies which
commend themselves to committees, but which cannot be sold
to the electorate.

New Socialist, Summer 1987

The single most important problem facing the left in
the post-war economy: the political implications of the
internationalisation of capital.

The Guardian, 28 May 1992

Philip Gould

1950–2011; political consultant and pollster

My death has become my life. And my life has gained a kind of
intensity and power that it had never had before.

Quoted in the *Daily Mail*, serialising his book *When I Die: Lessons from
the Death Zone*, 2 May 2012

I am enjoying my death. There is no question I am having the
most fulfilling time of my life.

Quoted in the *Daily Mail*, serialising his book *When I Die: Lessons from
the Death Zone*, 2 May 2012

The New Labour brand has been badly contaminated.

Internal memo leaked to the media, quoted in BBC News online,
19 July 2000

It is the object of constant criticism, and even worse, ridicule,
undermined by a combination of spin, lack of conviction and
apparently lack of integrity.

Internal memo leaked to the media, quoted in BBC News online,
19 July 2000

Antonio Gramsci

1891–1937; Marxist theorist

In Russia, Marx's *Das Kapital* was more a book of the
bourgeoisie than of the proletariat. It stood as the critical
demonstration of how events should follow a predetermined
course: how in Russia a bourgeoisie had to develop, and a

capitalist era had to open, with the setting-up of a Western-type civilisation, before the proletariat could even think in terms of its own revolt, its own class demands, its own revolution.

Selections from Political Writings (1988)

The state was everything, civil society was primordial and gelatinous; in the West, there was a proper relation between State and civil society, and when the State trembled a sturdy structure of civil society was at once revealed. The State was only an outer ditch, behind which there stood a powerful system of fortresses and earthworks: more or less numerous from one State to the next, it goes without saying – but this precisely necessitated an accurate reconnaissance of each individual country.

Selections from the Prison Notebooks (1971)

To link these institutions, co-ordinating and ordering them into a highly centralised hierarchy of competencies and powers, while respecting the necessary autonomy and articulation of each, is to create a genuine workers' democracy here and now – a workers' democracy in effective and active opposition to the bourgeois State, and prepared to replace it here and now in all its essential functions of administering and controlling the national heritage.

Presenting the Turin Workers' Council

John Gray

b. 1948; political theorist

The political fact of the age is the passing of social democracy.

The Guardian, 29 January 1996

Although many social democratic parties in government were content merely to contain or moderate the economic inequalities thrown up by market capitalism, their ideal remained that of compressing income and wealth inequalities.

After Social Democracy (1996)

The place we occupy is not a halfway house between rival extremes. Our position is not a compromise between two discredited ideologies. It is a stand on a new common ground.

Speech, *Guardian*/Nexus Conference, 1 March 1997

The first duty of political thought is to understand the present. The danger of the new social-democratic consensus is that it tracks a world which has now disappeared irretrievably.

After Social Democracy (1996)

Victor Grayson

1881–1920; socialist politician

If the people have no shrapnel, they have broken bottles.

Speech, Huddersfield, August 1907

I am simply a bullet fired by the Colne Valley workers against the established order.

Cited in R. Groves, *The Strange Case of Victor Grayson*

It leaves two courses open to the thinking animal …
Schopenhauer and suicide or socialism and struggle.

On living in the slums of Manchester, cited in R. Groves, *The Strange Case of Victor Grayson*

Graham Greene

1904–91; English novelist

Catholics and Communists have committed great crimes, but at least they have not stood aside, like an established society, and been indifferent. I would rather have blood on my hands than water like Pilate.

The Comedians (1966)

Germaine Greer

b. 1939; Australian feminist

Women's liberation, if is abolishes the patriarchal family, will abolish a necessary substructure of the authoritarian state, and once that withers away Marx will have come true willy-nilly, so let's get on with it.

The Female Eunuch (1970)

Womanpower means the self-determination of women, and that means that all the baggage of paternalist society will have to be thrown overboard. Woman must have room and scope to devise a morality which does not disqualify her from excellence, and a psychology which does not condemn her to the status of spiritual cripple.

The Female Eunuch (1970)

James Griffiths

1890–1975; Labour Party politician, deputy leader 1955–59

He [Gaitskell] knew that I belonged to the old tradition in socialist thought and practice, and that Clause Four was an article of faith to me and my generation. When I reminded him of this he replied sternly: 'Maybe, but you know that we do not intend, any of us, to implement Clause Four fully, and I regard it as my duty to say so to the Party and the country.'

Pages From Memory (1969)

Integrity, absolute integrity, that was the essential quality of Hugh Gaitskell's character. When he considered it was his duty to say or do something, nothing could stop him. The sharp edge of intellectual integrity would cut through all barriers.

Cited in P. Williams, *Hugh Gaitskell: A Political Biography* (1979)

Ernesto 'Che' Guevara

1928–67; Argentinian-born revolutionary

A revolution that does not continue to grow deeper is a revolution that is retreating.

Guerrilla Warfare: A Method (1961)

When asked whether or not we are Marxists, our position is the same as that of a physicist or a biologist who is asked if he is a 'Newtonian', or if he is a 'Pasteurian'.

'We Are Practical Revolutionaries', *Verde Olivo*, 8 October 1960

The true revolutionary is guided by feelings of great love.

Man and Socialism in Cuba (1965)

Whenever death may surprise us, let it be welcome, provided that this, our battle cry, may have reached some receptive ear, and another hand may be extended to wield our weapons, and other men be ready to intone the funeral dirge with the staccato chant of the machine gun and new battle cries of war and victory.

1967

Socialism is young and makes mistakes. We revolutionaries often lack the knowledge and the intellectual audacity to face the task of the development of a new man by methods different from the conventional ones.

Open letter, 1967

In a revolution one wins or dies.

Farewell letter from Che Guevara to Fidel Castro, 1 April 1965

If a man is willing and honest you can make a revolutionary of him. The question is one of fighting the causes and not just being satisfied with getting rid of the effects.

1953

A guerrilla fighter is ... a sort of guiding angel who has fallen into the area, always to help the poor and to bother the rich as little as possible.

Guerrilla Warfare: A Method (1961)

Each guerrilla must be prepared to die. Not to defend an ideal, but to transform it into a reality.

Guerrilla Warfare: A Method (1961)

Hatred is an element of the struggle, relentless hatred that impels us over and beyond the natural limitations of men and transforms us into effective, violent, selected and cold killing machines. It is a race of wolves. He who arrives does so only at the expense of the failure of others.

Man and Socialism in Cuba (1965)

H

Jürgen Habermas
b. 1929; political theorist

Today, difficulties that a mere two or three years ago would have passed for private matters – for conflicts between students and teachers, workers and employers, or marital partners, for conflicts between individual persons – now claim political significance and ask to be justified in political terms. Psychology seems to turn into politics – perhaps a reaction to the reality that politics, insofar as it related to the masses, has long been translated into psychology.

Towards a Rational Society (1969)

Lord Hailsham
1907–2001; Conservative politician

The Labour Party almost admittedly aims at the establishment of a single-party system; and it may be said at once that they are almost within striking distance of their goal ... Never since the days of Cromwell has a single force in this country constituted a more formidable menace to political liberty.

The Case for Conservatism (1947)

Peter Hain
b. 1950; Labour Party politician, Secretary of State for Wales 2009–10

It is only with interaction with others in political activity and civic action that individuals will fully realise their humanity.

Ayes to the Left (1995)

Now that the ghost of authoritarianism and command economies has been exorcised, socialism has the best opportunity for fifty years to win popular support in the democratic world.

Ayes to the Left (1995)

An extra-parliamentary dimension is necessary because it facilitates an intervention in the layers of society which surround or are below state institutions.

Ayes to the Left (1995)

Through joining direct action demonstrations, party members, MPs, and leaders will help to create the kind of extra-parliamentary pressure which will enormously assist the next Labour government in its commitment to cancel cruise.

The Guardian, 2 December 1982

The next Labour government should appoint only judges which have clear socialist or libertarian sympathies.

Tribune, 27 January 1984

We cannot stand on the fence over struggles by striking miners or direct action by opponents of cruise missiles.

The Guardian, 9 May 1984

Labour ministers should bring in scores of political aides drawn from the labour movement who will provide a link to the party and to extra-parliamentary forces.

New Statesman, 24 May 1985

Labour should announce that it will refuse to apply laws which are oppressive.

Sunday Telegraph, 20 July 1986

The concept of class, and of the working class in particular, may seem all too theoretical, but it is inextricably linked with politics. I don't think there should be any argument about class relations and a class analysis still being valid.

World Marxist Review, September 1989

We should not rely just on parliamentary, but also on extra-parliamentary forces, including the trade union movement, the women's movement, the peace movement, and the people in the community.

World Marxist Review, September 1989

The power of capitalism is international and can only be effectively challenged on an international basis.

Daily Telegraph, 21 May 1977

We cannot achieve Socialism through Parliamentary channels alone.

Morning Star, 27 April 1981

It is so critical that the whole [Labour] Party gives full support to the miners. The outcome of their battle will not only affect the future of workers in the mining industry. It will determine the terrain upon which other industrial struggles will have to be built.

Socialist Action, 11 May 1984

The organisation exists to perform a number of tasks: to facilitate internal Party business; to provide opportunities for members to discuss and to develop ideas; and to encourage the skills and the activities whereby the Party's political message can be taken to the broader electorate.

With Derek Fatchett, *A Stakeholder Party* (1997)

Observing Northern Ireland today, it's hard to recognise what was just a decade or so ago the theatre for such horror and barbarity, hate and bigotry.

Speech, Glucksman Ireland House, New York, 5 June 2008

The basic necessities of life are increasingly becoming luxuries even for people in the wealthiest nations.

Speech, BRICS Conference, London, 5 September 2012

I wish I hadn't stood for Labour deputy leader.

Interview, *The Guardian*, 4 March 2012

I thought the judge off his rocker.

Criticising a judge in Northern Ireland for which prosecution was threatened for 'scandalising the court', *Outside In* (2012)

I had become increasingly frustrated about the truly appalling quality of what passes for 'political debate' in Britain today.

Speech to the Institute for Public Policy Research, 29 July 2003

As a cabinet minister, I'm a believer in plain speaking and answering questions not ducking them.

Speech to the IPPR, 29 July 2003

Stuart Hall

b. 1932; co-founder of *Marxism Today*

If it is wrong for Britain to manufacture, store and test her own weapons, then it is surely wrong for her to be an inactive partner in a military alliance which is based on the use of nuclear weapons.

NATO and the Alliance (1961)

Has the Labour movement come through the fire and brimstone of the last fifty years to lie down and die before the glossy magazines? Has Labour no sense of the capacities, the potential of a society more various, more skilled, more literate, less cramped and confined, less beaten down and frustrated?

Cited in E. P. Thompson, *Out of Apathy* (1960)

A. H. Halsey
b. 1923; British sociologist

The Labour movement set out to nationalise democracy and welfare, to translate fraternity, equality and liberty from the local community to the national state.

Cited in T. Wright, *Socialisms: Old and New* (1996)

Keir Hardie
1856–1915; Scottish Labour Party politician

The demand of the Labour party is for economic freedom. It is the natural outcome of political enfranchisement.

Speech to the ILP Conference, 13 January 1893

We witness on every hand unchallenged male dominance, arrogant armament, harsh and unfeeling administration of the law. With the incoming of the mother element into politics this would be gradually changed.

On the participation of women in politics (1907)

Syndicalism is the direct outcome of the apathy and indifference of this House [of Commons] towards working class questions, and I rejoice at the growth of syndicalism. The more syndicalism we have outside, the quicker will be the pace at which this Chamber will move.

Hansard, 1912

Socialism makes war upon a system, not upon a class.

Labour Leader, September 1904

I take it that the aim of the Labour Party is to wean the workers from their allegiance to Liberalism and Toryism, and to unite them under a standard of their own raising.

Labour Leader, April 1883

Socialism, like every other problem of life, is at bottom a question of ethics or morals. It has mainly to do with the relationships which should exist between a man and his fellows.

From Serfdom to Socialism (1907)

[Socialism] is 'a handmaiden of religion', and as such entitled to the support of all who pray for the coming of Christ's Kingdom upon earth.

From Serfdom to Socialism (1907)

The fundamental fact which the working class is now beginning to recognise is that property, or at least its possession, is power. This is an axiom which admits of no contradiction.

From Serfdom to Socialism (1907)

[The worker] will use the political freedom which his fathers won for him to win industrial freedom for his children ... the real inward meaning of the rise of the Labour Party.

From Serfdom to Socialism (1907)

The friction does not lie between old-fashioned Trade Unionists who want to improve the condition of the worker and Socialists who want to change the industrial order. The friction lies between people, all of whom are Socialists, who want Socialism, who put Socialism before anything else.

My Confession of Faith in the Socialist Alliance (1909)

The outstanding value of the Labour Party is that it is what its name implies, an uprising of the working class, overseen and guided by that class, painfully and slowly working out its own emancipation.

My Confession of Faith in the Socialist Alliance (1909)

It is not so much Socialism, not the absence of it, which wins elections, as the fact that the candidate is representing a party which the average man who does not indulge over-much in theories, understands and approves.

My Confession of Faith in the Socialist Alliance (1909)

Socialism supplies the vision and a united working class satisfies the senses as a practical method of attaining its realisation.

Cited in F. Johnson, *Keir Hardie's Socialism* (1922)

Our work will be handicapped and our movement lopsided until women take their place with men as comrades and political equals in our great world-wide agitation for industrial and economic freedom.

My Confession of Faith in the Socialist Alliance (1909)

The life of one Welsh miner is of greater commercial and moral value to the British nation than the whole Royal Crowd put together, from the Royal Great Grand-mama down to this puling Royal Great Grand-child.

Labour Leader (1894)

Defeat is not in the Socialist dictionary.

Remark after losing election at Bradford East, 1896

It will take the British working man twenty years to learn to elect his equals to represent him. And then it will take him another twenty years not to elect his equals.

Cited in H. Nicolson in his diary, 27 February 1930

Born into the ranks of the working class, the new king's most likely fate would have been that of a street-corner loafer.

On George V, 1910

I understand what Christ suffered in Gethsemane as well as any man living.

Speaking to friends after hostility in Aberdare, 6 August 1914

The scientists, by sympathetic studies and laborious toil, have brought them within our ken. And so, in like manner, our socialist propaganda in revealing hidden and hitherto undreamed of powers and forces in human nature.

Speech, Bradford, 11 April 1914

A nation at war must be united, especially when its existence is at stake. With the boom of the enemy's guns within earshot, the lads who have gone forth to fight their country's battles must not be disheartened by any discordant notes at home.

Cited in C. F. Brand, *British Labour's Rise to Power* (1941)

Neither he [the miner] nor his union had any hand in shaping the circumstances which led to his being fully employed ... He feels himself to be under the sway of forces which work quite without his ken, and which have the power to make him the victim of their caprice.

From Serfdom to Socialism (1907)

Irksome as it is to endure the apathy of the [Liberal] government, it is tenfold more so to look at the inaction of these men. They are supposed to a special degree to represent labour, and so long as they are silent the Government can, with some show of justification, plead not guilty to the charge of neglect. If men who have been sent to Parliament holding a special brief for labour have nothing to say, why should a Cabinet drawn exclusively from the wealthy classes begin to make a fuss?

Labour Leader (1894)

I aim at a party which, on labour questions, shall lead Liberalism and the nation, and which shall not be content to play the part of a political Lazarus sitting at the gate of a rich man's party humbly begging crumbs from his table.

Labour Politics (1903)

For twenty-one years the SDF [Social Democratic Federation] has based its propaganda on the class-war theory, and the result is a dismal failure. How could it be otherwise? Mankind in the mass is not moved by hatred, but by love of what is right.

Keir Hardie (1975)

Harriet Harman

b. 1950; Labour Party politician, shadow deputy Prime Minister 2010–

My general approach is that you mustn't generalise.

BBC Radio 4, *Any Questions*, 1989

I am in the Labour Party because I am a feminist. I am in the Labour Party because I believe in equality.

Interview following her election as deputy leader of the Labour Party, *The Times*, 10 November 2007

I don't agree with all-male leaderships. Men cannot be left to run things on their own. I think it's a thoroughly bad thing to have men-only leadership.

Interview, *The Times*, 2 August 2009

For many young people, social mobility now means a bus down to the job centre.

On Nick Clegg's social mobility pledges, House of Commons, 5 April 2011

Tom Harris

b. 1964; Labour Party politician, Parliamentary Under-Secretary of State for Transport 2007–08

I love blogging because I love writing. I love politics, I love the Labour Party, I love writing about Labour Party politics. But the blog has become a burden. It's taking up too much time (though not as much as some might think – I am a very fast writer), it's getting me into too many squabbles with people I have never met and are likely never to meet. And increasingly

I've felt like I'm adopting stances simply for the sake of being confrontational and provoking a row. Basically, the bottom line: blogging is having a negative effect on my personal, family and political life for reasons too many and complicated to recount.

16 November 2010

The three years of his [Gordon Brown's] premiership were, on the whole, not a happy time for me, for my party or for my country.

Why I Am Right... And Everyone Else Is Wrong (2011)

Blogging shouldn't be the enemy of politics, it can actually be an ally.

Interview, *Total Politics*, 11 December 2009

Roy Hattersley

b. 1932; Labour Party politician, deputy leader 1983–92

Unless Labour addresses the issue of taxes it can say little that is positive and even less that is radical ... Radical decisions will certainly disadvantage some members of the higher-income groups.

The Observer, 15 January 1995

Unilateral nuclear disarmament, getting rid of our nuclear weapons when other countries did not get rid of theirs, was the most unpopular policy on which the Labour Party has ever fought a general election.

Interview, *Tribune*, 19 July 1983

Harold Wilson said Labour was a crusade or it was nothing. I try not to think about this assertion. The logical implications are too painful.

18 April 1997

Socialism is far more than a theory of economic organisation.

Foreword to E. Durbin, *New Jerusalems* (1985)

The forthcoming general election will be the most open battle in recent political history.

Speaking prior to the 1983 general election

In less than two years there will be a Labour government in Britain. I waste no time in justifying that assertion.

September 1986

You could fire a bazooka at her and inflict three large holes. Still she kept coming.

On Mrs Thatcher's performance at Prime Minister's Question Time, October 1990

He has built a Government which is untainted by dogma. Tony Blair is taking the politics out of politics.

The Guardian, 14 May 1997

The Labour Party as it now stands is ideologically the Labour Party I have wanted to see throughout my life.

New Statesman and Society, 26 July 1991

The true object of socialism is the creation of a genuinely free society in which the protection and extension of individual liberty is the primary duty of the state.

Choose Freedom (1987)

Socialism exists to provide – for the largest number of people – the ability to exercise effective liberty.

Choose Freedom (1987)

Socialists attempt to organise society in a way which allows increasing numbers of men and women to make ... choices for themselves.

Choose Freedom (1987)

In political folklore, April 29, 1995, will become the day when Labour turned itself into a social democratic party.

On the change of Clause IV, *The Guardian*, 27 April 1995

Socialists are not opposed to the market allocation of most goods and services.

Choose Freedom (1987)

To increase equality we need to create more equal primary incomes.

Choose Freedom (1987)

I believe in calling a spade a spade.

Following a speech against racism, August 1983

The curse of the British working class is their willingness to settle for so little. They are disciples not of the politics of envy but the politics of complacency. That is why they are so regularly ignored when the demands of the middle classes (who suffer from no such inhibition) increasingly dominate the policy agenda of both major parties.

1996

He loved being in government but wanted to govern on his own terms, not simply according to his own principles and policies but in a way consistent only with his unrealistic view of the world.

On Tony Benn, *The Observer*, 4 July 1999

A nation which is obsessed by the picture on its bank-notes rather than concerned about those bank-notes retaining their value, is a nation which is living in the past.

The Independent, 11 July 1999

In politics, being ridiculous is more damaging than being extreme.

Evening Standard, 9 May 1989

Bob Hawke

b. 1929; Australian trade union leader, Labor Prime Minister 1983–91

I find a fence a very uncomfortable place to squat my bottom.
  1976

Friedrich Hayek

1899–1992; Austrian-born political economist

The idea that a completely planned or directed economic system
could and would be used to bring about distributive justice
presupposes, in fact, the existence of something which does not
exist and has never existed: a complete moral code in which the
relative values of all human ends, the relative importance of all
the needs of all the different people, are assigned a definite place
and a definite quantitative significance.
  Freedom and the Economic System (1940)

Ron Hayward

1917–96; general secretary of the Labour Party 1972–82

The reason was that, for good or ill, the Cabinet, supported by
MPs, ignored Congress and Conference decisions.
  On the winter of discontent, speech to Labour Party Conference,
  1979

Denis Healey

b. 1917; Labour Party politician, Chancellor of the Exchequer 1974–79

Being attacked in the House by him is like being savaged by a
dead sheep.
  On being criticised by Sir Geoffrey Howe in the House of Commons,
  Hansard, 14 June 1978

The Prime Minister tells us that she has given the French president a piece of her mind – not a gift I would receive with alacrity.

On Margaret Thatcher, *The Independent*, 30 August 1997

She approached the problems of our country with all the one-dimensional subtlety of a comic strip.

On Margaret Thatcher, 1979

La Pasionaria of middle-class privilege.

On Margaret Thatcher ('La Pasionaria' was Dolores Ibárruri, a leading Spanish Communist during the civil war)

Rhoda the Rhino.

On Margaret Thatcher, October 1988

Pétain in petticoats.

On Margaret Thatcher

Economic forecasts are no better than the long-range weather forecasts.

On his time as Chancellor

The whole affair [the devaluation of sterling] was unnecessary. The Treasury had grossly overestimated the PSBR, which would have fallen within the IMF's limits without any of the measures they prescribed. Later figures showed that we managed to eliminate our current account deficit in 1977, before the IMF package had had time to influence it.

The Time of My Life (1989)

If we tighten our belt now we can start moving ahead next year and we'll be in better shape then than at any time since the war.

Budget broadcast, April 1975

We have no intention of ratting on any of our commitments. We intend to remain and still remain fully capable of carrying out

all the commitments we have at the present time, including the
Far East, the Middle East and Africa. We do intend to remain in
every sense a world power.

Canberra, 2 February 1966

I don't believe myself it is necessary for the people as a whole
to have their living standards lowered in order to conquer
inflation.

September 1974

I often compare the Prime Minister with Florence Nightingale.
She stalks through the wards of our hospitals as a lady with a
lamp – unfortunately it's a blow-lamp.

On Mrs Thatcher, speech, House of Commons, 25 November 1988

She is the Castro of the western world – an embarrassment to
all her friends. All she lacks is the beard.

On Mrs Thatcher, cited in I. Dale (ed.), *As I Said To Denis* (1998)

She adds the diplomacy of Alf Garnett to the economics of
Arthur Daley.

On Mrs Thatcher, cited in I. Dale (ed.), *As I Said To Denis* (1998)

Ted Heath in drag.

On Mrs Thatcher, cited in I. Dale (ed.), *As I Said To Denis* (1998)

It is now clear that the Prime Minister intends to become
the Ceausescu of the west and the main function of the Tory
chairman at the next Party Conference will be to arrange sixty-
nine standing ovations for her.

On Mrs Thatcher, November 1989

How do we know that next time, as always in the past, when
President Reagan says jump, she will not reply 'How high?'

Cited in I. Dale (ed.), *As I Said To Denis* (1998)

The standard of living has been deliberately reduced by the government over the last eighteen months in order that we should get ourselves financially straight. That should be a matter for congratulation and not for recrimination.

March 1977

The Russians are praying for a Labour victory.

Press conference in Moscow, 11 May 1987, on whether the Russians would prefer Mrs Thatcher or Neil Kinnock to win the next election

The winter of discontent was not caused by the frustration of ordinary workers after a long period of wage restraint. It was caused by institutional pressures from local trade union activists who had found their roles severely limited by three years of incomes policies agreed by their national leaders.

The Time of My Life (1989)

Power, of course, is not the only reality in world affairs. But it is a pervasive reality which has its own laws and fixes the limits within which moral criteria can operate.

New Fabian Essays (1952)

He had no sense of direction, and rarely looked more than a few months ahead. His short-term opportunism, allied with a capacity for self-delusion, which made Walter Mitty appear unimaginative, often plunged the government into chaos.

On Harold Wilson, *The Time of My Life* (1989)

I am afraid that a lot of things that many of us have said in the past three years are going to have to be unsaid.

Interview, BBC TV, 22 January 1968

I will consider selling off the Crown Jewels – but I am not absolutely certain that they are the property of Her Majesty's Government.

1976

I can't forgive [the Treasury] for misleading the Government, the country and the world for so many years about the true state of public spending in Britain. Indeed, I suspect that Treasury officials were content to overstate public spending in order to put pressure on governments which were reluctant to cut it.

The Time of My Life (1989)

I abandoned Keynesianism in 1975.

The Time of My Life (1989)

In many ways the Labour Party now is pursuing the line I recommended for it back in 1951.

Interview, *Anticipations*, Summer 1996

The thing that was branded on the inner core of everybody in the Labour Party was the need for loyalty. The memory went back to what was perceived as the desertion of Macdonald and Snowden which had destroyed the Party and kept us out. So whatever happened, we had to keep the thing together. We did feel we were part of a movement. It had got us where we were and it was our duty to go on working with it.

Cited in E. Pearce, *The Lost Leaders* (1997)

The great she-elephant, she who must be obeyed, the Catherine the Great of Finchley...

On Mrs Thatcher, speech, London, 27 February 1984

Eric Heffer

1922–91; Labour Party politician

Kinnock has proved to be a great cynical manipulator who has used the party's dislike and fear of Thatcher to get revisionist policies accepted. He has gone farther than Gaitskell in revising the party's principles, policies and organisation. He has got away with it because the party elected him in the belief that he was a left-wing leader who would carry out socialist policies. What an illusion that turned out to be.

Never A Yes Man (1991)

We were unanimous – in fact, we were all unanimous.

Following a meeting of Labour's National Executive Committee, 1982

My idea of a Labour government is one that fulfils its election pledges to build a new Jerusalem, which is not a corny ideal.

1975

Michael Heseltine

b. 1933; Conservative Party politician, deputy Prime Minister 1995–97

The self-appointed king of the gutter.

On Neil Kinnock, 7 June 1983

Patricia Hewitt

b. 1948; Labour Party politician, Secretary of State for Health 2005–07

We want places that are modern ... We do *not* want any closed factories, derelict housing sites, run-down hospitals ... or other wrecks of Thatcher's Britain. We also want *people* – bright, attractive people presenting an image of the broader base Labour has to capture – *not* people who present an image of old fashioned Labour die-hards.

Memo, 1986

It's obvious from our own polling, as well as from the doorstep that the 'London effect' is now very noticeable. The 'loony Labour left' is taking its toll: the gays and lesbians issue is costing us dear amongst the pensioners; and fear of extremism and higher taxes/rates is particularly prominent in the GLC area.

The Guardian, 6 March 1987

The essence of making Labour electable is trust. Trust in Labour's leadership, in the team, in Labour's ability to manage the economy competently. Trust that Labour knows where it is going – and trust in the policies to take it there.

New Statesman and Society, 4 August 1988

If the NHS is to meet the needs of the British people, and to reward them for the investment they are making in it, then the NHS must continue to change.

Speech, annual health and social care lecture, 13 December 2005

We have spent much too much time looking and sounding like managers and technocrats, and all the talk about 'what works', or 'delivery' and 'driving through change' – as though we were driving a herd of cattle or sheep. This is not why we came into politics. This isn't why people elected us into government.

Interview, 'Reviving the love Labour's lost', *The Guardian*, 29 September 2003

The accusation that we've lost our soul resonates with a very modern concern about authenticity.

Interview, 'Reviving the love Labour's lost', *The Guardian*, 29 September 2003

We're seeing quite a lot of people who really would like a return to class-based politics.

Interview, 'Reviving the love Labour's lost', *The Guardian*, 29 September 2003

Rudolf Hilferding

1877–1941; Austrian-born German socialist politician

Organised capitalism thus means in effect the replacement of the capitalist principle of free competition by the socialist principle of planned production. This planned, deliberately managed form of economy is much more susceptible to the conscious influence of society, which means to the influence of the *sole institution capable of the conscious*, compulsory organisation of the whole society, the state.

Speech to SPD conference (1927)

Joe Hill

1879–1915; American labour leader and songwriter

Don't mourn for me – Organise!

Last words before his execution, 18 November 1915

Leonard Hobhouse

1864–1929; philosopher

Liberty without equality is a name of noble sound and squalid result.

Liberalism (1911)

Eric Hobsbawm

1917–2012; political theorist

The future of Labour and the advance to socialism depends on mobilising people who remember the date of the Beatles' break-up, and not the date of the Saltley pickets; of people who have never read *Tribune* and who do not give a damn about the deputy leadership of the Labour Party.

The Forward March of Labour Halted? (1981)

The further we progress into the imperialist era, the more difficult does it become to put one's finger on groups of workers which did not, in one way or another, draw some advantage from Britain's position … Or … on workers who could not be made to feel that their interests depended on the continuance of imperialism.

Labouring Men (1972)

J. A. Hobson

1858–1940; political theorist

The economics of a hypothetical society in which the state, owning all the instruments of industry, need no longer take into account the categories of rent, interest and profit, with the economic analysis of current industry.

Political Science Quarterly (1925)

Its immanent conservatism recommends it, not only to timid academic minds, but to the general body of the possessing classes who, though they may be quite incapable of following its subtleties of reasoning, have sufficient intelligence to value its general conclusions.

Political Science Quarterly (1925)

Though ... my sympathies have been with the Labour Party, I have never quite felt at home in a body governed by trade union members and their finance, and intellectually led by full-blown Socialists. For neither section of this Labour Party avowedly accepts that middle course which seems to me essential to a progressive and constructive economic government in this country.

Confessions of an Economic Heretic (1938)

No general theory of socialism dependent for its working on some large view of the feasibility of social service as an adequate economic motive is likely to be adopted in this country.

Incentives In The New Industrial Order (1922)

S. G. Hobson

1870–1940; political theorist

The trade unions are undoubtedly the natural nuclei of future industrial organisation.

National Guilds (1914)

Political emancipation leaves the worker quite as much at the final disposition of the employer as was the Greek helot.

National Guilds (1914)

Thomas Hodgskin

1787–1869; political theorist

Those who have been masters, planners, contrivers, etc
... Have in general also been capitalists and have also had a command over the labour of those who have worked with their hands, their labour has been paid as much too high as common labour has been underpaid.

Labour Defended Against the Claims of Capital (1922)

The wages of the master, employer or contriver have been blended with the profit of the capitalist ... Masters are labourers as much as their journeymen. In this character, their interests are precisely the same as their men.

Labour Defended Against the Claims of Capital (1922)

Geoff Hodgson

b. 1946; political theorist

It is necessary to reject both the work-centred fatalism of the orthodox Marxists and the myopia of reformed socialism. The fudging, consensus politics that has predominated in the West has broken down. The future is in the hands of the radicals and visionaries.

The Democratic Economy (1984)

As the economic system becomes more and more complex and dependent on the efficient transmission of information, the market system becomes of less and less use for the purpose.

The Democratic Economy (1984)

Stuart Holland

b. 1940; political economist

The rise of managerial capitalism has not diluted the power of capitalism as a mode of production, but has increased the power of managers in the dominant mesoeconomic sector.

The Socialist Challenge (1975)

To ignore the techniques of state capitalism because they *are* state capitalist is not only to allow the devil some of the best tunes, but also to risk siren seduction of some sections of the working class, who would readily change job insecurity for job security, whatever the prevailing mode of production.

The Socialist Challenge (1975)

The edge of Thatcher's axe was not only ground in the treasury under a Labour administration, but fell and fell again in successive Labour budgets. The monetarism blue in tooth and claw which we now see ... was adopted against Party opinion by Labour Ministers in the Treasury and Cabinet.

In Ken Coates, *What Went Wrong?* (1979)

François Hollande

b. 1954; French Socialist politician, President 2012–

We have chased away the clouds, the sky is all 'rose'.

Speech to election rally, Palmer de Cenon park, 19 April 2012

In an election, one needs both hope and audacity.

Interview in SPIEGEL, 12 March 2012

The transatlantic relationship is vital for both our countries: France will remain a reliable ally of the United States. Nevertheless, ally does not mean aligned.

Interview with the *Huffington Post*, 26 January 2012

An education program is, by definition, a societal program.
Work should be done at school, rather than at home.

Quoted in ABC News on plans to ban homework, 17 October 2012

Austerity need not be Europe's fate.

Victory speech on winning the French presidency, 6 May 2012

As a president I will be like the candidate that I am, a respectful
candidate, a rallying candidate, a normal candidate for a normal
presidency, at the service of the Republic.

Final presidential campaign rally, May 2012

During a term in office there are highs and lows, but what
counts is that the goal is set as well as the means to achieve it,
and the force we put into getting results.

Press conference, 22 September 2012

Each country has a soul, and France's soul is equality.

Rally at Parisian suburb of Le Bourget, 22 January 2012

I am attached to the French language. I will defend the
ubiquitous use of French.

Quoted in the *Daily Mail*, 8 May 2012

I am for a clear distinction between public and private life. I
believe private matters should be regulated in private and I have
asked those close to me to respect this.

Bastille Day celebrations, 14 July 2012

I am proud to have been capable of giving people hope again.

Victory speech on winning the French presidency, 6 May 2012

I am the president of the youth of France.

Victory speech on winning the French presidency, 6 May 2012

I could have made a fortune in cheeseburgers, but I finally chose politics.

Interview, *New York Times*, 13 April 2012

I commit myself to serve my country.

Victory speech on winning the French presidency, 6 May 2012

I don't like indecent, unearned wealth. But it is legitimate for an entrepreneur who has created something to make a good living.

Interview in SPIEGEL, 12 March 2012

Our differences should not become divisive. Our diversity should not disunite us. The country needs reconciliation.

Speaking about reuniting France, inauguration ceremony, 21 May 2012

We have seen how heavy the price is when we are fragmented.

Comments to Associated Press, 23 April 2002

They failed because they did not start with a dream.

Citing Nicholas Shakespeare, journalist, novelist and biographer instead of his distant ancestor William, 25 January 2012

Geoff Hoon

b. 1953; Labour Party politician, Secretary of State for Transport 2008–09

One of the challenges I think which I am really looking forward to is sort of translating my knowledge and contacts about sort of international scene into something that bluntly, makes money.

Offering his lobbying services to an undercover investigative reporter, Channel 4, *Dispatches* programme, 'Politicians For Hire' with the *Sunday Times*, first broadcast 22 March 2010

George Howarth

b. 1949; Labour Party politician, Parliamentary Under-Secretary of State at the Home Office 1997–99

No one can remember a time since Neville Chamberlain, after Hitler invaded Norway, that anyone was so unpopular.

Quoted in the *Daily Telegraph* on then Prime Minister, Gordon Brown, 17 September 2008

Kim Howells

b. 1946; Labour Party politician, Minister of State for Education 2004–05

The Balkanisation of Britain … Pimply politics.

On Welsh devolution

The clique of spin doctors and party managers who foisted on us the anodyne policy statements and the gut-churning embarrassment of the Sheffield rally and others like it, all of which contributed so much to the decline in Labour's electoral appeal.

The Guardian, 14 April 1992

Victor Hugo

1802–85; French novelist

There is always more misery among the lower classes than there is humanity in the higher.

Les Misérables (1862)

Tristram Hunt

b. 1974; Labour Party politician and historian

Poverty was the challenge of 1945. Today's challenge is worklessness.

Interview, BBC TV, Newsnight, 11 March 2013

Will Hutton

b. 1950; journalist and author

The disintegration of family life and the decline in the public realm that disfigure contemporary Britain may seem far removed from London's financial markets, but they are linked to them as remote shocks are to the epicentre of an earthquake.

The State We're In (1995)

Britain needs what might be called a republican attitude to its culture and institutions.

The State We're In (1995)

The City of London and Whitehall and Westminster are symbiotic; one could not exist without the other, and none could have become what they are today without the other's support.

The State We're In (1995)

Not the static democracy of mass parties representing electorates in national parliaments, but a much more engaged democracy reviving the life of the citizen at work, home and play, offering a multiplicity of sites for association and community. There needs to be a whole new interlocking web of public agencies, ranging from training boards to development banks, from transport institutes to scientific laboratories, to which are delegated the job of setting boundaries to market behaviour.

In D. Miliband (ed.), *Re-inventing the Left* (1994)

For the Labour Party, some old-fashioned populism about the workings of foreign exchange speculators and life assurance salesman alike could pay dividends.

The Guardian, 29 September 1992

We cannot give up on reducing inequality. It would be a surrender too far, striking at the heart of the progressive tradition.

Marxism Today, November/December 1998

Thus from modest beginnings Mr Blair and his party have a chance of changing the structures of British democracy, sustaining the welfare state, lowering unemployment and creating a stakeholder business culture. Moreover, to do this in such a conservative country would be no mean achievement — and here there is a seismic shift under way that is not commonly recognised.

The State To Come (1997)

The moral and religious values which informed the socialist and social democratic movements of the twentieth century, along with their fierce advocacy of liberty, cannot be consigned to history without endangering the civilisation which we prize.

The State To Come (1997)

The instant you call yourself social democratic, you open up a conversation with the Left part of New Labour's coalition and dismay some on the Right.

The Observer, 20 September 1998

The curtain is being drawn on the interlude of Labour government within the conservative hegemony.

'Don't be naive about the brutal desire driving the Tories' lust for power', *The Observer*, 1 May 2011

My generation's opportunity squandered.

On the failure to deliver a balanced economy, interview in *The Guardian*, 3 October 2010

The heart of fairness is proportionality.

Interview, *The Guardian*, 3 October 2010

H. M. Hyndman

1842–1921; founder of the Social Democratic Federation

I may fairly claim to have done more than any man living
to spread knowledge of their [Marx's and Engels'] theories
amongst English-speaking peoples.
  1907

I

Dolores Ibárruri
1895–1989; Spanish Communist leader

Better to die on one's feet than to live on one's knees.
Speech, Valencia, 1936

J

Jean Jaurès
1859–1914; French socialist politician

Capitalism carries within itself war, as clouds carry rain.
Studies In Socialism (1902)

Douglas Jay
1907–96; Labour Party politician

One of the chief reasons that the poor are very poor is that the rich are very rich.
The Socialist Case (1937)

The tendency of socialists lately to think less of the dispossession of property and more of organisation, 'planning', efficiency and so on, is in many ways unfortunate. What society fundamentally needs is not so much planning as socialism.
The Socialist Case (1937)

Fair shares for all, is Labour's call.
Change and Fortune (1980)

In the case of nutrition and health, just as in the case of education, the gentleman in Whitehall really does know better what is good for people than the people know themselves.
The Socialist Case (1937)

He would never use one syllable when none would do.
On Clement Attlee

The poorer wage earners must always remain the real heart of socialism.

The Socialist Case (1937)

Massive redistribution is necessary if political freedom and other civilised values are to be preserved.

Socialism in the New Society (1962)

[Socialists have been] mistaken in making ownership of the means of production instead of ownership of inherited property the test of socialisation.

The Socialist Case (1937)

Socialists will thus be wise to recognise that the State monopoly form was devised to suit an earlier age which British manufacture and commerce have now largely outgrown.

Socialism in the New Society (1962)

It ought to be perfectly possible within a free society to ensure that private enterprise works according to the national interest; and when it does so work, it ought to be welcomed and complimented, not denounced.

Socialism in the New Society (1962)

There appears no evidence at all that the resources available for redistribution, even in Britain to-day, are negligible.

Socialism in the New Society (1962)

We believe in social ownership through the Co-operative Movement, municipal enterprise and public investment; but we do not believe in the extension of the public monopoly to manufacturing industry or distribution.

Cited in M. Foot, *Aneurin Bevan* (1973)

Clive Jenkins

1926–99; General Secretary of the Association of Scientific, Technical and Managerial Staffs 1961–88

Organising the middle classes.
> Entry in *Who's Who* under hobbies

Peter Jenkins

1934–92; British journalist

The keeper of the cloth cap.
> On Jim Callaghan, *The Battle of Downing Street* (1970)

Roy Jenkins

1920–2003; former Labour Party politician, co-founder of the SDP

The permissive society has been allowed to become a dirty phrase. A better phrase is the civilised society.
> Speech, Abingdon, 19 July 1969

A social democratic party without deep roots in the working class movement would quickly fade into an unrepresentative intellectual sect.
> 1972

The Labour Party is and always has been an instinctive part of my life.
> Speech, Oxford, 9 March 1973

The first duty of a party of the left is to be radical in the context of the moment, to offer a prospect of continuing advance and to preserve the loyalty of those whose optimistic humanism makes them natural supporters.
> *Pursuit of Progress* (1953)

The vocation of politicians ought to be to represent, to channel, to lead the aspirations of the electorate. These aspirations, not on every issue, but in essential directions, pull far more towards the centre than towards the extremes.

Cited in W. Kennett, *The Rebirth of Britain* (1982)

There is a lot of talk about a centre party – and that I might lead it. I find this idea profoundly unattractive.

Speech, Oxford, 9 March 1973

Traditionally, this British stability was considered a major national asset. Now the question is whether the stability has not turned into political rigidity, whether the old skin is not drawn too tight for effective national performance.

Cited in W. Kennett, *The Rebirth of Britain* (1982)

A substantial extension of public ownership is ... an essential pre-requisite of greater equality of earned incomes.

1952

It is now clear that techniques for managing the whole economy cannot solve detailed problems – even when the problem is that of a whole region rather than a single form. General demand management must be supplemented by more rigorous policies of direct intervention than those which we used between 1964 and 1970.

What Matters Now (1972)

There are always great dangers in letting the best be the enemy of the good.

Hansard, 1975

Each successive Labour government has been the most rapacious, doctrinaire and unpatriotic conspiracy to be seen this side of the iron curtain.

Speech, London, 22 November 1979

I am sure Mr Heath thinks he is honest but I wish he didn't have to have his friends say it so often.
    1970

The fact is that Harold [Wilson] is a person no one can like, a person without friends.
    Cited in J. Morgan (ed.), *The Backbench Diaries of Richard Crossman*
    (1981)

The case for public ownership is essentially a political case tied up with the stability of the whole economy and the transference of a great concentration of economic power from private to public control.
    In Pursuit of Progress (1953)

We should seek to hive off parts of the private sector to the nationalised sector and to encourage the nationalised sector to diversify wherever it sees the opportunity.
    What Matters Now (1972)

We have underestimated the scale of poverty in Britain.
    What Matters Now (1972)

The politics of the left and centre of this country are frozen in an out-of-date mould which is bad for the political and economic health of Britain and increasingly inhibiting for those who live within the mould. Can it be broken?
    Speech to the Parliamentary Press Gallery, 9 June 1980

We must not expect a full-scale peaceful revolution every time a Labour Government is elected.
    Speech, Blackpool, 1970

Alan Johnson

b. 1950; Labour Party politician, Home Secretary 2009–10

[Trade unions] cannot connect to a whole swath of the
workforce that thinks they died out with the ark.

Interview, 'Militant Moderate', *Progress*, February 2013

I really admire our frontbench in opposition. To me it was
horrible, sitting there on the government benches one minute
and then sitting on the opposition benches.

Interview, 'Militant Moderate', *Progress*, February 2013

Jack Jones

1913–2009; General Secretary of the Transport and General Workers'
Union 1969–78

I have never doubted the values of the Social Contract, which
I saw as a major step towards economic equality and better
conditions for working people, and used every democratic
means to gain the co-operation of fellow trade unionists.
Sometimes I felt that political leaders did not appreciate the
hard work involved in influencing rank-and-file opinion.

Union Man (1986)

Units of industry [would] eventually be seen as a series of self-
governing communities within which working people [would]
assume the role of policy-making and controlling.

The Right to Participate (1970)

Tessa Jowell

b. 1947; Minister for the Olympics 2005–10

Just as forever those who lost their lives will be remembered as
part of the Olympics and the Olympic dream that will take us
through to 2012, so too will the fortitude, solidarity, strength

and resilience of London and Londoners see us through the next seven years until the games begin in 2012.

Celebrating the 2012 win in Trafalgar Square, 1 September 2005

I started as a sceptic, but I looked at the case and I believed it was do-able… My job then was to persuade every member of Cabinet.

'The day Coe won gold', *The Observer*, 10 July 2005

K

Gerald Kaufman

b. 1930; Labour Party politician, shadow Foreign Secretary 1987–92

The longest suicide note in history.
> Considering the Labour Party's 1983 election manifesto, cited in
> D. Healey, *The Time of My Life* (1989)

You can't make socialist omelettes without breaking capitalist eggs.
> Attributed

The task of British Socialism must be, wherever possible, to save the smaller nations from this futile ideological warfare and to heal the breach between the USA and the USSR. But we cannot do this if we ourselves have taken sides either in a Communist bloc or in an anti-Bolshevik axis.
> Attributed

A socialist Britain cannot prosper so long as Europe is divided. The goal we should work for is a federation which binds together the nations now under eastern domination with the peoples of western Europe.
> Attributed

The attitude of some members of the Labour Party raises anew the fundamental question of whether we are determined to reshape the character of the British economic and social system or whether we are going to be satisfied with the coalition Government's doctrine of relying on intermittent budgetary policy to counteract the instability and injustice of an uncontrolled market and price system.
> 1950

Karl Kautsky

1854–1938; socialist theorist

Social democracy is a revolutionary party, but not a revolution-making party. We know that our objective can only be reached through revolution. But we also know that it is no more in our power to make this revolution than it is in the power of our enemies to prevent it. We have no wish either to stir up or to prepare the ground for one.

The Road to Power (1909)

Knowledge is still today a privilege of the property-owning classes: the proletariat cannot create out of itself a strong and living socialism. It must have it brought to it.

Cited in T. Wright, *Socialisms: Old and New* (1996)

Socialist consciousness is represented as a necessary and direct result of the proletarian class struggle. But this is absolutely untrue... Socialism and the class struggle arise side by side and not one out of the other; each arises under different conditions. Modern socialist consciousness can arise only on the basis of profound scientific knowledge ... The vehicle of science is not the proletariat, but the bourgeois intelligentsia: it was in the minds of individual members of this stratum that modern socialism originated, and it was they who communicated it to the more intellectually developed proletarians who, in their turn, introduced it into the proletarian class struggle where conditions allow that to be done. Thus, socialist consciousness is something introduced into the proletarian class struggle from without, and not something that arises within it spontaneously.

Cited by V. I. Lenin, *What Is To Be Done?* (1902)

John F. Kennedy

1917–63; US President 1961–63

If a free society cannot help the many who are poor, it cannot save the few who are rich.

Inaugural address, 20 January 1961

Political sovereignty is but a mockery without the means of meeting poverty and illiteracy and disease. Self-determination is but a slogan if the future holds no hope.

Address to the United Nations General Assembly, 25 September 1961

Communism has sometimes succeeded as a scavenger, but never as a leader. It has never come to power in any country that was not disrupted by war or internal corruption or both.

Address to NATO, 3 July 1963

Those who make peaceful revolution impossible will make violent revolution inevitable.

Speech at the White House, 13 March 1962

Robert F. Kennedy

1925–68; Attorney General 1961–64

Far from being a classless society, Communism is governed by an elite as steadfast in its determination to maintain its prerogatives as any oligarchy known to history.

The Pursuit of Justice (1964)

John Maynard Keynes

1883–1946; economist

Leninism is a combination of two things which Europeans have kept for some centuries in different compartments of the soul – religion and business.

Essays in Persuasion (1933)

Capitalism is the extraordinary belief that the nastiest of men, for the nastiest of reasons, will somehow work for the benefit of us all.

Attributed

[Labour] is a class party and the class is not my own. If I am going to pursue sectional interests at all, I shall pursue my own … I can be influenced by what seems to me to be justice and good sense, but the class war will find me on the side of the educated bourgeoisie.

Essays in Persuasion (1931)

[Ignorant trade unionists] once the oppressed, now the tyrants, whose selfish and sectional pretensions need to be bravely opposed.

Essays in Persuasion (1931)

The Labour Party has got tied up with all sorts of encumbering and old-fashioned luggage. They respond to anti-Communist rubbish with anti-capitalist rubbish. The consequence of all this is that, whether in or out of office, the business of orderly evolution seems likely to remain in Liberal hands.

Liberalism and Industry (1927)

We are brought to my heresy – if it is a heresy. I bring in the State. I abandon *laissez-faire* – not enthusiastically, not from contempt for that good old doctrine, but because, whether we like it or not, the conditions for its success have disappeared.

A Drastic Remedy for Unemployment (1924)

If communism achieves a certain success, it will achieve it not as an improved economic technique, but as a religion.

> *Laissez-Faire and Communism* (1926)

The Labour Party should be something more than an almshouse for the retired agitators.

> 1939

Financial Dunkirk.

> On what the 1945 Labour government faced, cited in A. Cairncross, *Years of Recovery* (1985)

Great changes will not be carried out except with the active aid of Labour. But they will not be sound or enduring unless they have first satisfied the criticism and precaution of Liberals.

> *Essays in Persuasion* (1931)

Robert Kilroy-Silk

b. 1942; former Labour Party politician; TV presenter

The conference floor erupted. And that bastard Heffer, the prima donna to outdo all prima donnas, got up and lumbered off the platform and out of the hall. The shit. The absolute shit. And that's just what I called him: the language from my parliamentary colleagues standing around me was still more colourful and apt. He'd been waiting for the opportunity, of course.

> On Eric Heffer's reaction to Neil Kinnock's anti-Militant speech at the 1985 Labour Party Conference, *Hard Labour* (1986)

Neil Kinnock

b. 1942; Labour Party leader, 1983–92

An enabling state which is at the disposal of the people … a servant state.

> Speech to Labour Party Conference (1985)

There are no circumstances in which I would order or permit the firing of a nuclear weapon.

New Socialist, October 1983

I would die for my country. But I would never allow my country to die for me.

Speech to Labour Party Conference, 30 September 1986

That appalling woman.

On Mrs Thatcher

We will govern as we have campaigned – strongly, positively, looking to the future. The contrast with the Tories could not be more sharp. They are a spent force.

Party election rally, Sheffield, 1992

We're all right. We're all right. We're all right. We're all right:

Party election rally, Sheffield, 1992

We cannot remove the evils of capitalism without taking its source of power – ownership.

Tribune, 5 December 1975

We are definitely in the last few weeks of Thatcherism – the last weeks of that job-destroying, oil-wasting, truth-twisting, service-smashing, nation-splitting bunch of twisters under a one-person government.

On 1987 general election, which Labour went on to lose

Mrs Thatcher has a great sense of propriety and she believes, as many women from her particular class believe, and certainly women with important positions believe, that it's part of their duty to be solicitous and kindly in an official way, and she is fastidious in following that through.

The Thatcher Phenomenon (1986)

'No such thing as society,' she says.
No obligation to the community.
No sense of solidarity.
No principles of sharing or caring.
'No such thing as society.'
No sisterhood, no brotherhood.
No neighbourhood.
No honouring other people's mothers and fathers.
No succouring other people's little children.
'No such thing as society.'
No number other than one.
No person other than me.
No time other than now.
No such thing as society, just 'me' and 'now'.
That is Margaret Thatcher's society.

> Speech to Labour Party Conference, 1988

May I pay tribute to you on your decision this morning. You
showed by that that you amount to more than those who have
turned against you in recent days.

> To Mrs Thatcher at Prime Minister's Questions, 22 November 1990

The Labour Party has a non-nuclear defence policy and a Labour
government will implement that policy.

> *Daily Telegraph*, 27 May 1983

We cannot engage in the expenses and risks that go with trying
to sustain ourselves as a nuclear power.

> BBC Radio, *The World This Weekend*, 1 January 1984

She only went to Venice because somebody told her she could
walk down the middle of the street.

> On Mrs Thatcher's trip to the Venice economic summit during the
> general election campaign, 9 June 1987

There is nothing in the Labour Party constitution that could or should prevent people from holding opinions which favour Leninist-Trotskyism.

Broad Left Alliance journal, October 1982

The government has neither the means nor the judgement to make large-scale manufacturing investment.

The Guardian, 2 May 1990

We can curse the irresponsibility, prejudice and power of the currency movers. All of that is justifiable. It is also idle.

Making Our Way (1986)

A lot of what Mrs Thatcher did I only blame her in part for. I blame [the Cabinet] for letting her get away with it.

11 May 1991

The press jeopardise British democracy.

Reforming the Labour Party (1994)

If Margaret Thatcher wins on Thursday, I warn you not to be ordinary, I warn you not to be young, I warn you not to fall ill, and I warn you not to grow old.

Speech, 7 June 1983

Yesterday was hers, tomorrow is ours.

On the tenth anniversary of Mrs Thatcher's election of May 1979

It's a pity others had to leave theirs on the ground at Goose Green to prove it.

In response to heckler who said Mrs Thatcher had 'shown guts' over the Falklands War, 6 June 1983

It is inconceivable that we could transform this society without a major extension of public ownership.

Marxism Today, 1983

Maggot extremists.

Describing activists with Militant tendencies, February 1986

Why am I the first Kinnock in a thousand generations to be
able to get to university? Was it because *all* our predecessors
were 'thick'? Did they lack talent – those people who could
sing, and play, and recite poetry; those people who could make
wonderful, beautiful things with their hands; those people who
could dream dreams, see visions; those people who had such a
sense of perception as to know in times so brutal, so oppressive,
that they could win their way out of that by coming together?

Speech, Llandudno, 15 May 1987

The market is potentially a powerful force for good. It can
be a remarkable co-ordinating mechanism. [It] can stimulate
innovation and productive efficiency, and provide an economic
environment in which individuals can experiment.

Making Our Way (1986)

We've stopped all that nonsense.

When considering some of the Labour Party's 'unpopular' polices

If anyone wants to know why we must conduct in this fashion,
just remember at all times … how you, each and every one of
you, sitting in this hall, each and every Labour worker watching
this conference, each and every Labour voter, yes, and some
others as well, remember how you felt on that dreadful morning
of June 10. Just remember how you felt then, and think to
yourselves: 'June the Ninth, 1983; never ever again will we
experience that'.

Speech to Labour Party Conference, 1983

In my case, of course, the managerial role was a matter of
necessity … the condition of the party made management an
obligation – so I got on with it.

Reforming the Labour Party (1994)

[The] object past, present and future of democratic socialism [is] individual freedom. And the means which democratic socialism has chosen to protect that freedom are equality and democracy.

The Future of Socialism (1985)

Collective provision has not been the enemy of individual freedom, it has been the agent of individual emancipation and for that reason it will occupy a central position in the forging of the future of socialism.

The Future of Socialism (1985)

[I was] never sure the whole party was with me. I was always dragging it, inch by inch, advancing a little, fighting more, advancing. I had to choose my ground so carefully.

Asking Around (1993)

I'll tell you what happens with impossible promises. You start with far-fetched resolutions. They are then pickled into a rigid dogma, a code, and you go through the years sticking to that, out-dated, misplaced, irrelevant to the real needs, and you end in the grotesque chaos of a Labour council – a *Labour* council – hiring taxis to scuttle round a city handing out redundancy notices to its own workers. I am telling you, no matter how entertaining, how fulfilling to short-term egos – I'm telling you, and you'll listen – you can't play politics with people's jobs and with people's services or with their homes.

Speech to Labour Party Conference, 1985

If you make change at a speed that is not agreed or acceptable to the Labour movement, then you smash into the wall of the block vote or uproar in the constituencies.

Remaking the Labour Party (1996)

The essence of social democracy is that it is not concerned with the structure of property ownership, or the transfer of economic power; it is defined in terms not of social change, but social relief, not of eradicating inequality, but relieving its most gross manifestations.

The Future of Socialism (1985)

Unity is the price of victory. Not unity for four weeks before the general election, not unity for four weeks before the European Assembly elections, but unity here and now and from henceforth, not a cosmetic disguise, but a living, working unity of a movement, of a belief and conviction, who want to win in order to save our country and our world.

Cited in C. Hughes and P. Wintour, *Labour Rebuilt* (1990)

People who are entirely defensive about the possibility of change are simply not in touch with the fact that people's opinions in this country are much more dynamic and forward-looking than some politicians give them credit for.

Interview, BBC Radio 4, 5 January 1992

Under Labour governments the City does very well and so does profitability in industry.

The Economist, 11 April 1992

Young people by definition have their future before them.

The Economist, 11 April 1992

I naturally feel a strong sense of disappointment. Not for myself ... for I am very fortunate in my personal life. But I feel dismay and sorrow for so many people in our country who do not share this personal good fortune.

Speech following the election defeat of 9 April 1992

I'm not going to be bloody kebabbed!

Temporarily suspending the interview with James Naughtie with the tape still rolling, BBC Radio 4's *The World At One*, May 1989

Spin was invented by the press, not the government.

Commenting on Alastair Campbell's resignation, quoted in *The Guardian*, 30 August 2003

Nikita Khrushchev

1894–1971; Soviet Communist politician, First Secretary 1953–64

A Communist has no right to be a mere onlooker.

Report to Communist Party Central Committee, 14 February 1956

Everyone can err, but Stalin considered that he never erred, that he was always right. He never acknowledged to anyone that he made any mistake, large or small, despite the fact that he made not a few mistakes in the matter of theory and in his practical activity.

Cited in T. H. Rigby (ed.), *Stalin* (1966)

Every year humanity takes a step towards Communism. Maybe not to you, but at all events your grandson will surely be a Communist.

Speaking to a British ambassador, 1 June 1956

Whether you like it or not, history is on our side. We will bury you.

To Western diplomats, 26 November 1956

We occupy second place in the world. We have left England behind … We have also left France behind, and comrade, there is only America left. She can be compared to a worn-out runner. United States scientists have reported that Russia will overtake America in 1970. They are quite right. That is our date.

1959

Comrades! The cult of the individuals acquired such monstrous size chiefly because Stalin himself, using all conceivable methods, supported the glorification of his own person.

Speech to the Communist Party, 25 February 1956

Politicians are the same all over. They promise to build a bridge even where there is no river.

Comment to reporters, October 1960

We are not ignorant savages anymore. You cannot frighten us as you would have done thirty years ago.

In conversation with Labour Party politicians, 24 April 1956

Everything is fluid and everything is progress towards Communism.

In conversation with American trade union leaders, 20 September 1959

If someone hits me on the left cheek, I would not turn my own. I would hit him on the right cheek, and so hard it would knock his head off.

Attributed

Comrades! We must abolish the cult of the individual decisively, once and for all; we must draw the proper conclusions concerning both ideological, theoretical and practical work.

Speech, Moscow, 25 February 1956

If you feed the people just with revolutionary slogans they will listen today, they will listen tomorrow, they will listen the day after tomorrow, but on the fourth day they will say 'To hell with you!'

New York Times, 4 October 1964

Life is short, live it up.

New York Times, 3 August 1958

In a fight you don't stop to choose your cudgels.
If we should promise people nothing better than only revolution, they would scratch their heads and say 'Isn't it better to have a good goulash?'

1 August 1964

If you live amongst the wolves, you have to act like a wolf.

The Observer, 20 September 1964

Those who wait for that must wait until a shrimp learns to whistle.

On speculation that the USSR may abandon Communism, 1955

L

Labour Party

[Labour's aim is to] bring about a fundamental and irreversible shift in the balance of power and wealth in favour of working people and their families.

Labour's Programme (1973)

A fundamental and irreversible shift in the balance of power and wealth in favour of the working class people and their families.

The aim of a Labour government as stated in the 1983 election manifesto, *New Hope for Britain* (1983)

Yesterday's Men

Slogan beneath a caricature of Conservative Party leaders, 1970

The market and competition are essential in meeting the demands of the consumer, promoting efficiency and stimulating innovation, and often the best means of securing all the myriad, incremental changes which are needed to take the economy forward.

Meet the Challenge, Make the Change (1989)

Our social and economic objectives can be achieved only through an expansion of common ownership substantial enough to give the community decisive power over the commanding heights of the economy.

Labour's Programme (1982)

Business where appropriate: government where necessary.

Looking to the Future (1990)

Two worlds, one white, well fed and free, the other coloured, hungry and struggling for equality, cannot live side by side in friendship.

Election manifesto (1959)

The true purpose of democratic socialism and, therefore, the true aim of the Labour party, is the creation of a genuinely free society in which the fundamental objective of the government is the protection and extension of individual liberty.

Democratic Socialist Aims and Values (1988)

To secure for the workers by hand or by brain the full fruit of their industry, and the most equitable distribution thereof that may be possible, upon the basis of the common ownership of the means of production, distribution and exchange, and the best obtainable system of popular administration and control of each industry and service.

Clause IV, Part IV of the Labour Party's Constitution

The Labour Party is a democratic socialist party. It believes that by the strength of our common endeavour we achieve more than we achieve alone, so as to create for each of us the means to realise our true potential and for all of us a community in which power, wealth and opportunity are in the hands of the many not the few, where the rights we enjoy reflect the duties we owe, and where we live together, freely, in a spirit of solidarity, tolerance and respect.

The 'New' Clause IV

In such an epoch of revolutionary change, those who identify laissez-faire with liberty are enemies, however unwitting, of democracy. The enlargement of freedom which we all desire cannot be achieved by opposing State intervention but only by assuring that national resources are wisely allocated and community serves humanely planned.

Signposts for the Sixties (1961)

The Labour Party is a Socialist Party, and proud of it. Its ultimate purpose at home is the establishment of the Socialist Commonwealth of Great Britain.

Let Us Face the Future (1945)

There is no wealth but life.

Labour and the Nation (1928)

Labour will plan from the ground up.

Let Us Face the Future (1945)

Oskar Lafontaine

b. 1943; German Social Democratic politician, Finance Minister 1998–99

The Social Democratic future is international.

Cited in S. Lightfoot, 'Prospects for Euro Socialism', *Renewal*, Spring 1999

David Lammy

b. 1972; Labour Party politician, Minister of State for Innovation, Universities and Skills 2008–10

Black History is too often taught in isolation.

From an article which is an adaption of two articles written by Lammy: one used as part of the foreword for Haringey's Black History Month magazine and the other published by the Young Fabians, www.davidlammy.co.uk, October 2012

While the state must provide financial support, the community must provide male role models for young men to learn from. Corporations should be encouraged to offer mentors to young men, not just sign cheques.

'Youth violence is not about race', *New Statesman*, 14 August 2008

Politicians who grew up enjoying structure, consistency, responsible male role models and an abundance of opportunities for education and enrichment need to do more than lecture others when they reach adult life.

'Youth violence is not about race', *New Statesman*, 14 August 2008

In our public life there is a palpable lack of hope, ambition and imagination. After the riots, we must ask ourselves a deeper and more searching question as a society. Out of the ashes, what kind of country do we want to build?

Out of the Ashes: Britain After the Riots (2012)

George Lansbury
1859–1940; Labour Party politician, leader 1932–35

I have no right to preach pacifism to starving people in this country and preach something else in relation to people elsewhere. And that has been a fundamental state, it has not been something of an expediency. It has been a belief that we should sooner or later in the world win our way with waiting.

Labour Party Annual Conference Report (1935)

It is certain as the day that a Labour town council, a Socialist or Communist government, would not for a day tolerate strikes in social or other services necessary for the life of the nation.

1934

Harold Laski
1893–1950; Labour Party politician, chairman 1945–46

I now recognise ... that the pluralist attitude to the State and law was a stage on the road to a Marxist understanding of them.

Grammar of Politics (1941)

The first duty of a political philosophy [is] to examine the character of the State in its actuality rather than in its idea.

The State in Theory and Practice (1935)

[The State is] an instrument, not of the community as a whole – that is an abstract entity devoid of intellectual expression – but of the class which owns the instruments of economic power.

Parliamentary Government in England (1932)

The State is their [the owners of economic power] State; and its supreme coercive power can only be directed to those objects of which they are willing to approve.

Parliamentary Government in England (1932)

The British Constitution ... is the expression of a politically democratic government; it is not the expression of a democratic society.

Parliamentary Government in England (1932)

I believe that it is the duty of the citizen to exhaust the means placed at his disposal by the constitution of the State before resorting to revolution.

The State in Theory and Practice (1935)

The fulfilment of the state-purpose can only be accomplished when the incidence of its actions is unbiased.

The State in Theory and Practice (1935)

Yes my friend, we are both Marxists. You in your way and I in Marx's.

To a heckler

The meek do not inherit the earth unless they are prepared to fight for their meekness.

Attributed

We must plan our civilisation or we must perish.

1945

We live under a system by which the many are exploited by the few, and war is the ultimate sanction of that exploitation.

Plan or Perish (1945)

Neal Lawson

b. 1963; Former lobbyist, chair of pressure group Compass

Labour's attitude to immigration will define its future.

'Come On Labour. Be Brave On Immigration For Once', *The Guardian*, 8 March 2013

Charles Leadbeater

Political theorist, author and former adviser to Tony Blair

The loss of trust in the state's ability to act as the guardian of collective social interests: the decay of traditional sources of solidarity and common identity forged through work; the growth in the importance of individual choice in consumption, the revolt against centralising sameness, the pursuit of diversity.

'Power to the Person', *Marxism Today*, October 1988

Jennie Lee

1904–88; Labour Party politician, former Minister of State at the Department of Education and Science, partner of Aneurin Bevan

Nye was born old and died young.

On Bevan

Vladimir Ilyich Lenin

1870–1924; Russian Communist leader

The European bourgeoisie has its reasons to be frightened. The proletariat has its reasons to rejoice.

Cited in A. Deutscher, *Stalin: A Political Biography* (1949)

Do we in practice pay sufficient attention to this question, which in theory every Communist considers indisputable? Of course not. Do we take proper care of the *shoots* of communism which already exist in this sphere? Again the answer is *no*. Public catering establishments, nurseries, kindergartens – here we have examples of these shoots … which can *really emancipate women* … These means are not new (like all the material prerequisites for socialism); they were created by large-scale capitalism.

A Great Beginning (1919)

The conditions for direct, open, really mass and really revolutionary struggle *do not yet exist*.

Left Wing Communism (1920)

Class political consciousness can be brought to the workers *only from without*, that is, only from the economic struggle, from outside the sphere of relations between workers and employers. The sphere from which alone it is possible to obtain this knowledge is the sphere of relationships of *all* classes and strata to the state and the government, the sphere of the interrelations between *all* classes.

What Is To Be Done? (1902)

Social Democracy is not a seminar where different ideas are compared. It is the fighting class organisation of the revolutionary proletariat … There is only one answer to revisionism: smash its face in!

Cited in N. Volsky, *Encounters with Lenin* (1968)

Internationalism (kindly note) consists in the workers of all countries shooting at each other in the name of the 'Defence of the Fatherland'.

Letter to A. G. Shlyapnikov, 27 October 1914

The idea of a lawful separation between one nationality and the other ... is a reactionary idea.

Socialism and War (1915)

Dear comrades, soldiers, sailors and workers! I am happy to hail in you the victorious Russian revolution! ... The hour is not far off when at the summons of our comrade, Karl Liebknecht, the German people will turn their weapons against their capitalist exploiters. The sun of the world socialist revolution has already risen.

Speech at the Finland Station, Petrograd, 16 April 1917

By its economic essence imperialism is monopolist capitalism. This fact alone determines the place of imperialism in history.

Imperialism, the Highest Form of Capitalism (1917)

A good man fallen among Fabians.

On George Bernard Shaw, cited in A. Ransome, *Six Weeks in Russia in 1919* (1919)

Capitalists are no more capable of self-sacrifice than a man is capable of lifting himself by the bootstraps.

Letter From Afar (1917)

Comrades, either the louse defeats socialism, or socialism defeats the louse.

Speech to the Congress of Soviets, November 1919

In one country it is impossible to accomplish such a work as a socialist revolution.

Speech, 24 October 1920

Communism is Soviet power plus the electrification of the whole country.

Report to the Congress of Soviets, 22 December 1920

This cook will give us nothing but spicy dishes.
On Stalin's election as General Secretary of the Communist Party, cited in L. Trotsky, Political Quarterly, July 1932 We cannot outline socialism. What socialism will look like when it takes on its final form we do not know and cannot say.

Cited in M. Lasky, *Utopia and Revolution*

I can't listen to music too often. It affects your nerves; you want to say nice, stupid things and stroke the heads of people who could create such beauty while living in this vile hell. And now you must not stroke anyone's head – you might get your hand bitten off. You have to hit them on the head, without any mercy.

Cited in M. Lasky, *Utopia and Revolution*

A democracy is a state which recognises the subjection of the minority to the majority. That is, an organisation for the systematic use of violence by one class against another, by one part of the population against another.

The State and Revolution (1917)

Imperialism is the monopoly stage of capitalism.

Imperialism as the Last Stage of Capitalism (1916)

Freedom is a bourgeois notion devised as a cloak for the spectre of economic slavery.

Speech, quoted in the Bolshevik Press, July 1920

The bourgeoisie is many times stronger than we. To give it the weapon of freedom of the press is to ease the enemy's cause, to help the class enemy. We do not desire to end in suicide, so we will not do this.

Pravda, 1912

To decide once every few years which member of the ruling class is to repress and crush the people through parliament – this is the real essence of bourgeois parliamentarianism, not only in parliamentary–constitutional monarchies, but also in the most democratic republics.

State and Revolution (1917)

We have said that there could not have been social-democratic consciousness among the workers. It would have had to be brought to them from without. The history of all countries shows that the working class, exclusively by its own effort, is able to develop only trade union consciousness.

What Is To Be Done? (1902)

We now stand, not only as the representatives of the proletarians of all countries but as the representatives of the oppressed peoples as well.

Attributed

During a revolution millions and tens of millions people learn in a week more than they do in a year of ordinary, somnolent life.

Attributed

We say that our morality is entirely subordinated to the interests of the proletariat's class struggle … Morality is what serves to destroy the old exploiting society and to unite all the working people around the proletariat, which is building up a new, a communist society … To a Communist all morality lies in this united discipline and conscious mass struggle against the exploiters. We do not believe in an eternal morality and we expose the falseness of all fables about morality.
The dictatorship of the proletariat is nothing else than power based upon force and limited by nothing – by no law and absolutely no rule!

Cited in G. P. Maximoff, *The Gullotine at Work* (1940)

Whenever the cause of the people is entrusted to professors, it's lost.

Attributed

The state is a special cudgel, nothing more.

The State and Revolution (1917)

It is true that liberty is precious – so precious that it must be rationed.

Cited in S. and B. Webb, *Soviet Communism: A New Civilisation?* (1935)

Revolutions are the locomotives of history. Drive them full speed ahead...

Attributed

As an ultimate objective, 'peace' simply means communist world control.

Attributed

While the State exists there is no freedom, where there is no freedom there will be no State.

The State and Revolution (1917)

After taking over the position of Secretary-General Comrade Stalin accumulated in his hands immeasurable power and I am not certain whether he will be always able to use this power with the required care.

Letter to the Communist Party Congress, December 1922

Stalin is excessively rude, and this defect, which can be freely tolerated in our midst and in contacts among communists, becomes a defect which cannot be tolerated in one holding the position of Secretary-General. Because of this I propose that the comrades consider the method by which Stalin would be removed from this position and by which another man would be selected for it, a man who, above all, would differ from Stalin in only one quality, namely, greater tolerance, greater loyalty, greater kindness and more considerate attitude towards the comrades, a less capricious temper.

Letter to the Communist Party Congress, December 1922

Pope Leo XIII
1810–1903

The present age handed over the workers, each alone and defenceless, to the unbridled greed of competitors … so that a very few and exceedingly rich men have laid a yoke of almost slavery on the unnumbered masses of non-owning workers.

Rerum Novarum (1891)

Joan Lestor
1931–98; Labour Party politician

Mrs Thatcher likes to portray herself as Mother Earth. To the poor children of this country she is Mother Hubbard and her cupboard is always bare.

October 1990

Harold Lever
1914–95; Labour Party politician, Chancellor of the Duchy of Lancaster 1974–79

Labour's leadership … knows as well as any businessman that an engine which runs on profit cannot be made to run faster without extra fuel … For their part businessmen should show less sensitivity and more sense. It is time they realised that a ringing political slogan is often used as a sop to party die-hards or as an anaesthetic while doctrinal surgery is being carried out.

Cited in L. Panitch, *Socialist Register* (1988)

Bernard Levin
1928–2004; British journalist

The Minister of Technology flung himself into the Sixties technology with the enthusiasm (not to say the language) of a newly enrolled Boy Scout demonstrating knot-tying to his indulgent parents.

On Tony Benn, *The Pendulum Years* (1976)

Karl Liebknecht
1871–1919; German socialist

The basic law of capitalism is you or I, not both you and I.

Speech to the Fourth Socialist Young People's Conference, Stuttgart, 1907

Abraham Lincoln
1809–65; US President 1861–65

These capitalists generally act harmoniously, and in concert, to fleece the people.

Speech to the Illinois legislature, 1837

Tom Litterick
1929–81; Labour Party politician

Governments and only governments win or lose elections. Oppositions do not.

Speech to Labour Party Conference, 1979

Ken Livingstone
b. 1945; Labour Party politician; Mayor of London 2000–08

One of the major problems facing Tony Blair's new Labour government is that for twelve years London has been the only capital city in Europe without a democratically elected government.
Speech, Barcelona, 19 March 1999

In politics nothing is ever wholly a defeat or a victory. Even when you are coasting home to a great victory, things are probably happening as a by-product of your success which are laying the seeds for future problems and which might mushroom into future defeats.
Cited in P. Seyd, *The Rise and Fall of the Labour Left* (1987)

Granted that all of us make an endless number of mistakes and errors, the structure of the Left is such that before you've really had time to think through that you've made a mistake, admit it to yourself and then to others, you've been denounced in the most bitter fashion.
Cited in P. Seyd, *The Rise and Fall of the Labour Left* (1987)

I'm the sort of person Mrs Thatcher's parents warned her not to talk to as a little girl. I'm quite proud of that.
8 July 1995

Historically, it was the left of the party that was most bitterly opposed to the use of professional advertising agencies and it was only after the death of Aneurin Bevan in 1960 that the Labour Party turned to professional ad men for (usually) free advice.
The Independent, 6 January 1999

He asked to see me again. I think he wants me for my body.
Remarks made to the media after meeting Secretary of State for Transport Norman Fowler (18 June 1981), cited in *Citizen Ken* (1984) by John Carvel

I take a much more pragmatic view than many people on the Left about working with Neil Kinnock. Kinnock represents the best vehicle possible for achieving socialism now.

Ham and High, 21 February 1986

The British judiciary is one of the most corrupt in the world because of politically active judges.

Daily Telegraph, 17 May 1986

If Voting Changed Anything They'd Abolish It.

Title of his autobiography, published 1987

I urge everybody to stay inside the Labour Party and fight to ensure that nothing like this ever happens again.

Statement following the London Labour Party's ballot for a Mayoral candidate in which Livingstone was defeated by Frank Dobson, *The Guardian*, 20 February 2000

George Bush is just about everything that is repellent in politics.

Quoted in the *Daily Mirror*, 9 May 2003

I just long for the day I wake up and find that the Saudi royal family are swinging from lampposts and that they've got a proper government that represents the people of Saudi Arabia.

Interview, *The Guardian*, 8 April 2004

You are just like a concentration camp guard.

Comment made to *Evening Standard* journalist Oliver Finegold, 8 February 2005. Livingstone was subsequently suspended from office

It would actually be quite nice if the American ambassador in Britain could pay the charge that everybody else is paying and not actually try and skive out of it like some chiselling little crook.

Interview, ITV, *London Today*, 27 March 2006

I want to say one thing specifically to the world today. This was not a terrorist attack against the mighty and the powerful. It was not aimed at Presidents or Prime Ministers. It was aimed at ordinary, working-class Londoners – black and white, Muslim and Christian, Hindu and Jew, young and old – an indiscriminate attempt to slaughter, irrespective of any considerations for age, for caste, for religion or whatever.

That isn't an ideology, it isn't even a perverted faith, it is just an indiscriminate attempt at mass murder – and we know what the objective is. They seek to divide Londoners. They seek to turn Londoners against each other.

Response to London bombings, 7 July 2005

In this city 300 languages are spoken and the people that speak them live side by side in harmony. This city typifies what I believe is the future of the human race and a future where we grow together and we share and we learn from each other.

Press conference, 8 July 2005

As I was saying before I was so rudely interrupted fourteen years ago…

Victory speech on being elected Mayor of London, 5 May 2000

Anybody who enjoys being in the House of Commons probably needs psychiatric help.

Quoted in *Total Politics*

[The public] should be allowed to know everything, except the nature of private relationships – unless there is hypocrisy, like some Tory MP denouncing homosexuality while they are indulging in it.

'The world is run by monsters', *New Statesman*, 9 February 2012

I think he has real ability, real intelligence, and he just never achieves his potential with it.

On Boris Johnson, 'The world is run by monsters', *New Statesman*, 9 February 2012

Clinically insane.

On Margaret Thatcher, 'The world is run by monsters', *New Statesman*,
9 February 2012

This is my last election. Forty-one years ago almost to the day,
I won my first election on a manifesto promising to build good
council housing and introduce a free bus pass for pensioners.
Now I've lived long enough to get one myself. I didn't think I
necessarily would at the time. And since then, I've won eleven
more elections and lost three. But the one I most regret losing
is this. This is the defeat I most regret, because these are the
worst times for eighty years, and Londoners needed a mayor to
get them through this very difficult period by cutting fares, by
cutting energy prices and putting people back to work building
good council homes. I am sincerely sorry to those Londoners
who desperately wanted us to win that I failed to do that and
they will continue to bear the pain of this recession without any
help from here in City Hall.

Concession speech after losing the 2012 London Mayoral election,
4 May 2012

Ken Loach

b. 1936; film director

Capitalism will never provide work or a decent life for the vast
majority of its people.

Interview, BBC TV, *Newsnight*, 11 March 2013

William Lovett

1800–77; Chartist leader

So long as the people of any country place their hopes of
political salvation *in leadership of any description*, so long will
disappointment attend them.

Public letter to Daniel O'Connell, 1843

Rosa Luxemburg
1871–1919; Polish-born socialist revolutionary

Not a man, not a farthing for this system; instead war to the knife.

Spartakusbriefe, 22 April 1916

Freedom only for the supporters of the government, only for the members of one party – however numerous they may be – is no freedom at all. Freedom is always and exclusively for one who thinks differently. Not because of any fanatical concept of 'justice' but because all that is instructive, wholesome and purifying in political freedom depends on this characteristic.

The Russian Revolution (1918)

That is why people who pronounce themselves in favour of the method of legislative reform *in place* of and in *contradistinction* to the conquest of political power and social revolution, do not really choose a more tranquil, calmer and slower road to the *same* goal, but a *different* goal. Instead of taking a stand for the establishment of a new society, they take a stand for surface modifications of the old society. If we follow the political conceptions of revisionism, we arrive at the same conclusion that is reached when we follow the economic theories of revisionism. Our programme becomes not the realisation of socialism, but the reform of capitalism; not the suppression of the system of wage labour, but the diminution of exploitation, that is, the suppression of the abuses of capitalism instead of the suppression of capitalism itself.

Reform or Revolution (1900)

M

Ramsay MacDonald

1866–1937; Labour Party politician, Prime Minister 1924, 1929–35

With the discussion of general strikes and Bolshevism and all that kind of thing, I have nothing to do at all. I respect the Constitution as much as Sir Robert Horne does.

House of Commons, 3 May 1926 on the eve of the general strike

The democratic state is an organisation of the people, democratic government is self-government, democratic law is an expression of the will of the people who have to obey the law – not perhaps the will of every individual, but the communal will voicing the need of all classes in their relation to the community.

Socialism and Society (1905)

[Practical policy must be based] not on functions [like labour], but on the complete civic unity to which functions are only contributory, and upon the citizen, of whom the worker is only a differentiated and specialised aspect ... The community idea must be the dominant note; the thought must be of the co-operation of citizens, not of workmen nor of consumers.

Parliament and Democracy (1920)

Let [the French and the Germans] put their demands in such a way that Great Britain can say that she supported both sides.

On disarmament and security in Europe, December 1932

Tomorrow every duchess in London will be wanting to kiss me!

After forming the National Government, 25 August 1931

If God were to come to me and say, 'Ramsay, would you rather be a country gentleman than a Prime Minister?' I should reply, 'Please God, a country gentleman.'

In conversation, October 1930

The civilisation of the idle or uselessly employed rich, and the civilisation of the industrious poor.

On two civilisations created by private interests, *Socialism and Society* (1905)

Parliament is a laboratory; its legislative experiences must be undertaken in precisely the same scientific frame of mind as those of the chemist or the physicist.

Socialism and Society (1905)

Socialism marks the growth of a society, not the growth of a class. The consciousness which it seeks to quicken is not one of economic class solidarity, but one of ... growth towards organic wholeness.

Socialism and Society (1905)

Poverty rather than property is the reward of labour today.

Socialism (1907)

Capital creates values too ... Therefore, labour's quarrel with capitalism is not in the sphere of production, but in that of distribution.

Socialism (1907)

There must be co-operation and not conflict between labour and capital.

Socialism: Critical and Constructive (1921)

The field upon which it [the trade union conflict] has to be fought out is the State, not the workshop; the weapon is to be the ballot box and the Act of Parliament, not collective bargaining.

The Social Unrest (1913)

If the new Labour movement were simply an attempt of Trade
Unionists to use their political power for purely sectional ends
… it would be a menace to all the qualities that mark public
life with distinction and honour… Trade Unionism in politics
must identify itself with something higher and wider than Trade
Union industrial demands. It must set those demands into a
system of national well-being; the wage earner must become
the citizen; the Union must become the guardian of economic
justice.

> Cited in D. Marquand, *Ramsay MacDonald* (1977)

There is just as much security in a political agreement as in a
regiment of soldiers or a fleet of battleships.

> 1929

As long as I hold any position in the Parliamentary Labour Party
– and I know I can speak for my colleagues also – we are not
going to take our instructions from any outside body unless we
agree with them.

> Speech to Labour Party Conference, 1928

Socialist change must be gradual and must proceed in stages,
just as the evolution of an organism does.

> *Socialism* (1907)

When the tendencies begun by scores of experiments – factory
laws, public health laws, municipalisation – are followed out,
joined together, systematised, Socialism is the result.

> *Socialism* (1907)

There can be no steadiness of industry as long as there is anarchy
in production.

> *Socialism and Society* (1905)

The life of the coming epoch germinates in the bosom of the
order which is maturing.

> *Socialism and Society* (1905)

Our pledges are the pledges of men and women who are Socialists, our pledges are the pledges of men and women who know that this system of society cannot and will not work smoothly, and that the great task of statesman of vision is to transform that system of society from the 'is' until it has become the 'is to be'; and in the course of that transformation, rightly or wrongly, my creed, and I think, the creed of the great majority, if not all my colleagues, has been evolution – evolution applied in precisely the same way as the sacrifice medical man, the scientific healer applies his knowledge and his art to the frail and ailing body.

Speech, Llandudno, 7 October 1930

John Mackintosh
1929–78; Labour Party politician

It is, I fear, basically unhealthy for a country to depend on a political system which is not backed by positive conviction and understanding, and whose original principles have become corrupted and confused.

Cited in D. Marquand, *John P. Mackintosh: On Parliament and Social Democracy* (1982)

The denial of legitimacy is a clear consequence of two concepts. First, that passage by the House of Commons is not itself an adequate indication of the consent of the community, and second, that prior consultation with recognised groups has become an essential part of the legitimising process.

Cited in D. Marquand, *John P. Mackintosh: On Parliament and Social Democracy* (1982)

Harold Macmillan

1894–1986; Conservative Party politician, Prime Minister 1957–63

He enjoys prophesying the imminent fall of the capitalist system, and is prepared to play a part, any part, in its burial, except that of mute.

On Aneurin Bevan, address to the House of Commons, 1934

If Harold Wilson ever went to school without any boots, it was merely because he was too big for them.

Reacting to Wilson's tales of childhood poverty

Denis MacShane

b. 1948; former Labour Party politician, Minister of State for Europe 2002–05

Labour may not always be able to learn from its own defeats.

French Lessons for Labour, Fabian Society (1986)

All the talk is Blair, Blair, Blair. SPD people say: 'BMW brought Rover, how can we buy Blair?' If Schmidt was the European left figure of the Seventies, and Felipe Gonzalez for the Eighties, it's Blair for the Nineties.

The Independent, 1 April 1996

John Major

b. 1943; Conservative Party politician, Prime Minister 1990–97

His idea of policy is to spend, spend, spend. He is the Viv Nicholson of politics.

On Michael Foot, comparing him to a sixties pools winner

Nelson Mandela

b. 1918; South African black liberation leader, President 1994–99

The communist bogey is an American stunt to distract the attention of the people of Africa from the real issue facing them, namely, American imperialism.

Liberation, March 1958

Peter Mandelson

b. 1953; Labour Party politician, European Commissioner for Trade 2004–08

We must ensure that our message is simply encapsulated in memorable phrases and policies explained in terms people can understand.

The Proposed Campaign On Social Policy (1995)

[Labour should] set out to unite the country by polarising opinion between those who can afford the Tories and the rest of us who can't, those who profit from the status quo and the majority who need change ... Those who like Thatcher and those who can't take any more of that boring, sanctimonious voice.

General election strategy, 27 October 1986

TV is putting tremendous pressure on us ... to turn out strong visuals so that they have interesting pictures for their news bulletins ... to have that special exclusive shot, that interesting angle that their rivals don't have.

Tribune, 29 January 1989

I'll be lucky to be offered any job, to serve in any capacity.

3 April 1997

Unemployment can never be a price worth paying.

Speech to Labour Party Conference, 1998

Totally unashamedly, we have used the Conference to project the Party to make an impact on the public.

The Guardian, 6 December 1990

Let everyone be clear. There is no complacency at the heart of New Labour. Instead a driving ambition to secure lasting and effective change.

Labour's Next Steps (1997)

Communications means throwing your net much wider than publicity. It means deciding what we say, how we say it, and which spokesmen and women we chose to say it.

Interview, *The Guardian*, 25 November 1985

You have to remember that most people lead very humdrum lives.

The Observer, 25 April 1999

The job of the centre of government is to make sure departments work together: failure of government machinery means failing the people who elected us.

The Independent, 17 September 1997

I am the nicest person I know and what I say is the truth as I see it.

Attributed

For Labour, modernisation is about far more than red roses, seductive sound-bites and fancy packaging, however, important these may be in the modern media age. It is about a fundamental reinvention of what Labour offers to the British people.

With R. Liddle, *The Blair Revolution* (1996)

The old Labour Party never sought to modernise its structures in the light of changes in society.

With R. Liddle, *The Blair Revolution* (1996)

I was born into the Labour Party, brought up in the Labour
Party and worked in the Labour Party all my adult life.

Daily Telegraph, 1 July 1999

I think I'm a cross between a crab and an ox rather than just a
crab. I'm made of strong stuff. I have got a tough hide and I can
carry a lot of weight behind me. Perhaps I'm really a bit of a
pussycat – that's how my mother would see me, anyway.

Interview with the *Daily Mirror*, 21 August 1997

I know that Tony said our project would only be complete when
the Labour Party learned to love Peter Mandelson. I think
perhaps he set the bar a little too high. Though I am trying my
best.

Speech to Labour Party Conference, 28 September 2009

Big beast in the jungle.

On John Prescott, interview with the *Daily Mirror*, 21 August 1997

I'm a fighter, not a quitter.

On being re-elected at the 2001 general election

The markets don't like instability and they don't like
uncertainty.

Interview with United Press International, 25 April 2005

I have moved on from being a British parliamentarian, I have
moved on from being a New Labour politician, I have moved on
from being the supporter in the active day-to-day sense of Tony
Blair.

Comments to European Parliament Trade Committee, 4 October 2004

I understand why the Tories will be gunning for Alastair
Campbell: because they fear his campaigning skills.

BBC Radio, *Today* programme, 7 February 2005

In my experience of these things, parties which shout about dirty tricks and the like tend to do so because they fear a direct hit in some vulnerable part of their political anatomy.

> BBC Radio, *Today* programme, 7 February 2005

It's a very good idea that we have a third-term Labour government led by Tony Blair for a full term.

> BBC Radio, *Today* programme, 27 December 2004

I have Bridget moments myself all the time.

> On being a fan of the film *Bridget Jones's Diary*, quoted in the *Daily Telegraph*, 23 November 2010

I stood up for myself, I'm not to be bullied.

> On his disagreement with Nicolas Sarkozy, the President of France, BBC News, 8 July 2008

I tend not to rule out anything in politics.

> Interview with Iain Dale in *Total Politics*, November 2010

Gordon ... you have a problem in not appearing to be the front-runner ... You have to either escalate rapidly or you need to implement a strategy to exit with enhanced position, strength and respect.

> Letter to Gordon Brown on 16 May 1994 on Brown and Blair's positions in the aftermath of the death of Labour leader John Smith

[New Labour is] intensely relaxed about people getting filthy rich as long as they pay their taxes.

> The quote first emerged in *The Guardian* in Victor Keegan's 'Economics Notebook: Raising the risk stakes', 26 October 1998 but has been variously misquoted especially removing the tax element. This was clarified by John Rentoul, *Eagle Eye*, 12 February 2013

I must return to the people whence I came.

> Mandelson's way of saying he was going to his parliamentary
> consistency, Hartlepool. Cited by J. Rentoul, *Eagle Eye*, 12 February
> 2013

I'm leaving the campaign to join pig, Peppa Pig.

> After Peppa Pig's withdrawal from a Labour Party election event,
> Labour Party news conference, 24 April 2010

I feel intensely pig sick about it.

> On Peppa Pig's withdrawal from a Labour Party election event,
> Labour Party news conference, 24 April 2010

I didn't mislead people. I know I didn't lie and I have got to
establish that.

> Commenting on his resignation from government over the Hinduja
> passport affair, *Independent on Sunday*, 4 February 2001

Stop walking away. Stop the silence. Stop the name calling. Stop
the blame game.

> News conference urging the recommencement of peace talks in
> Northern Ireland, 16 March 2000

I am told I am the PM's Willy, but he already has a pair of Balls
in the Cabinet.

> Press gallery lunch quoted in the *Daily Mail*, 14 July 2009

If people started to like me too much, I would lose all my power.

> Quoted in *The Guardian*, 'The Ministry of Truth', 9 August 1997

I think I probably did inhale a bit too much.

> On taking too much pleasure from publicity, interview with Piers
> Morgan, BBC TV, *Tabloid Tales*, 8 May 2003

I am, and always have been, a member of the Labour family –
and when times get tough, families pull together.

> *The Guardian*, 6 October 2008, quoting an interview with Sky News

From now on, we're joined at the hip.

> On his relationship with Gordon Brown, quoted in *The Guardian*,
> 18 February 2009

I do think he [Gordon] is a winner. He has got a very solid body of beliefs. There is nothing surface or superficial about Gordon Brown. He has real depth and I think people want to see that in their nation's leader.

> On the Blair/Brown deal, September 2006, quoted in *The Guardian*,
> 'In quotes: Mandelson on Brown', 3 October 2008

The reason why Gordon's speech at conference [2008] was a success was that it opened more of a window on to Gordon Brown ... The public want to feel a connection, a personal one, with their prime ministers. They know he has a full head of policy ideas and experience. But they also want to know more about him. These are serious times. But that doesn't mean he has to be only about policy, and he showed another side of him.

> Supporting Gordon Brown, quoted in *The Guardian*, 'In quotes:
> Mandelson on Brown', 3 October 2008

Why should I have that guy running down the country? Who the **** is he?

> Following Starbucks CEO Howard Schultz's complaints about the
> UK economy saying that 'the concern for us is Western Europe and
> specifically the UK. The UK is in a spiral' cited in the *Daily Telegraph*,
> 'Peter Mandelson launches fierce attack on Starbucks chief over UK
> economy', 18 February 2009

That's why voters who flirt with Nick Clegg are likely to end up married to David Cameron.

> Commenting in his fourth 'State of the Race' memo to Labour Party
> members and supporters about voting for the Liberal Democrats,
> 26 April 2010

Some of that guacamole.

> Buying supper at a chippie in his former Hartlepool constituency, Mandelson allegedly asked for haddock, chips and 'some of that guacamole' – mistaking the mushy peas for the avocado dip. However, the same story was being used years before by Militant about various Labour right-wingers in Liverpool. The Mandelson story was first reported in the 'John North' column in the Northern Echo and was similar to stories told about Harold Macmillan when he was MP for Stockton before the war. Mandelson dismisses the whole story in his autobiography, *The Third Man*

Rumours, rumours, rumours.

> On allegations made in Julia Langdon's biography of Mo Mowlam, speaking on BBC TV's *Breakfast With Frost*, 10 September 2000

I am still a new Labour man.

> Speech, CBI London annual dinner, 21 March 2013

Thomas Mann
1875–1955; German author and critic

Every reasonable human man should be a moderate Socialist.
> *New York Times*, 18 June 1950

Tom Mann
1856–1941; syndicalist

The outlook for the future is not that of a centralised official bureaucracy giving instructions and commands to servile subordinates (but) ... the coming of associations of equals. As a collectivist and a member of the ILP, I know for a certainty that the greatest hindrance to the democratic movement of the present time is the lack of effective industrial organisation, backed up by equally effective political organisation, for purposes of industrial change.

What is the ILP Driving At? (1894)

There is no possibility of achieving economic freedom unless the workers themselves are conscious that what they suffer from, as a class, is economic subjugation. Workers must organise at the point of production.

The Industrial Syndicalist (1910)

The engines of war to fight the workers' battle to overthrow the capitalist class, and to raise the general standard of life while so doing, must be of the workers' making. The unions are the workers' own.

The Industrial Syndicalist (1910)

The Industrial Syndicalist declares that to run industry through Parliament, i.e. by State machinery would be even more mischievous to the working class than the existing method, for it would assuredly mean that the capitalist class would, through Government departments, exercise over natural forces, and over the workers, a domination even more rigid than is the case today.

The Industrial Syndicalist (1910)

It [Parliament] was not brought into existence to enable the working class to obtain ownership and mastery over the means of production. Parliament was brought into existence by the ruling class to have more effective means of dominating and subjugating the working class.

The Industrial Syndicalist (1910)

With the experience of Russia to guide us, I entirely agree that there will be a period, short or long, when the dictatorship of the proletariat must be resorted to.

Tom Mann's Memoirs (1923)

David Marquand
b. 1934; political scientist; former Labour Party politician; founder
member of the SDP

Britain's adjustment problems have as much to do with politics
as with economics, and with tacit political understandings as
with political institutions.

The Unprincipled Society (1988)

It was the capitalism of the long post-war boom, the capitalism
of *Mitbestimmung* and the Commissariat Général du Plan, the
capitalism of the paid holidays, the tight labour markets and the
rising welfare expenditures that won the race with the regimes
of eastern Europe, not the capitalism of the Great Depression.
If the contest had been between Herbert Hoover and the
command economy, the command economy might have won.
Labour's class appeal has always been fundamental to it.

The Progressive Dilemma (1991)

The capitalist free market is a marvellous servant, but a
disastrous master. In one of the greatest achievements of the
second half of the twentieth century, a few favoured societies
learned to convert it from master to servant. The danger now is
that a smug and vainglorious capitalism will not remember the
lesson.

After Socialism (1993)

How can a fragmented society make itself whole? How can a
culture permeated by possessive individualism restore the bonds
of community?

The Unprincipled Society (1988)

Among left-of-centre Keynesian social democrats, equality came
to be seen as a good in itself, irrespective of the uses to which
the fruits of egalitarian policies were put.

The Ideas That Changed Post-War Britain (1996)

Labour ministers discovered – or thought they had discovered – that, in good hands, the Westminster model could be the engine of a social revolution. For social democrats of Crosland's generation, the point of political activity was to get back into the engine room and reach for the levers. There was no need to worry about the finer points of its design.

Times Literary Supplement, 1 April 1997

Labour's institutional revolution should go wide and deep, taking in all those institutions whose unreformed condition blocks the path to a more decent, dynamic and democratic society. Financial institutions have to be harnessed to the needs of the real economy. Company structures should be remodelled to incorporate the interests of an enlarged range of stakeholders. The privatised utilities need to be reorganised as public interest companies. New institutions are required to run a reformed welfare state. The public schools have to be opened up. The institutions of professional power must have clearer and stronger public accountability.

With T. Wright, *The Guardian*, 23 October 1995

Pluralism is not a panacea.

Must Labour Win? (1998)

'Keynesian social democracy' became, for most of the time, a technocratic philosophy rather than a political one: a philosophy of social engineering, rather than of persuasion, negotiation and debate.

Beyond Social Democracy (1987)

Don Marquis

1878–1937; journalist

When a man tells you that he got rich through hard work, ask him whose.

O Rare Don Marquis (1962)

Karl Marx

1818–83; German political theorist

Communism as a complete naturalism is humanism, and a complete humanism is naturalism. It is the *definitive* resolution of the antagonism between man and nature, and between man and man. It is the true solution of the conflict between existence and essence, between objectification and self-affirmation, between freedom and necessity, between individual and species. It is the solution of the riddle of history and knows itself to be the solution.

Economic and Philosophical Manuscripts (1844)

By bourgeoisie is meant the class of modern capitalists, owners of the means of social production and employers of wage labour. By proletariat, the class of modern wage labourers who, having no means of production of their own, are reduced to selling their labour power in order to live.

With F. Engels, *Manifesto of the Communist Party*, Footnote (1848)

Constant labour of one uniform kind destroys the intensity and flow of a man's animal spirits, which find recreation and delight in mere change of activity.

Das Kapital (1867–94)

Capital produces essentially capital.

Das Kapital (1867–94)

Communism is for us not a stable state which is to be established, an *ideal* to which reality will have to adjust itself. We call communism the *real* movement which abolishes the present state of things.

With F. Engels, *The German Ideology* (1846)

Accumulate, accumulate! That is Moses and the prophets! ... Accumulation for accumulation's sake, production for production's sake; by this formula classical economy expressed the historical missions of the bourgeoisie, and did not for a single instant deceive itself over the birth-throes of wealth.

Das Kapital (1867–94)

Religion is the sigh of the oppressed creatures, the heart of a heartless world, just as it is the soul of soulless conditions. It is the opium of the people.

A Contribution to the Critique of Hegel's Philosophy of Right (1844)

Always but momentary and forcible solutions of the existing contradictions. They are violent eruptions which for a time restore the disturbed equilibrium.

On crises, *Das Kapital* (1867–94)

A spectre is haunting Europe – the spectre of Communism.

With F. Engels, *Manifesto of the Communist Party* (1848)

The history of all hitherto existing society is the history of class struggles.

With F. Engels, *Manifesto of the Communist Party* (1848)

The proletariat alone is a really revolutionary class. The other classes decay and finally disappear in the face of modern industry; the proletariat is its special essential product.

With F. Engels, *Manifesto of the Communist Party* (1848)

The essential condition for the existence and the sway of the bourgeois class is the formation and augmentation of capital; the condition for capital is wage labour. Wage labour rests exclusively on competition between labourers. The advance of industry, whose involuntary promoter is the bourgeoisie, replaces the isolation of labourers, due to competition, by their revolutionary combination, due to association. The development of modern industry, therefore, cuts from under its feet the very foundation on which the bourgeoisie produces and appropriates products. What the bourgeoisie, therefore, produces, above all, is its own gravediggers. Its fall and the victory of the proletariat are equally inevitable.

With F. Engels, *Manifesto of the Communist Party* (1848)

Political power, properly so called, is merely the organised power of one class for oppressing another.

With F. Engels, *Manifesto of the Communist Party* (1848)

Let the ruling classes tremble at a Communist revolution. The proletarians have nothing to lose but their chains. They have a world to win. WORKING MEN OF ALL COUNTRIES UNITE!

With F. Engels, *Manifesto of the Communist Party* (1848)

What I did that was new was to demonstrate:
1: that the *existence of classes* is merely linked to *particular phases in the development of production*;
2: that class struggle necessarily leads to the *dictatorship of the proletariat*;
3: that this dictatorship itself constitutes the transition to the abolition of *all classes* and a *classless society*.

Letter to J. Weydemeyer, 1852

The philosophers have only interpreted the world in various ways; the point is to change it.

Theses on Feuerbach (1888)

Capital is dead labour that, vampire-like, lives only by sucking living labour, and lives the more, the more labour is sucks.

Das Kapital (1867–1894)

Social progress can be measured exactly by the social position of the fair sex.

Selected Correspondence, 1846–1895 (1934)

If new money, according to Augier, 'comes into the world with a congenital bloodstain on one cheek', capital comes dripping from head to foot, from every pore, with blood and dirt.

Das Kapital (1867–1894)

Labour in a white skin cannot be free so long as labour in a black skin is branded.

Das Kapital (1867–1894)

The English have all the material requisites for the revolution. What they lack is the spirit of generalisation and revolutionary ardour.

Private circular against the Bakuninists, January 1870

The working men's Paris, in the act of its heroic self-holocaust, involved in its flames buildings and monuments. While tearing to pieces the living body of the proletariat, its rulers must no longer expect to return triumphantly into the intact architecture of their abodes ... The bourgeoisie of the whole world, which looks complacently upon the wholesale massacre after the battle, is convulsed by horror at the desecration of brick and mortar.

The Civil War in France (1871)

All I know is that I am not a Marxist.

Letter from Friedrich Engels, 5 August 1890

Between capitalist and communist society lies the period of the revolutionary transformation of the one into the other. Corresponding to this is also a political transition period in which the state can be nothing but the revolutionary dictatorship of the proletariat.

Critique of the Gotha Programme (1875)

From each according to his abilities, to each according to his needs.

Critique of the Gotha Programme (1875)

All the houses, in our time, are marked with a mysterious red cross. The judge is history, the executioner is the proletariat.

Cited in A. Camus, *The Rebel* (1951)

The arch-philistine Jeremy Bentham was the insipid, pedantic, leather-tongued oracle of the bourgeois intelligence of the nineteenth century.

Das Kapital (1867–94)

History does nothing. It does not possess immense riches, it does not fight battles. It is men, real, living men who do all this … History is nothing but the activity of men in pursuit of their ends.

A Contribution to the Critique of Political Economy (1859)

The ultimate aim of this most bourgeois of lands would seem to be the establishment of a bourgeois aristocracy and a bourgeois proletariat, side by side with the bourgeoisie … The revolutionary energy of the British workers has oozed away. Better the whole world should be destroyed and perish utterly than that a free man should refrain from one act to which his nature moves him.

Cited in I. Berlin, *Karl Marx: His Life and Environment* (1939)

In the social production of their life, men enter into definite relations that are indispensable and independent of their will, relations of production which correspond to a definite stage of development of their material productive forces. The sum total of these relations of production constitutes the economic structure of society, the real foundation, on which rises a legal and political superstructure and to which correspond definite forms of social consciousness. The mode of production of material life conditions the social, political, and intellectual life process in general. It is not the consciousness of men that determine their being, but, on the contrary, their social being that determines their consciousness.

A Contribution to the Critique of Political Economy (1859)

So long as the proletariat is yet insufficiently developed to constitute itself as a class, these theoreticians are merely utopians who, to meet the wants of the oppressed classes, improvise systems and go in search of a regenerating science. But in the measure that history moves forward, and with it the struggle of the proletariat assumes clearer outlines, they no longer need to seek science in their minds; they have only to take note of what is happening before their eyes and become its mouthpiece ... From this moment, science which is a product of the historical movement, has associated with it, has ceased to be doctrinaire, and has become revolutionary.

Poverty of Philosophy (1847)

Individuals are dealt with only in so far as they are the personification of economic categories, embodiments of particular class relations and class interests. My standpoint, from which the evolution of the economic formation of society is viewed as a process of natural history, can less than any other make the individual responsible for relations whose creature he socially remains.

Das Kapital (1867–94)

Force is the midwife of every old society pregnant with a new one.

On violent revolution, *Das Kapital* (1867–94)

The emancipation of the working classes must be conquered by the working classes themselves.

Provisional Rules of the First International

We know of the allowances we must make for the institutions, customs and traditions of the various countries; and we do not deny that there are countries such as America, England, and I would add Holland if I knew your institutions better, where the working people may achieve their goal by peaceful means. If that is true, we must also recognise that in most of the continental countries it is force that will have to be the lever of our revolutions.

Speech, Amsterdam, 1872

The task of the really revolutionary party is to carry through the strictest centralisation.

March address, 1850

The political form at last discovered under which to work out the economic emancipation of labour.

The Civil War in France (1871)

The existence of religion is the existence of a defect ... Religion for us no longer has the force of a basis of secular deficiencies, but only that of a phenomenon. We do not change secular questions into theological ones. We change theological ones into secular ones. History has for long enough been resolved into superstition. We now resolve superstition into history.

On the Jewish Question (1843)

There is no greater stupidity than for people of general aspirations to marry and so surrender themselves to the small miseries of domestic and private life.

Letter to Engels, 1856

History repeats itself, the first time as tragedy, the second time as farce.

Talking about Hegel's remarks that all great world-historic facts and personages appear, so to speak, twice. *The Eighteenth Brumaire of Louis Napoleon* (1852)

Pierre Mauroy

b. 1928; French socialist politician, Prime Minister 1981–84

One does not salute the victory of the Left with devaluation.

C'est ici le chemin (1982)

James Maxton

1885–1946; Labour Party politician

All I say is, if you cannot ride two horses you have no right in the circus.

> Opposing the disaffiliation of the Scottish Labour Party from the Labour Party, *Daily Herald*, 12 January 1931

Sit down man, you're a bloody disgrace.

> To Ramsay MacDonald as he made his last speech in the House of Commons

Margaret McDonagh

b. 1961; General Secretary of the Labour Party 1998–2001

For me success will be to complete the modernisation of our party.

> Speech to Labour Party Conference, 1998

Jimmy McGovern

b. 1949; award-winning scriptwriter

It's very hard to be a real socialist.

> Interview, *Big Issue*, 9 October 2012

Michael Meacher

b. 1939; Labour Party politician, Minister for the Environment 1997–2003

[There is] no socialist objection to the technical conception of a market.

> *Tribune*, 4 December 1987

Personally I think that she has the qualities of a very great politician. I believe she has tremendous conviction, she has drive, she has a commitment, she is totally genuine.

On Mrs Thatcher, 1985

In the last analysis socialism in Britain means using resources in a planned way to serve the needs of the people. For this to be possible Britain must become more self-reliant.

Socialism with a Human Face (1982)

James Meade

1907–95; socialist theorist

The problem of unemployment is capable of solution without any revolutionary changes in our economic system.

An Introduction to Economic Policy and Analysis (1937)

In those industries in which there is least perfect competition … there is greatest need for state control of industry.

Cited in E. Durbin, *New Jerusalems* (1985)

Ian Mikardo

1908–93; Labour Party politician

Men sometimes behave like lemmings, but we're not lemmings: when we get to the cliff we take a peek over the edge before we decide whether to jump. And there are rapidly increasing numbers of us who don't like, and are drawing back from, what we've seen in that peek over the edge.

Back-bencher (1988)

If they [members of the Labour Left] get together and organise they are condemned as sectarian and as a threat to the solidarity of the Movement, and they are thereby crushed, and if they remain informal and unorganised they are out-manoeuvred and picked off one at one at a time.

Cited in P. Seyd, *The Rise and Fall of the Labour Left* (1987)

George Mikes

1912–87; Hungarian-born journalist and author

The one class you do *not* belong to and are not proud of at all is the lower-middle class. No one ever describes himself as belonging to the lower-middle class.

How to be Inimitable (1966)

David Miliband

b. 1965; former Labour Party politician, Foreign Secretary 2007–10

To reinvent the left is to give to its practice a cutting edge that the old formulas no longer possess, and to make possible radical changes that are badly needed.

Reinventing the Left (1995)

Governments now recognise that the market is a good servant, but not a good master. Market mechanisms should further public purposes.

Daily Telegraph, 15 July 1999

Hooey and nonsense.

On reports of a rift with his brother, Ed, Labour Party Conference fringe event, 25 September 2011

I promise you the soap opera is not back and certainly not back for daily episodes with me in frontline politics. The really important thing is that the country sees that the Labour party is renewing itself, which it is under Ed's leadership, and that it is able to have real discussion about the future of the country ... I think he's doing it with purpose, with conviction, with some success actually in a number of areas ... There is not going to be [a leadership contest]. Ed has been elected to fight the next election and I think he is going to fight it with real courage and conviction.

BBC TV, *BBC Breakfast*, 6 February 2012

Gordon is the best qualified and will be the best Prime Minister and best leader of the party.

Quoted in *The Guardian*, 2 March 2007

Social justice is what gets me up in the morning.

Quoted in *The Guardian*, 2 March 2007

Our generation has the chance to play with new ideas. Those sticking to the Left have to believe in something. I think you have to believe that your friends will get it together again.

Profile, *Daily Telegraph*, 30 July 2008

I believe in the potential of inclusion, the power of opportunity and our responsibility to extend it to all.

Maiden speech in the House of Commons, 25 June 2001

I think it's about good judgement and I think I did the right thing for the country, because it was important in the middle of an economic crisis to have a strong government, but I also think I did the right thing for the party because I wasn't willing to make a bad situation worse.

On not challenging Gordon Brown for the leadership of the Labour Party, profile, BBC online, 29 September 2010

I have had the extraordinary privilege to represent my constituents in Parliament; to lead major change in schools, local government and environmental policy; and, for three years, to represent our country in the wider world as Foreign Secretary.

Letter of resignation to Chair of South Shields Labour Party, 27 March 2013

A moral economy. A good society. An open, creative, campaigning, united Labour Party.

> Speech drafted in event of being elected Labour Party leader, published in *The Guardian*, 10 June 2011

I feared being a distraction in whatever role I played in Westminster.

> On his resignation from Parliament, interview with Nick Robinson, BBC, 27 March 2013

Ed Miliband

b. 1969; Labour Party politician, leader 2010–

We've got to take politics back to where it belongs: to you.

> Speech, 'One Nation Labour', 23 March 2013

On charities, the reality is that the Prime Minister is not making the rich worse off. He is making charities worse off. Over the past month we have seen the charity tax shambles, the churches tax shambles, the caravan tax shambles and the pasty tax shambles, so we are all keen to hear the Prime Minister's view on why he thinks, four weeks on from the Budget, even people within Downing Street are calling it an omnishambles Budget.

> Prime Minister's Questions, 18 April 2012, helping to popularise the term 'omnishambles' first heard in the BBC political satire, *The Thick of It*

Sad to hear that Bob Holness has died. A generation will remember him fondly from Blackbusters.

> Deleted tweet, 6 January 2012, should have read *Blockbusters*

My beliefs will run through everything I do. My beliefs, my values are my anchor and when people try to drag me, as I know they will, it is to that sense of right and wrong, that sense of who I am and what I believe, to which I will always hold.

> Speech to Labour Party Conference, 28 September 2010

Freedom and opportunity are precious gifts and the purpose of our politics is to expand them, for all our people.
Speech to Labour Party Conference, 28 September 2010

I suppose not everyone has a dad who wrote a book saying he didn't believe in the Parliamentary road to socialism.
Speech to Labour Party Conference, 28 September 2010

I don't believe in God personally but I have great respect for those people who do and different people have different religious views in this country.
Interview, BBC Radio 5 Live, 29 September 2010

I come from a generation that suffered school lessons in portacabins and crumbling hospitals. I tell you one thing, for the eighteen years they were in power the Tories did nothing to fix the roof when the sun was shining.
Speech to Labour Party Conference, 28 September 2010

Let the message go out – a new generation has taken charge of Labour which is optimistic about our country, optimistic about our world, optimistic about the power of politics. We are optimistic and together we will change Britain.
Speech to Labour Party Conference, 28 September 2010

The most important lesson of New Labour is this: every time we made progress we did it by challenging the conventional wisdom.
Speech to Labour Party Conference, 28 September 2010

The new generation of Labour is different. Different attitudes, different ideas, different ways of doing politics.
Speech to Labour Party Conference, 28 September 2010

Look, of course it was a bruising leadership contest and as time goes on that sort of recedes and that's good for our relationship.

I wouldn't take it as indication about a change in his view, he's not coming back to the shadow Cabinet – but the door is open.

Interview, *Daily Mirror*, 9 January 2013

I'm my own man.

Speech to Labour Party Conference, 27 September 2011

I think that those labels don't help … that's not the way I would see my leadership. It's not about some lurch to the Left, absolutely not. Look, I'm for the centre ground of politics, but it's about defining where the centre ground is. You see my issue about what happened to New Labour is that at the beginning, we were a radical and reforming government. We were people who were hungry for change in Britain. We said there are injustices, there are problems in our society, we need to sort them out. I'm afraid we became the Establishment.

BBC TV, interview with Andrew Marr, 26 September 2010

I aspire to be your Prime Minister not for more of the same. But to write a new chapter in our country's history. The promise of Britain lies in its people The tragedy of Britain is that it is not being met. My mission. Our mission. To fulfil the promise of each so we fulfil the promise of Britain

Speech to Labour Conference, 27 September 2011

I had a deviated septum and it needed repositioning. Typical Labour leader. He gets elected and everything moves to the centre.

Speech to Labour Conference, 27 September 2011

David is very supportive of me, we talk a lot, he's an asset to our party and our relationship is good.

On the relationship with his brother, David. Interview with *Grazia*, 11 December 2012

I don't really watch *Downton*. But I would probably choose it over *Strictly*.

On *Downton Abbey* vs. *Strictly Come Dancing*, interview with *Grazia*, 11 December 2012

Proud? I'm not sure. Sort of accepting. Look, one thing is, you don't try and pretend to be something you're not.

On being called a geek, interview with *Grazia*, 11 December 2012

I think I'm a pretty normal guy. It's in the eye of the beholder. Interview, BBC Radio, Today programme, 28 September 2011 It is about substance. It is absolutely about substance.

Interview, BBC Radio, *Today* programme, 28 September 2011

Predistribution is about saying, 'We cannot allow ourselves to be stuck with permanently being a low-wage economy and hope that through taxes and benefits we can make up the shortfall.

Speech at the Stock Exchange, 6 September 2012

One Nation: a country where everyone has a stake. One Nation: a country where prosperity is fairly shared. One Nation: where we have a shared destiny, a sense of shared endeavour and a common life that we lead together. That is my vision of One Nation. That is my vision of Britain. That is the Britain we must become.

Speech to Labour Party Conference, 2 October 2012

It will be to Labour that [this] squeezed middle must look to understand their hopes. They and their concerns will be at the heart of our policy review and plans to change Britain.

'Ed Miliband: Labour must be a force for optimism', *Daily Telegraph*, 26 November 2010

My late father would have loved the idea of Red Ed. He would have been disappointed that it's not true.

On his nickname and his Marxist historian father Ralph Miliband, speech to Labour Party Conference, 2 October 2012

A new generation has taken over and it's not about the old labels anymore.

BBC TV, interview with Andrew Marr, 26 September 2010

These strikes are wrong at a time when negotiations are going on.

Interview with Damon Green, which included the same basic quote repeated six times in response to a series of different questions, 30 June 2011

Ralph Miliband

1924–94; Marxist theorist

Of political parties claiming socialism to be their aim, the Labour Party has always been one of the most dogmatic – not about socialism but about the parliamentary system.

Parliamentary Socialism (1961)

Social democracy, for the most of its existence, has been primarily engaged in political brokerage between labour and the established order. This is a function which is of crucial importance to modern capitalism.

New Reasoner (1958)

What the present Labour leaders are basically about is … the more efficient and … the more humane functioning of British capitalism. What distinguishes them from their Tory and Liberal political colleagues and competitors is not their will to create a socialist society on the basis of the social ownership and control of economic power … but a greater propensity to invoke state intervention in economic and social life than these competitors are willing to accept.

The Socialist Register (1966)

A party of modest social reform in a capitalist system within whose
confines it is ever more firmly and by now irrevocably rooted.

On the Labour Party, *Parliamentary Socialism* (1961)

This is the belief that because of A and B are not *totally* different,
they are not *really* different at all.

On Marxists, cited in T. Wright, *Socialisms: Old and New* (1996)

The available classical writings are simply silent or extremely
perfunctory over major issues of politics and political theory.

Marxism and Politics

Lewis Minkin

Writer on the Labour movement, lecturer

The Conference set the principles; the parliamentarians
applied them. The Conference took the policy decisions, the
parliamentarians decided upon their timing and application.
The parliamentarians were an arm of the movement but they
remained an autonomous body regulating their own affairs.

The Labour Party Conference (1978)

Austin Mitchell

b. 1934; Labour Party politician

With the re-emergence of the old problems, there is even
greater need for the old Labour Party.

The Case for Labour (1983)

Altruism is generated by affluence.

The Case for Labour (1983)

It seems almost unbelievable that intelligent men in responsible
governments should make such impossible plans.

Four Years in the Death of the Labour Party (1983)

To lead was to betray. Leadership itself was an anti-social act, an indictable offence. Leaders would sell out – unless they were stopped.

Four Years in the Death of the Labour Party (1983)

Policy would be formulated through the wishes of the activists coming up in resolutions passed by Conference, then wedded into a Manifesto, not by the parliamentary party which had abused its independence, but by a National Executive dependent on the Party activists. That Manifesto would then become a binding mandate.

Four Years in the Death of the Labour Party (1983)

An ermine-lined dustbin, an up-market geriatric home with a faint smell of urine.

On the House of Lords

Parliament's role is like that of the Mothers' Union in the governance of the Church of England, and our debates about as relevant. We are there to be used, abused or ignored. It's a dog's life.

Attributed

François Mitterrand
1916–96; French Socialist politician, President 1981–95

You, Attali, are a mere chapter. I am the entire volume.

To his adviser, Jacques Attali, *The Observer*, 29 December 1991

To have great designs is the privilege of great nations. In today's world there can be no greater exigency for our country than to forge a new alliance between socialism and freedom and no greater ambition than to be able to offer it to tomorrow's world.

Speech, 21 May 1981

John Monks
b. 1945; General Secretary of the Trades Union Congress, 1993–2003

My biggest mistake was to believe so long in conflict being inevitable in the world of work.
The Independent, 14 April 1999

British entry to the Euro is both inevitable and, on balance, an advantage.
The Observer, 9 May 1999

Bernard Law Montgomery
1887–1976; Field Marshal

Anyone who votes Labour ought to be locked up.
Speech, 1959

Jo Moore
b. 1963; special adviser to Stephen Byers 1999–2002

It is now a very good day to get out anything we want to bury. Councillors' expenses?
Memo written on 11 September 2001, often referred to as 'a good day to bury bad news'

Rhodri Morgan
b. 1939; Labour Party politician

The Sir Humphreys have drawn the covered wagons of Whitehall into a circle in order to deny information.
On the Freedom of Information Bill, 24 May 1999

Estelle Morris

b. 1952; Labour Party politician, Secretary of State for Education and
Skills 2001–02

I've learned what I'm good at and also what I'm less good at.
I'm good at dealing with the issues and in communicating to the
teaching profession. I am less good at strategic management of a
huge department and I am not good at dealing with the modern
media. All this has meant that with some of the recent situations
I have been involved in, I have not felt I have been as effective as
I should be, or as effective as you need me to be.

> Resignation letter, resigning as Secretary of State for Education and
> Skills, 23 October 2002

Bill Morris

b. 1938; General Secretary of the Transport and General Workers' Union
1992–2003

I believe that there are four issues which should concern us most
of all – full employment, ending low pay, repairing the welfare
state and scrapping the anti-trade union laws passed by the
Tories. These four issues stand together.

> *Socialist Campaign News*, June 1995

William Morris

1834–96; social reformer

So long as the system of competition in the production and
exchange of the means of life goes on, the degradation of the
arts will go on; and if that system is to last for ever, then art is
doomed, and will surely die; that is to say, civilisation will die.

> *Art Under Plutocracy* (1883)

The chief accusation I have to bring against the modern state of society is that it is founded on the art-lacking or unhappy labour of the greater part of men.

Art Under Plutocracy (1883)

The very essence of competitive commerce is waste; the waste that comes of the anarchy of war.

Art Under Plutocracy (1883)

The most grinding poverty is a trifling evil compared with the *inequality* of classes.

Letter to Andreas Scheu, 5 September 1883

It is not revenge we want for poor people, but happiness; indeed, what revenge can be taken for all the thousands of years of the sufferings of the poor?

How We Live and How We Might Live (1884)

When our opponents say, as they sometimes do, How should we be able to procure the luxuries of life in a Socialist society? answer boldly, We could not do so and we don't care, for we don't want them and won't have them; and indeed, I feel sure that we cannot if we are all free men together.

'The Society of the Future' (1887)

Not one, not one, nor thousands must they slay
But one and all if they would dusk the day.

A Death Song (1887)

I call myself a Communist ... All genuine Socialists admit that Communism is a necessary development of Socialism.

Socialism and Anarchism (1889)

Truth to say, my friends, I do not know what Marx's Theory of Value is, and I'm damned if I want to know. Truth to say, my friends, I have tried to understand Marx's theory, but political economy is not in my line, and much of it appears to me to be dreary rubbish. But I am, I hope, a Socialist none the less. It is enough political economy for me to know that the idle rich class is rich and the working class is poor, and that the rich are rich because they rob the poor.

Cited in J. B. Glasier, *William Morris and the Early Days of the Socialist Movement* (1921)

Forever must the rich hate the poor.

The Earthly Paradise, 'Bellerephon at Argos' (1868–70)

This living death of Commercialism ... no rest, no beauty, no leisure ... all England become like the heart of Lancashire is now: a breeding sty for flesh and blood machines.

Art and the People (1883)

Everything made should be a joy to the maker and a joy to the user.

Useless Work and Useless Toil (1884)

Why should one third of England be stifled and poisoned with smoke ... why must Yorkshire and Lancashire rivers run with filth and dye?

At a Picture Show (1884)

A transition period during which people would be getting rid of the habits of mind bred by the long ages of tyranny and commercial competition and be learning that it is to the interest of each that all should thrive.

On State Communism, *What Socialists Want* (1888)

We should have so much leisure from the production of what are called 'utilities' that any group of people would have leisure to satisfy its craving for what are looked on as superfluities, such as enjoying works of art, research ... literature.

Why I Am A Communist (1894)

Herbert Morrison

1888–1965; Labour Party politician, Lord President of the Council, 1945–51

Work is the call. Work at war speed. Goodnight – and go to it.
  Broadcast as Minister of Supply, 22 May 1940

We have turned our backs on the economics of scarcity.
  Speech to Labour Party Conference, 1946

An enemy of reasonable culture.
  On commercial television

It is essential that Socialism should be sound public business as
well as being healthy in its social morality.
  Socialisation and Transport (1933)

Don't trust that man, he is wicked.
  On Aneurin Bevan, cited in D. Marquand, *The Progressive Dilemma*
  (1991)

Socialism is what a Labour government does.
  Attributed

Advance must be followed by detailed consolidation, and by
exploiting the territory that had been gained. That is the state
we are now reaching. And if we go on always stretching out our
hands for more and not making good the gains we have claimed,
only disaster can follow.
  Speech to Labour Party Conference, 1948

Oswald Mosley

1896–1980; former Labour Party politician, English fascist leader

I am not, and never have been, a man of the right. My position
was on the left and is now in the centre of politics.
  Letter to *The Times*, 26 April 1968

Could a wage giving a civilised standard be paid until reorganisation had taken place or a credit policy on Socialist lines be operated? How could we win the Socialist Commonwealth by operating the capitalist system of finance?

ILP Annual Conference Report (1926)

Dedicated communists are highly-trained political soldiers, equally prepared to sing in the choir of churches open to their infiltration, or to use machine-guns in the streets, which are conveniently carried beneath surplices.

My Life (1968)

It may well be an error to use the term socialism because it is an emotive word which repulses many people, and is capable of so many different interpretations that in the end it has come to mean almost nothing except a mild shock to complacent guardians of the status quo.

My Life (1968)

Dr Mo Mowlam

1949–2005; Labour Party politician, Secretary of State for Northern Ireland, 1997–99

Until the Labour Party can mentally make the leap that says aspiring to be middle class is positive, the public will always have trouble believing that we want to help anyone less fortunate.

Cited in A. McSmith, *John Smith: A Life* (1994)

Didn't you know? I'm the new tea lady around here.

Comment to US President Bill Clinton on being sidelined during peace negotiations in Northern Ireland, BBC News online, 'Mowlam "sidelined by Blair"', 10 September 2000

He makes decisions with a small coterie of advisers, just like the President of the United States.

Criticising Tony Blair, BBC TV documentary, *Cabinet Confidential*, 17 November 2001

I believe there is the determination and the will to do it and I believe we will have a good day.

Quoted by CNN, 9 April 1998

Some of the changes can happen quickly, some will need legislation, and some will take years.

On reform of the police service in Northern Ireland, 9 September 1999

Malcolm Muggeridge
1903–90; journalist

There is no snobbishness like that of professional egalitarians.

Chronicles of Wasted Time (1978)

Geoff Mulgan
b. 1961; founder of Demos, former director of policy at No. 10 Policy Unit

The changing balance between public and private sector, state and market solutions, cannot be separated from the organisational forms and competencies which each brings to bear. It is with these, and with public and private organisations' practical ability to recognise and solve problems in everything from energy to prisons and from universities to childcare, that any useful argument now has to begin.

Cited in C. Crouch and D. Marquand (eds.), *Ethics and Markets* (1993)

State responsibility does not, however, imply that national systems will work best ... Success in developing new ways of creating work and improving welfare will depend crucially on much greater scope for local experiment.

New Statesman, 17 January 1997

Chris Mullin

b. 1947; Labour Party politician

I have been in this place twenty-three years. I hope that, during that time, I have left the occasional footprint in the sand, but I am under no illusion. Only a handful of those who currently strut these corridors will still be remembered ten or twenty years from now and I do not expect to be among them.

Speech, House of Commons, 26 March 2010

The great thing about democracy is that, although harsh things are sometimes said, we are not actually trying to kill each other. Differences are ultimately resolved at the ballot box. One side wins; one side loses and the loser lives to fight another day.

Speech, House of Commons, 26 March 2010

The Sunderland South Labour Party selected me as their candidate in the summer of 1985, two years before I was elected. Rejoicing was not universal. A few days later an editorial appeared in the *Daily Mail* which began as follows: 'Poor Sunderland. First their football team is relegated and now comes even worse news...' A year or so later, *The Sun* published a page of photographs of what it described as 'Labour's Top Ten Loony Tunes'. I was number eight.

Speech, 8 June 2007

Jim Murphy

b. 1967; Labour Party politician, shadow Secretary of State for Defence 2010–

Those who have been lost will always be remembered and loved by their families. Street naming will be a chance for their names to live publicly and forever.

Labour urges councils to rename streets after war heroes, BBC online, 21 February 2012

Len Murray

1922–2004; General Secretary of the Trades Union Congress 1973–84

The British disease is old age – old institutions, old industrial assets, and old attitudes. You could call it maturity, but there is only a thin line between maturity and senility.

The Times, 16 May 1980

O

Barack Obama

b. 1961; Democratic Party politician, President of the United States of America 2009–

In the end, that's what this election is about. Do we participate in a politics of cynicism or a politics of hope?
  Speech, Democratic National Convention, 27 July 2004

Change will not come if we wait for some other person or some other time. We are the ones we've been waiting for. We are the change that we seek.
  Speech, Chicago, Illinois, 5 February 2008

We need to steer clear of this poverty of ambition, where people want to drive fancy cars and wear nice clothes and live in nice apartments but don't want to work hard to accomplish these things. Everyone should try to realize their full potential.
  Cited in *Daily Southtown*, 19 February 2005

Focusing your life solely on making a buck shows a poverty of ambition. It asks too little of yourself. And it will leave you unfulfilled.
  Speech, 12 July 2006

There is not a liberal America and a conservative America – there is the United States of America. There is not a black America and a white America and Latino America and Asian America – there's the United States of America.
  Speech, Democratic National Convention, 27 July 2004

These are Americans who still believe in an America where anything's possible – they just don't think their leaders do. These are Americans who still dream big dreams – they just sense their leaders have forgotten how.

Speech, 14 June 2006

The thing about hip-hop today is it's smart, it's insightful. The way they can communicate a complex message in a very short space is remarkable.

Interview, 8 January 2008

I think when you spread the wealth around it's good for everybody.

Defending his tax plan to Joe the Plumber, Toledo, Ohio, 12 October 2008

If you're looking for the safe choice, you shouldn't be supporting a black guy named Barack Obama to be the next leader of the free world.

Piers Morgan, CNN, *Piers Morgan Tonight*, 20 July 2011

What Washington needs is adult supervision.

Fundraising letter, October 2006

I'm a warrior for the middle class.

Speech in Cincinnati, 22 September 2011

Money is not the only answer, but it makes a difference.

Referenced in Management Today, 1 February 2011

The Internet didn't get invented on its own. Government research created the Internet so that all the companies could make money off the Internet. The point is, is that when we succeed, we succeed because of our individual initiative, but also because we do things together.

Speech to supporters, Roanoke, VA. 15 July 2012

A change is brought about because ordinary people do extraordinary things.

> Quoted on Examiner.com

Yes We Can!

> Campaign slogan, 2008

We don't ask you to believe in our ability to bring change, rather, we ask you to believe in yours.

> Speech, 2 August 2011

Nothing can stand in the way of the power of millions of voices calling for change.

> Speech to supporters following the New Hampshire primary, 8 January 2008

No one is pro-abortion.

> Presidential debate, 15 October 2008

You can put lipstick on a pig. It's still a pig.

> Comments on efforts to change John McCain's campaign approach, 9 September 2008

While we breathe, we will hope.

> Speech following victory in the South Carolina primary, 26 January 2008

You can't let your failures define you. You have to let your failures teach you.

> National address to America's schoolchildren, 8 September 2009

Where we are met with cynicism and doubt and fear and those who tell us that we can't, we will respond with that timeless creed that sums up the spirit of the American people in three simple words – yes, we can.

> Speech following victory in the South Carolina primary, 26 January 2008

Hope – Hope in the face of difficulty. Hope in the face of uncertainty. The audacity of hope! In the end, that is God's greatest gift to us ... A belief in things not seen. A belief that there are better days ahead.

Speech, Democratic National Convention, 27 July 2004

I wish the country had fewer lawyers and more engineers.

The Audacity of Hope: Thoughts on Reclaiming the American Dream (May 2007)

It was a creed written into the founding documents that declared the destiny of a nation: Yes we can.
It was whispered by slaves and abolitionists as they blazed a trail toward freedom through the darkest of nights: Yes we can.
It was sung by immigrants as they struck out from distant shores and pioneers who pushed westward against an unforgiving wilderness: Yes we can.
It was the call of workers who organized; women who reached for the ballot; a President who chose the moon as our new frontier; and a King who took us to the mountaintop and pointed the way to the Promised Land.
Yes we can to justice and equality. Yes we can to opportunity and prosperity. Yes we can heal this nation. Yes we can repair this world. Yes we can.

Speech to supporters following the New Hampshire primary, 8 January 2008

If they bring a knife to the fight, we bring a gun.

Speech at fundraising event in Philadelphia, 13 June 2008

Change has come to America.

Victory speech on winning the presidential election, Chicago, 5 November 2008

I inhaled, frequently – that was the point.

November 2011

I'm the President, but he's The Boss.

On Bruce Springsteen, 6 December 2009

Change doesn't come *from* Washington. Change comes *to* Washington.

Speech to Democratic National Congress, 28 August 2008

We're all in this together. That's how we campaigned, and that's who we are. This happened because of you. Thank you.

Tweet, following his re-election as President, 6 November 2012

Four more years.

Tweet, following his re-election as President, 6 November 2012

Forward.

Campaign slogan, 2012

Stanley (Stan) Orme

1923–2005; Labour Party politician, Secretary of State for Social Security, 1976–79

When I worked in industry, to wear overalls almost had a social stigma.

Cited in G. Kaufman (ed.), *Renewal: Labour's Britain in the 1980s* (1983)

George Orwell

1903–50; novelist and essayist

The 'Communism' of the English intellectual is something explicable enough. It is the patriotism of the deracinated.

Inside The Whale (1940)

Political language – and with variations this is true of all political parties, from Conservatives to Anarchists – is designed to make lies sound truthful and murder respectable, and to give an appearance of solidity to pure wind.

Shooting an Elephant (1950)

Probably the battle of Waterloo *was* won on the playing fields of Eton, but the opening battles of all subsequent wars have been lost there.

The Lion and the Unicorn (1941)

An army of unemployed led by millionaires quoting the Sermon on the Mount – that is our danger ... The lazy in the Rolls-Royce is more damaging to morale than a fleet of Goering's bombing planes.

The Lion and the Unicorn (1941)

All animals are equal, but some animals are more equal than others.

Animal Farm (1945)

Big brother is watching you.

Nineteen Eighty-Four (1949)

There are certain people like vegetarians and communists whom one cannot answer. You just have to go on saying your say regardless of them, and then the extraordinary thing is that they may even start listening.

In conversation with Stephen Spender, 11 January 1950

We shall get nowhere until we start by recognising that political behaviour is largely non-rational, that the world is suffering from some kind of mental disease which must be diagnosed before it can be cured.

1946

A socialist United States of Europe seems to me the only worthwhile political objective today.

Partisan Review, 1947

Capitalism leads to dole queues, the scramble for markets, and war. Collectivism leads to concentration camps, leader worship and war. There is no way out of this unless a planned economy can somehow be combined with the freedom of the intellect.

Review of Hayek's *Road to Serfdom*

The typical socialist ... a prim little man with a white-collar job, usually a secret teetotaller and often with vegetarian leanings.

The Road to Wigan Pier (1937)

In our time there is no such thing as 'keeping out of politics'. All the issues are political issues and politics itself is a mass of lies, evasions, folly, hatred and schizophrenia.

Politics and the English Language (1946)

He reminds me of nothing so much as a dead fish before it has had time to stiffen.

On Clement Attlee

A family with the wrong members in control – that, perhaps, is as near as one can come to describing England in a phrase.

The Lion and the Unicorn (1941)

As with the Christian religion, the worst advertisement for Socialism is its adherents.

The Road to Wigan Pier (1937)

David Owen

b. 1938; Labour Party politician, Foreign Secretary 1977–79; co-founder of the SDP, 1981

We are fed up with fudging.

Speech to Labour Party Conference, 1980

To talk of Mrs Thatcher glorying in Falklands slaughter is to move the politics of the gutter to the politics of the abattoir.

> After Denis Healey had accused her of glorifying in slaughter, 2 June 1983

I have never considered Margaret Thatcher to be a Tory. In some senses she is a populist, she's an instinctive politician, she's not afraid of change, she's not afraid to challenge vested interests and doesn't mind if they are Tory interests – this is where she has an appeal. You cannot deny her political acumen and skills.

> *Time To Declare* (1991)

She is a heady mix of whisky and perfume.

> Cited in I. Dale (ed.), *As I Said to Denis* (1998)

The most foolish course now for those who are determined to swing the Labour Party back to sensible socialism would be to abandon the struggle within the Labour party, to talk of founding new parties, to break out from the Labour party just at the very moment when, at long last, we are beginning to fight back from within.

> 1979, cited in I. Crewe and A. King, *SDP: The Birth, Life and Death of the Social Democratic Party* (1995)

An 'enabling society' is one where individuals have declared rights and can achieve their full potential, where a sense of community thrives in the open acceptance of duties, obligations and responsibility for others, and where effort is respected no less than altruism is encouraged.

> Cited in W. Kennet (ed.), *The Rebirth of Britain* (1982)

The price of championing human rights is a little inconsistency from time to time.

> 1977

Without the return of a fresh spirit to enliven our national life, nothing will revive Britain's economic fortunes.

With D. Steel, *The Time Has Come* (1987)

He is the acceptable face of opportunism.

On Roy Hattersley

Robert Owen

1771–1858; social reformer

Courts of law, and all the paraphernalia and folly of law ... cannot be found in a rational state of society.

Speech, 1 May 1833

If we cannot yet reconcile all opinions, let us endeavour to unite all hearts.

The Crisis, motto

The mission of my life appears to be, to prepare the population of the world to understand the vast importance of the second creation of Humanity, from the birth of each individual, through the agency of man, by creating entirely new surroundings in which to place all through life, and by which a new human nature would appear to arise from these new surroundings.

The Life of Robert Owen, written by Himself (1857)

P

Christabel Pankhurst
1880–1958; suffragette

We are here to claim our rights as women, not only to be free, but to fight for freedom.
Speech, London, 23 March 1911

Emmeline Pankhurst
1858–1928; suffragette

I am what you call a hooligan.
Speech, New York, 25 October 1909

We are here, not because we are lawbreakers; we are here in our efforts to become lawmakers.
Speech, London, 21 October 1908

The militancy of men, through all the centuries, has drenched the world with blood, and for these deeds of horror and destruction men have been rewarded with monuments, with great songs and epics. The militancy of women has harmed no human life save the lives of those who fought the battle of righteousness.
My Own Story (1914)

If we women are wrong in destroying private property in order that human values may be restored, then I say, in all reverence, that it was wrong for the founder of Christianity to destroy the private property, as He did when He lashed the money changers out of the Temple and when He drove the Gadarene Swine into the Sea.
My Own Story (1914)

We in the Suffragette Army have a great mission: the greatest
mission the world has ever known – the freeing of one half of
the human race and through that freedom the saving of the other
half. I incite this meeting to rebellion!

Attributed

Nothing is more horrible than wars of aggression. But I believe
that, whatever faults we have had in the past, now we are engaged
in a righteous war. Much as I love peace, I believe there are
times when it is right to fight. And I say to young men: There are
women today who never thought to envy men their manhood,
but who would, at least for this purpose, be glad to be men.

Speech, London, 30 November 1914

Tony Parsons

1922–96; British diplomat

They are the real class traitors, betrayers of the men who fought
the Second World War, those who fought for Churchill but voted
for Clement Attlee. But in the tattooed jungle they have no
sense of history. The true unruly children of Thatcherism, they
know their place and wallow in their peasanthood.

Arena (1989)

The death of the grammar schools – those public schools
without the sodomy – resulted in state education relinquishing
its role of nurturing bright young working class kids.

Arena (1989)

Chris Patten

b. 1944; former Conservative politician, EU Commissioner 1999–2004;
Chairman BBC Trust 2011–

A kind of walking obituary for the Labour Party.

On Michael Foot

Arthur Penty

1875–1937; Guild socialist

The nature of the reform is such as to place the centre of gravity of the reform movement outside the sphere of politics.

Restoration of the Guild System (1906)

To medieval social arrangements we shall return, not only because we shall never be able to regain complete control over the economic forces in society except through the agency of restored Guilds, but because it is imperative to return to a simpler state of society.

Guilds and the Social Crisis (1919)

Eva Perón

1919–52; wife of Juan Perón, First Lady of Argentina 1946–52

Almsgiving tends to perpetuate poverty; aid does away with it once and for all. Almsgiving leaves a man just where he was before. Aid restores him to society as an individual worthy of all respect and not as a man with a grievance. Almsgiving is the generosity of the rich; social aid levels up social inequalities. Charity separates the rich from the poor; aid raises the needy and sets him on the same level with the rich.

Speech to the American Congress of Industrial Medicine, 5 December 1949

Juan Perón

1895–1974; Argentinian politician, President 1946–55 and 1973–74

The order of the day for every Peronist … is to answer a violent action with another action still more violent.

Speech, Buenos Aires, September 1958

You cannot oppose violence with anything but violence.
 1974

Morgan Phillips

1902–63; Labour Party politician, General Secretary of the Labour Party

The Labour Party owes more to Methodism than to Marxism.
 Cited in J. Callaghan, *Time and Chance* (1987)

Raymond Plant

b. 1945; political theorist

There are difficulties with a grass-roots or communitarian
socialism, and it is an illusion to think that criticisms of state
power in a redistributive welfare society can be refuted by
invoking the values of decentralisation and community.
 Equality, Markets and the State (1985)

Sometimes strategic decisions overriding market considerations
taken by democratic governments may well reflect the strategic
choice of individuals rather than the tyranny of small decisions
in the market.
 Equality, Markets and the State (1985)

We lack a rich conception of political community, and with it
a sense of membership and citizenship, and therefore of the
way in which the state could embody the moral purpose of the
community.
 With A. Vincent, *Philosophy, Politics and Citizenship* (1984)

The market itself needs a framework of civic responsibility
within which to operate just as interest groups like unions do.
Unless such a civic vision is articulated and defended, not just
as a matter of altruism but as something which is in all our

interests, then the political community will fall victim to strong special interests whether in politics or in markets.

Citizenship, Rights and Socialism (1988)

Plato

c. 427–347 BC; political philosopher

Any city, however small, is in fact divided into two, one the city of the poor, the other of the rich; these are at war with one another.

The Republic (370 BC)

Laurens van der Post

1906–96; South African writer and philosopher

No new ideas have come out of the Labour Party since the manifesto of 1848. There is nothing that is of the modern age – not their structure, their concept of life or their concept of society. Their concept of society is a partial society ruled by social workers.

A Walk with a White Bushman (1986)

Eugene Pottier

1816–87; French revolutionary socialist

Arise, you prisoners of starvation!
Arise, you wretched of the earth!
For justice thunders condemnation
A better world's in birth.
No more tradition's chains shall bind us.
Arise you slaves no more in thrall
The earth shall rise on new foundations.
We have been naught, we shall be all.
Tis the final conflict

Let each stand in his place
The international working class
Shall be the human race
Words to *The Internationale*

John Prescott
b. 1938; Labour Party politician, deputy Prime Minister, 1997–2007

I believe we will have to set ourselves a target [on employment] … I don't think the public are going to be satisfied with rhetoric.
The Guardian, 13 June 1994

I have quite fundamental disagreements with Tony [Blair].
25 June 1994

John Prescott: I am still a socialist.
Heckler, in crowd: You could have fooled me.
General election campaign, April 1997

They are gnats on an elephant's backside.
On workers in Labour's Millbank HQ, 7 April 1997

The basic ideas of socialism – full employment, redistribution of wealth and power, equality, public ownership, collective provision – are as relevant in the 1990s as they were in 1945.
June 1988

I believe in Clause Four – I think there is a role for it.
July 1994

To be fair, you were either with Kinnock or against him. Same with me. So we were against each other.
Esquire, June 1994

It's the fourth election we've lost running under, as I understand it, these people – I call them the 'beautiful people' – who have, in fact, run the elections that last two times and we've still lost.

Interview, ITV, 14 June 1992

The spin-doctors may have triumphed, but they didn't do much good for the Labour Party.

Interview, ITN, 25 May 1992

I had to peer in on the television to see who was on the campaign strategy team and who was making decisions.

The Guardian, 18 June 1992

If you question the relationship between the trade unions and the Labour Party, then you question the very fundamental being of the Labour Party.

The Times, 4 June 1994

Public ownership is a distinguishing feature between a left-of-centre party and a right-of-centre party.

The Times, 25 February 1993

I'm afraid of being rejected, of being put down.

Interview, *Sunday Telegraph*, 15 May 1994

The green belt is a Labour achievement, and we mean to build on it.

Discussing the merits of the green belt, BBC Radio, 19 January 1998

The contribution of the local authorities and the public sector did much to civilise this century in which we live and I believe will do so in the next century.

The Guardian, 8 July 1999

Let us never forget our heritage or our roots.

Speech to Durham Miners' Gala, 10 July 1999

Can we do that again? I made that crap.

> Giving up midway through a sentence during a live interview on *BBC News 24* with Nick Robinson, 7 March 2000

I will have failed if in five years' time there are not ... far fewer journeys by car. It's a tall order but I urge you to hold me to it.

> Speech to the Royal Geographical Society, 6 June 1997

Because of the security reasons for one thing and second, my wife doesn't like to have her hair blown about. Have you got another silly question?

> On using a car to drive the short distance between his hotel and the Labour Party Conference venue, BBC online, 30 September 1999

What a load of crap ... what the bloody hell are you on about?

> Commenting on Tony Blair creating 'New Labour', *Daily Telegraph*, 9 December 2009

I don't think I'll stand for election again but I will forever be a politician and campaigner.

> Following his defeat in election to be Police and Crime Commissioner, *Hull Daily Mail*, 20 November 2012

It is who I am and the party I am in. I'm not going to be sitting around in my slippers. I will be campaigning in my coffin.

> Following his defeat in election to be Police and Crime Commissioner, *Hull Daily Mail*, 20 November 2012

All I could feel was this warm liquid running down my neck. You automatically think it's blood, it's all in split seconds, so I decided I didn't agree with him.

> Before he hit a protester, interview, ITV, *Piers Morgan's Life Stories*, 14 May 2011

Perhaps they thought I was on a fact-finding mission, never for one moment thinking that a man of my age and build could be suffering from bulimia nervosa, but that's what the consultant said I had.

Sunday Times, 20 April 2008

She's not forgiven me, but we have a wonderful life from our family and that's the nature and quality of that woman that she can say that.

On his affair with Tracey Temple, interview, ITV, *Piers Morgan's Life Stories*, 14 May 2011

There was only one punch. Tony Blair rang me and he said 'Are you OK?' and I said 'Yes', and he said 'Well, what happened?' and I said 'I was just carrying out your orders. You told us to connect with the electorate, so I did.'

On hitting a protestor, interview, ITV, *Piers Morgan's Life Stories*, 14 May 2011

Can you keep your mouth shut for a moment, love?

To a woman heckler during a live interview on the BBC News channel, 11 May 2010

If we can't make this work, we're not much of a government.

On the Millennium Dome, June 1997

Disunity kills political parties.

Interview, BBC Radio, *Today* programme, 18 September 2008

A bus is a good way to get over to campaigning. You know I'm into Facebooks and all that kind of new technology now. But I'm into face to face. You've got to go out in the market square.

Interview, BBC Radio, *Today* programme, 2 May 2009

You know what his name is? He's called Peter. Do you think you will get on the executive, Peter?

Speaking to a crab called Peter (Mandelson), quoted in the *Daily Mirror*, 19 August 1997

I know in the last year I let myself down, I let you down. So Conference, I just want to say sorry.

Speech to Labour Party Conference, 28 September 2006

I don't pursue vendettas or punch people on the nose.

The Guardian, 1994

It's great to be back on terra cotta.

1999

I can tell you I'm pretty middle-class.

Interview, BBC Radio, *Today* programme, 12 April 1996

Pierre-Joseph Proudhon

1809–65; French political theorist

Property is theft.

What Is Property? (1840)

Communism is inequality, but not as property is. Property is exploitation of the weak by the strong. Communism is exploitation of the strong by the weak.

What Is Property? (1840)

As man seeks justice in equality, so society seeks order in anarchy.

What Is Property? (1840)

Whoever puts his hand on me to govern me is an usurper and a tyrant; I declare him my enemy.

Confessions of a Revolutionary (1849)

All parties, without exception, in so far as they seek power, are varieties of absolutism.

Confessions of a Revolutionary (1849)

Universal suffrage is counter-revolution.
The General Idea of the Revolution in the Nineteenth Century (1851)

To be governed is to be watched, inspected, spied upon, directed, law-ridden, regulated, penned-up, indoctrinated, preached at, checked, appraised, seized, censured, commanded by beings who have neither title, nor knowledge, nor virtue.

The General Idea of the Revolution in the Nineteenth Century (1851) James Purnell

b. 1970; Labour Party politician, Secretary of State for Work and Pensions 2008–09

I now believe your continued leadership makes a Conservative victory more, not less likely. That would be disastrous for our country. This moment calls for stronger regulation, an active state, better public services, an open democracy. It calls for a government that measures itself by how it treats the poorest in society.
Resignation letter to then Prime Minister, Gordon Brown, 4 June 2009

The cancer at the heart of the Labour party.
On fellow MP, Tom Watson, *The Guardian* diary, 23 March 2010

R

Giles Radice

b. 1936; Labour Party politician

[Labour's] failure to accept the market economy fully has been a major handicap.

Southern Discomfort (1992)

Labour cannot win by relying on its 'core' voters amongst the unskilled manual workers because there are not enough of them.

Southern Discomfort (1992)

[The Labour Party] has to show it understands the concerns and aspirations of upwardly mobile, home-owning, 'middle' Britain.

With S. Pollard, *More Southern Discomfort* (1993)

Labour is seen as the party that is likely to 'clobber' people.

With S. Pollard, *More Southern Discomfort* (1993)

The role of government is not to try to run industry or 'second guess' business but to act as an enabler, as a midwife of change.

Labour's Path to Power (1989)

Future spending commitments, if they have to be made, should be made very cautiously indeed and always with the maximum attention to electoral advantage.

Southern Discomfort (1992)

Attitude surveys can help Labour to find out how to win their [voters'] support.

With S. Pollard, *Any Southern Comfort?* (1994)

John Rawls

1921–2002; political theorist

The guiding idea is that the principles of justice for the basic
structure of society are the object of the original agreement.
They are the principles that free and rational persons concerned
to further their own interests would accept in an initial
position of equality as defining the fundamental terms of their
association.

A Theory of Justice (1972)

Phil Redmond

b. 1949; television producer and screenwriter

Everywhere you looked there were big schools, big hospitals,
big housing estates. St Kevin's itself, in the heart of Kirkby new
town, stood opposite a row of five twenty-two-storey tower
blocks. It was part of the great socialist utopia, and that was the
problem. Everything was too big.

On his school days, *Mid Term Report* (2012)

Merlyn Rees

1920–2006; Labour Party politician, Home Secretary 1976–79

Our priority is full employment. The need to rethink the
meaning of full employment in the context of the latter years of
the twentieth century emphasises the lack of a fixed blueprint
for our plans. We must constantly reassess our progress, for we
know that it is not that problems end but that the nature of the
problems changes.

G. Kaufman (ed.), *Renewal: Labour's Britain in the 1980s* (1983)

Rachel Reeves

b. 1979; Labour Party politician, shadow Chief Secretary to the Treasury
2011–

Modest incomes.

> LBC Radio, interview with Iain Dale, in which she repeated the same
> phrase eight times in 80 seconds, 14 February 2013

Dr John Reid

b. 1947; Labour Party politician, Home Secretary 2006–07

I want to be straight with the Committee today and honest with
you because I believe that, despite these advances, in the wake
of the problems of mass migration that we have been facing
our system is not fit for purpose. It is inadequate in terms of its
scope; it is inadequate in terms of its information technology,
leadership, management, systems and processes.

> On the UK's immigration system, appearance before the Home Affairs
> Select Committee, 23 May 2006. Dr Reid later revealed that the
> 'not fit for purpose' phrase was coined by a civil servant, speaking to
> Andrew Neil, BBC TV, 17 November 2011

Terrorists love a vacuum. I know that from my own experience
in Northern Ireland. And it's the same throughout the world.

> 7 April 2006

All government departments will be smoke-free … All enclosed
public places and workplaces … will be smoke free. All
restaurants will be smoke free. All pubs and bars preparing and
serving food will be smoke free.

> House of Commons, 16 November 2004

She could prick the pomposity of the powerful with the same
ease with which she could communicate with the mass of
ordinary folk.

> In tribute to Mo Mowlam, *Daily Telegraph*, 19 August 2005

I freely admit to you that I expect that the terrorists will get more frenetic, more frantic.

20 September 2005

We are promoting the opportunity for healthy living in a manner and scale unseen before.

Discussing a health White Paper, quoted in *The Sun*, 1 August 2007

It's not my job to manage this department – it's my job to lead this department.

On the Home Office, BBC News, 23 May 2006

Leadership isn't a zero sum game. When one of us shines it doesn't diminish the others, it reflects on all of us.

Speech to Labour Party Conference, 28 September 2006

Until Roy Hattersley said he would shoot himself if I became Prime Minister, I had not been able to see any possible advantage in standing.

Speech to Labour Party Conference, 28 September 2006

You don't have to love everything George W. Bush stands for to hate everything that Osama Bin Laden stands for.

Speech to Labour Party Conference, 28 September 2006

Jules Renard

1864–1910; French author

Socialism must come down from the brain and reach the heart.

Journal, August 1905

David Ricardo
1772–1823; economist

There is no way of keeping profits up but by keeping wages down.
On Protection in Agriculture (1820)

Maximilien de Robespierre
1758–94; French Revolutionary leader

In politics nothing is just save what is honest; nothing is useful except what is just.
Speech to the National Assembly, May 1791

I prefer the individual whom chance, birth, and circumstance have given us for a king to all those kings whom the people wish to give us.
Speech to the Jacobin Society, March 1792

Citizens, do you want a revolution without revolution?
Speech to the National Convention, 5 November 1792

The government of the Revolution is the despotism of liberty against tyranny.
Speech to the National Convention, 5 February 1794

Terror is nothing other than justice, prompt, secure and inflexible.
Speech to the National Convention, 5 February 1794

Bill Rodgers
b. 1928; Former Labour Party politician, Secretary of State for Transport 1976–79, co-founder of the SDP

Throughout the 1960s and 1970s, no serious attempt was made by the leadership of the Labour Party to ensure its relevance to the problems that Britain faced in the remaining years of the century. This failure created the opportunities for those who cared little for the Labour Party's tradition of tolerance and commitment to Parliamentary democracy, or, alternatively, chose to pursue policies remote from the facts of political life.

The Politics of Change (1982)

The trade union leadership [had] abrogated its responsibility to lead.

The Politics of Change (1982)

We are the heart of the party. We are what the Labour movement is all about. We are going to win and we are going to keep it that way.

On being a Labour moderate, 1977

Will Rogers

1879–1935; American humorist

England elects a Labour government. When a man goes in for politics over here, he has no time to labour, any man that labours has no time to fool with politics. Over there politics is an obligation; over here it's a business.

The Autobiography of Will Rogers (1949)

Communism is like Prohibition, it's a good idea but it won't work.

The Autobiography of Will Rogers (1949)

Franklin Delano Roosevelt

1882–1945; US President 1933–45

I pledge you, I pledge myself to a new deal for the American people.

Speech, 2 July 1932

If I went to work in a factory, the first thing I'd do would be to join a union.

As quoted on a CIO recruiting poster, c. 1936

It is one of the characteristics of a free and democratic nation that it has free and independent labour unions.

Address before the Teamsters' Union Convention, Washington, DC, 11 September 1940

First of all, let me assert my firm belief that the only thing we have to fear is fear itself – nameless, unreasoning, unjustified terror.

Inaugural address, 4 March 1933

A conservative is a man with two perfectly good legs who, however, has never learned to walk forwards ... A reactionary is a somnambulist walking backwards ... A radical is a man with both feet firmly planted – in the air.

Radio broadcast, 26 October 1939

We look forward to a world founded upon four essential human freedoms. The first is freedom of speech and expression – everywhere in the world. The second is the freedom of every person to worship God in his own way – everywhere in the world. The third is freedom from want ... everywhere in the world. The fourth is freedom from fear ... anywhere in the world.

Address to Congress, 6 January 1941

I see one-third of a nation ill-housed, ill-clad, and ill-nourished.

Inaugural address, 1937

Jean-Jacques Rousseau

1712–78; French political philosopher

Man is born free, and everywhere he is in chains.

The Social Contract (1762)

Joan Ruddock

b. 1943; Labour politician; former CND chairperson

We [CND] have to create a position where people who support our stance cannot vote Conservative.

The Times, 18 April 1983

The threat comes from the United States having made Europe the front line in its conflict with the Soviet Union.

Morning Star, 7 September 1984

John Ruskin

1819–1900; socialist theorist

It is a good and desirable thing, truly, to make many pins in a day. But if we could only see with what crystal sand their points are polished – sand of human soul – we should think there might be some loss in it also. We blanch cotton and strengthen steel and refine sugar and shape pottery; but to brighten, to strengthen, to refine or to form a single living spirit never enters into our estimate of advantages.

The Stones of Venice (1851)

Government and co-operation are in all things the laws of life; anarchy and competition the laws of death.

Unto This Last (1862)

Bertrand Russell

1872–1970; British philosopher

Marx's *Das Kapital* is in essence, like the Bryce Report, a collection of atrocity stories designed to stimulate martial ardour against the enemy. Very naturally, it also stimulates the martial ardour of the enemy. It thus brings about the class-war which it prophesies.

Speech, 10 October 1923

Advocates of capitalism are very apt to appeal to the sacred principles of liberty, which are embodied in one maxim: *The fortunate must not be restrained in the exercise of tyranny over the unfortunate*.

Sceptical Essays (1928)

Dora Russell

1894–1986; author and campaigner

We have never yet had a Labour Government that knew what taking over power really means; they always act like second-class citizens.

The Observer, 30 January 1983

S

Jean-Paul Sartre

1905–80; French philosopher

When the rich wage war, it's the poor who die.
Le Diable et le Bon Dieu (1951)

I hate victims who respect their executioners.
Les Séquestrés d'Altona (1960)

In the France of today, the only class with a doctrine is the
working class, the only one whose 'particularism' is in full
harmony with the interests of the nation; a great party
represents it, the only one which has included in its programme
the safeguarding of democratic institutions, the re-establishment
of national sovereignty, and the defence of peace, the only one
which pays attention to economic rebirth and an increase in
purchasing power, the only one, in fact which is *alive*, which
crawls with life when the others are crawling with worms.
The Communists and Peace (1969)

Hugh Scanlon

1913–2004; President of the Amalgamated Engineering Union 1968–78

The leadership of the trade union movement is now almost a
part of the Establishment – more important still, is a recognised
part of the Establishment. That wasn't as apparent during the
thirties and during the war. It's more a phenomenon of full
employment and employers utilising the trade union leadership
rather than the heavy stick of unemployment.
In *New Left Review* (1967)

Of course liberty is not licence, liberty in my view is conforming to majority opinion.

Television interview, 9 August 1977

Arthur Scargill

b. 1938; leader of the National Union of Mineworkers 1981–2002

It appeared to me that, irrespective of what I did politically in the ... Labour Party or the Communist Party or any other political organisation, the *real power* – and I say that in the best possible sense – the real power lay either with the working classes or the ruling classes.

In *New Left Review* (1975)

We haven't demanded anything. What we have demanded is that the coal board withdraw their demands.

During the strike of 1984–85

There *is* a class conflict, we *do* live in a class society – those who own and control the means of production, distribution and exchange, and those who work by hand and by brain. There is no middle class as is suggested by those academics and intellectuals who would like to stratify society. There are only two classes in the strict personal sense.

Interview, *Marxism Today*, April 1981

If the church to which you went decided to stop worshipping God and started worshipping the devil, you would have second thoughts. The leadership of New Labour has abandoned their socialist faith and embraced capitalism which is tantamount to embracing the devil!

The Guardian, 4 May 1996

I'm sure if I have plans, the Press will inform me.

Attributed

Parliament itself would not exist in its present form had people not defied the law.

Evidence to a House of Commons Select Committee, 2 April 1980

Margaret Thatcher has been absolutely clear in recognising *her* enemy – it is socialism and she has openly declared her intention of wiping it off the British agenda.

Speech, Merthyr Tydfil, 30 October 1987

I have never been an idealist, that implies you aren't going to achieve anything.

1974

Joseph Schumpeter

1883–1950; American economist

The cold method of economic theory is in Marx's pages immersed in such a wealth of steaming phrases as to acquire a temperature not naturally its own.

Capitalism, Socialism and Democracy (1942)

Economic progress, in capitalist society, means turmoil.

Capitalism, Socialism and Democracy (1942)

I for one cannot visualise in the conditions of modern society, a socialist organisation in any form other than that of a huge and all embracing bureaucratic apparatus.
An institutional pattern in which the control over means of production and over production itself is vested with a central authority – or, as we may say, in which, as a matter of principle, the economic affairs of society belong to the public and not the private sphere.
What may be termed Centralist Socialism seems to me to hold the field so clearly that it would be a waste of space to consider other forms.

Capitalism, Socialism and Democracy (1942)

Bill Shankly

1913–81; football manager, Liverpool Football Club 1959–74

The socialism I believe in is not really politics. It is a way of living. It is humanity. I believe the only way to live and to be truly successful is by collective effort, with everyone working for each other, everyone helping each other, and everyone having a share of the rewards at the end of the day.

Cited on www.shankly.com

Burns was early socialist – the first was Jesus Christ of course. He didn't think that God made people to be unequal, he thought everyone should share in the work and the rewards.

Cited on www.shankly.com

George Bernard Shaw

1856–1950; Irish Fabian socialist and author

No man is good enough to be another man's master.

Major Barbara (1905)

The greatest of evils and the worst of crimes is poverty ... our first duty – a duty to which every other consideration should be sacrificed – is not to be poor.

Major Barbara (1905)

The Socialism advocated by the Fabian Society is State Socialism exclusively.

On the state machinery of army, police and law courts, *The Impossibilities of Anarchism* (1893)

Give women the vote, and in five years there will be a crushing tax on bachelors.

Man and Superman (1903)

My last word for the present is – read Jevons and the rest for your economics; and read Marx for the history of their working in the past, and the conditions of their application in the present.

Bernard Shaw and Karl Marx (1930)

A Bolshevik as far as I can tell is nothing but a socialist who wants to do something about it. To the best of my knowledge I am a Bolshevik myself.

Interview in *The Liberator*, 1919

The more Communism, the more civilisation.

The Intelligent Woman's Guide to Socialism, Capitalism, Sovietism and Fascism (1937)

A life spent in making mistakes is not only more honourable but more useful than a life spent in doing nothing.

Doctor's Dilemma (1909)

An election is a moral horror, as bad as a battle except for the blood; a mud bath for every soul concerned in it.

Back to Methuselah (1921)

Assassination is the extreme form of censorship.

The Rejected Statesman (1916)

Liberty means responsibility. That is why so many men dread it.

Man And Superman (1903)

Kings are not born, they are made by universal hallucination.

Man and Superman (1903)

Under fully developed Capitalism civilisation is always on the verge of revolution. We live as in a villa on Vesuvius.

Man and Superman (1903)

How great, of all that human hearts endure,
That part Factory Acts alone can cure!

Man and Superman (1903)

Socialism means equality of income or nothing.

Man and Superman (1903)

When democratic Socialism has achieved sufficiency of means,
equality of opportunity, and national inter-marriageability
for everybody, with production kept in its natural order from
necessities to luxuries, and the courts of justice unbiased by
mercenary barristers, its work will be done.

Everybody's Political What's What? (1944)

Unimaginative people disparage Socialism because it will, they
fear, reduce life to a dead level. Never was an apprehension less
plausible. Millions of well-fed bumptious citizens with plenty of
leisure for argument will provide all the excitement the most
restless spirits can desire.

Everybody's Political What's What? (1944)

The great corruption of Socialism which threatens us at present
... calls itself Fascism in Italy, National Socialism (Nazi for
short) in Germany, New Deal in the United States, and is
clever enough to remain nameless in England; but everywhere
it means the same thing: Socialist production and Unsocialist
distribution.

Everybody's Political What's What? (1944)

Very few people can afford to be poor.

Cited in S. Winsten, *Days with Bernard Shaw* (1949)

Democracy substitutes election by the incompetent many for
appointment by the corrupt few.

Maxims for Revolutionists (1913)

I'm one of the undeserving poor.

Pygmalion (1912)

The British soldier can stand up to anything except the British War Office.

The Devil's Disciple (1897)

He knows nothing and thinks he knows everything. That points clearly to a political career.

Major Barbara (1905)

Bring a friend if you have one.

Sending an invitation to his new play, *St Joan*, to Winston Churchill. Churchill replied, 'I cannot come. Would it be possible for you to let me have tickets for the second night – if there is one?'

A drama critic is a man who leaves no turn unstoned.

New York Times, 1950

Englishmen never will be slaves; they are free to do whatever the government and public opinion allow them.

Man and Superman (1903)

Our laws make law impossible, our liberties destroy all freedom, our property is organised robbery, our morality is an impudent hypocrisy, our wisdom is administered by inexperienced or mal-experienced dupes, our power wielded by cowards and weaklings and our honour false in all its points. I am an enemy of the existing order for good reasons.

Major Barbara (1905)

Nowadays, a parlour-maid as ignorant as Queen Victoria was when she came to the throne would be classed as mentally defective.

On Queen Victoria

Hartley Shawcross

1902–2003; Labour Party politician, Attorney General 1945–51

'But,' said Alice, 'the question is whether you can make a word mean different things.' 'Not so,' said Humpty-Dumpty, 'the question is which is to be the master. That's all.' We are all masters at the moment, and not only at the moment, but for a very long time to come.

Hansard, 2 April 1946

I thought we were the masters at that time – as undoubtedly we were. But it was an unwise thing to say. If you are the masters in politics it's rather tactless to emphasise the matter too much. You want to exercise the powers of mastership and leadership but not brag about it. It's what you do that matters.

Cited in A. Mitchell, *Election '45: Reflections on the Revolution in Britain* (1995)

No word in the vocabulary has been so debased and abused as democracy.

1977

Emanuel Shinwell

1884–1986; Labour Party politician, Secretary of State for War 1947–50, Minister of Defence 1950–51

We know that the organised workers of the country are our friends. As for the rest they don't matter a tinker's cuss.

Speech to the Electrical Trades Union Conference, Margate, 7 May 1947

I went to the House of Lords because I had nowhere else to go.

1977

Peter Shore

1924–2001; Labour Party politician, Secretary of State for Trade 1974–76

The old argument about nationalisation and private enterprise was left behind when Wilson advanced the new role of public enterprise, to be pressed forward to apply science and technology to new industries and processes which the private sector had neglected. Far from saying that public ownership was outmoded and irrelevant, Wilson championed public enterprise as an essential tool for the modernisation of British industry.

Leading the Left (1993)

A month ago, I said that what Mr Benn was about was the creation of a New Model Party to be created not out of new policies – for the differences here are certainly reconcilable – but out of a radical new doctrine and practice for party democracy.

On Tony Benn's plans for the Labour Party, speech, Cardiff, 5 June 1981

Clare Short

b. 1946; former Labour Party politician, Secretary of State for International Development 1997–2003

We should not be cowards … maybe that includes taxing and selling cannabis.

TV interview, October 1995

I think that in a fair tax system, people like me would pay a bit more tax.

TV interview, 14 April 1996

We go to the shadow Cabinet. We go to the National Executive Committee. Everything we do is in the light. They live in the dark. It is a good place for them.

On the use of advisers by her leader, Tony Blair, August 1996

It is my view that our political system is in trouble and that the exaggerated majorities in the House of Commons have led to an abject parliament and a concentration of power in Number 10 that has produced arrogant, error prone government.

Resignation letter from sitting in the House of Commons as a Labour member, 19 October 2006

I do think, however, that the errors we are making over Iraq and other recent initiatives flow not from Labour's values, but from the style and organisation of our government, which is undermining trust and straining party loyalty in a way that is completely unnecessary.

In our first term the problem was spin – endless announcements, exaggeration and manipulation of the media that undermined people's respect for the government and trust in what we said.

It was accompanied by a control freak style, which has created many of the problems of excessive bureaucracy and centralised targets that is undermining the success of our public sector reforms.

In the second term, the problem is centralisation of power into the hands of the Prime Minister and an increasingly small number of advisers who make decisions in private without proper discussion.

Speech, House of Commons, on her resignation as Secretary of State for International Development, 12 May 2003

There is no real collective responsibility because there is no collective, just diktats in favour of increasingly badly thought through policy initiatives that come from on high.

Speech, House of Commons, on her resignation as Secretary of State for International Development, 12 May 2003

Robert Skidelsky

b. 1939; economist

Without any adequate theory of the transition, the Labour Party was bound to be defeatist in the circumstances of 1929. Socialism was impossible and capitalism was doomed: there was nothing to do but govern without conviction a system it did not believe in but saw no real prospect of changing.

Politicians and the Slump (1967)

The failures of collectivism everywhere led to the mistaken view that the state could do almost everything.

The World After Communism (1995)

Dennis Skinner

b. 1932; Labour Party politician

Is the Prime Minister aware that his Cabinet reshuffle of his B team has not raised a ripple with the general public? On the other hand, those loud boos that greeted the Chancellor of the Exchequer will haunt the posh boys for ever. Why does the Prime Minister not be a man, do the decent thing and call a general election?

Prime Minister's Question Time, 5 September 2012

My life hasn't been all about politics.

Interview, *The Guardian*, 17 June 2012

When posh boys are in trouble, they sack their servants.

House of Commons, 25 April 2012

I was formed in the pits and the war.

Interview, *The Guardian*, 17 June 2012

I don't believe in patronage.

Interview, *The Guardian*, 17 June 2012

The only thing growing were the lines of coke in front of boy George [Osborne] and the rest of them.

> Commenting on growth and unemployment in the 1980s, 8 December 1995

Any Tory moles at the palace?

> Referencing the arrest of Damian Green MP, House of Commons, 3 December 2008

I realised that you could get into trouble with a dull speech. But if you can keep them laughing, you can get away with murder.

> Andrew Roth profile, *The Guardian*, 20 March 2001

You'll never be able to trust him because he's broken his pledge and his loyalty to his party.

> On Ken Livingstone, speech, 19 April 2000

The personality cult of the ego does not work down a coal mine and it does not work in the Labour party.

> Speech, 19 April 2000

Jubilee year, double dip recession, what a start.

> Jibe before the start of the Queen's Speech, 9 May 2012

The miners have once again secured a victory that will be historic ... This is the turning point of industrial power in this country.

> Comment on TV news following clashes outside Ogreave during the miners' strike, 1984 (YouTube)

My job as a Member of Parliament, and as a miner for twenty-one years before I went to Parliament, is to back those who are fighting for the right to work.

> TV news coverage of visit to Shirebrook, 1984 (YouTube)

Adam Smith

1723–90; political economist

The rich only select from the heap what is most precious and agreeable. They consume little more than the poor, and in spite of their natural selfishness and rapacity, though they mean only their own convenience, though the sole end which they propose from the labours of all the thousands whom they employ, be the gratification of their own vain and insatiable desires, they divide with the poor the produce of all their improvements. They are led by an invisible hand to make nearly the same distribution of the necessities of life, which would have been made, had the earth been divided into equal portions among all its inhabitants; and thus without intending it, without knowing it, advance the interest of the society, and afford means to the multiplication of the species.

The Theory of Moral Sentiments (1759)

No society can surely be flourishing and happy, of which the far greater part of the members are poor and miserable.

The Wealth of Nations (1776)

Labour, therefore, it appears evidently, is the only universal, as well as the only accurate, measure of value, or the only standard by which we can compare the values of different commodities, at all times, and at all places.

The Wealth of Nations (1776)

Chris Smith

b. 1951; Labour Party politician, Secretary of State for Culture, Media and Sport 1997–2001

Unorganised, it lacks direction, it hasn't any coherent definition and it has precious little influence on Neil [Kinnock].

On the 'soft' Left, *The Guardian*, 11 November 1985

I've always considered that being green is at the heart of being a socialist.

Tribune, 26 March 1993

Democratic socialism in Britain has always been about this simple task: ensuring that we all can live and act as citizens in society.

New Questions for Socialism (1996)

There are some who argue that the best test of how progressive a welfare policy is, is the amount of money that is spent on it. I disagree. High social spending is a sign of failure, not a sign of success.

The Guardian, 7 May 1996

Good afternoon, I'm Chris Smith, I'm the Labour MP for Islington South and Finsbury. I'm gay, and so for that matter are about a hundred other members of the House of Commons, but they won't tell you openly.

Speech, Rugby, November 1984, making him the first openly out homosexual politician in the UK parliament

I did not feel the need to tell people, except for a very, very few, as it was not in any way affecting my work.

On revealing that he is HIV positive, *Mail on Sunday*, 'MP Chris Smith: I've had HIV for 17 years', 30 January 2005

John Smith
1938–94; Labour Party leader 1992–94

We can't spend what we haven't earned. We intend to earn it before we spend it. That will be the guiding light of the next Labour Government's economic policy.

The Guardian, 2 October 1989

Whether we like it or not interdependence is the reality of the modern world. Matters of vital importance to our lives such as our economic prosperity and the protection of our environment all depended on international collaboration. These days no country can go it alone.

'No One Can Go It Alone', *Socialist Affairs* (1993)

Clearly the Prime Minister's devious hand is afoot.

1989

Strengthening the Labour Party's democracy does not mean weakening our relationship with the trade union movement. Our values and principles are shared with the trade unions, as is our history. In modernising our systems of election and in reforming the block vote I believe we can build a new partnership with the trade union movement that will be stronger because it is fairer between Party and unions.

Labour's Choice: The Fabian Debates (1992)

Labour must and will not sever its links with the trade union movement.

Cited in A. McSmith, *John Smith: A Life* (1994)

One trade union general secretary casting millions of votes will not happen in the future.

Preparing for the One Member One Vote reforms, interview, BBC TV, 9 January 1993

The goal of full employment remains at the heart of Labour's economic vision. Labour's economic strategy will ensure that all instruments of macroeconomic management, whether it concerns interest rates, the exchange rate or the level of borrowing will be geared to sustained growth and rising employment.

Speech, TUC Congress, 7 September 1993

Just as the Christian stands by the fundamental tenets of Christianity, so the socialist should stand by the tenets of socialism. For me, socialism is largely Christian ethical values ... Politics is a moral activity. Values should shine through at all times. You could either call it evangelism or salesmanship. I want the spirit of the evangelic but the success of the good salesman.

Cited in A. McSmith, *John Smith: A Life* (1994)

I've defended some of the worst murderers in Scotland – I can always find something good to say about a Labour politician.

Cited in A. McSmith, *John Smith: A Life* (1994)

The opportunity to serve – that is all we ask.

His last public words, 11 May 1994

The Laurel and Hardy of British politics.

On John Major and Norman Lamont after Black Wednesday, speech to Labour Party Conference, 29 September 1992

Ethel Snowden

1881–1951; suffragette

We were behind the 'iron curtain' at last!

Through Bolshevik Russia (1920)

Philip Snowden

1864–1937; Labour Party politician; Chancellor of the Exchequer 1924 and 1929–31

I hope you have read the election programme of the Labour Party. It is the most fantastic and impracticable programme ever put before the electors ... This is not socialism. It is Bolshevism run mad.

After joining the National Government, BBC radio broadcast, 17 October 1931

It would be desirable if every government, when it comes into power, should have its old speeches burned.

Attributed

It would be unwise on the part of the community to deprive private enterprise of the opportunity of proving its superiority over nationalisation. But private enterprise could not be permitted to exist unless it conformed to the standard of wages, hours, and conditions prevailing under public employment.

Labour and the New World (1921)

[This spirit of co-operation] will permeate everybody from the most responsible manager to the humblest worker, and each will feel that in doing his best he is not only contributing to the common good, but is promoting his own personal interests.

The Way to Industrial Peace (1927)

I have been active in political life for forty years, and my only object has been to improve the lot of the toiling millions. That is still my aim and object, and, if I ask for some temporary suspensions, some temporary sacrifices, it is because that is necessary to make future progress possible.

Hansard, 1930–31

The line of advance to which socialists attach greatest importance is by way of public ownership. All other ways are merely palliative.

Socialism and Syndicalism (1913)

Competition has served the purpose of weeding out the incompetent and ill-equipped capitalists.

Socialism and Syndicalism (1913)

The enlightened self-interest and ethical impulses of all classes would abolish industrial slavery.

Socialism and Syndicalism (1913)

SPD

German Social Democratic Party

The market when possible, planning where necessary.
Bad Godesberg (1959)

Joseph Stalin

1878–1953; Soviet Communist politician, General Secretary of the Party
1922–52

Only on the bones of the oppressors can the people's freedom
be founded – only the blood of the oppressors can fertilise the
soil for the people's self-rule.
Appeal for the Tiflis Social Democratic committee, 1905

Objectively, Social Democracy is the moderate wing of fascism.
Cited in I. Deutscher, *Stalin. A Political Biography* (1949)

The revolution is incapable either of regretting or of burying its
dead.
Cited in I. Deutscher, *Stalin, A Political Biography* (1949)

The State is an instrument in the hands of the ruling class, used
to break the resistance of the adversaries of that class.
Foundations of Leninism (1924)

We will stay friends with you, whatever happens.
Speaking to a German military attaché, August 1939

The principal task of socialism – the organisation of socialist
production – has still to be fulfilled. Can this task be fulfilled,
can the final victory of socialism be achieved in one country,
without the joint efforts of the proletarians in several advanced
countries? No, it cannot.
The Foundations of Leninism (1924)

What do we mean by the possibility of the victory of socialism in one country? We mean the possibility of solving the contradictions between the proletariat and the peasantry with the aid of the internal forces of our country, the possibility of the proletariat's assuming power, and using that power to build a complete socialist society in one country ... without the preliminary victory of the proletarian revolution in other countries.

Problems of Leninism (1924)

The Pope! How many divisions has he got?

In conversation with Pierre Laval, 13 May 1935

We are under no illusion that they [the Russian people] are fighting for us [the Communist Party]. They are fighting for Mother Russia.

In conversation with Averell Harriman, September 1941

In the Soviet Army it takes more courage to retreat than to advance.

In conversation with Averell Harriman, September 1941

Communism fits Germany as a saddle fits a cow.

In conversation with Mikolajczyk, August 1944

There is really nothing more delightful than carefully plotting a trap into which your enemy in the party is bound to fall, and then going to bed.

Cited in I. Silone, *The School For Dictators* (1963)

There are no fortresses that Bolsheviks cannot capture. We have solved a number of most difficult problems, we have overthrown capitalism. We have assumed power. We have built up a huge socialist industry. We have transformed the middle peasants on to the path of socialism.

Speech, Moscow, 4 February 1931

A grave danger hangs over our country.
>On the threat of Hitler, speech, Moscow, 3 July 1941

This war with Fascist Germany cannot be considered an ordinary war. It is not only a war between two armies, it is also a great war of the entire Soviet people against the German Fascist forces.
>Speech, Moscow, 3 July 1941

Print is the sharpest and the strongest weapon of our party.
>1935

You cannot make a revolution with silk gloves.
>1935

Gaiety is the most outstanding feature of the Soviet Union.
>1935

The undesirable classes never liquidate themselves.
>When asked by Lady Astor 'When are you going to stop killing people?', 1935

A single death is a tragedy, a million deaths is a statistic.
>1958

A reactionary petty-bourgeois absurdity worthy of some primitive sect of ascetics.
>Report to the Seventeenth Party Congress of the CPSU, 26 January 1934

John Strachey

1901–63; Labour Party politician, Secretary of State for War 1950–51

[Marx] under-rated the element of liberty and over-rated the element of necessity in man's condition even within a given social and economic system. His categories were altogether too hard and fast.

Contemporary Capitalism (1956)

The social ownership of the decisive parts of the means of production is the only permanent basis for a Socialist, classless society.

New Statesman, 6 October 1956

They will cease, in a very real sense, to be Socialists at all: they will subside into the role of well intentioned, amiable, rootless, drifting social reformers.

On the consequences of abandoning public ownership, *New Statesman*, 6 October 1956

The market mechanism will be neither retained as the tyrannical arbiter of the economy nor yet done away with and replaced by a pre-determined plan, but ... transformed until it itself becomes an instrument of the plan.

Left News (1941)

Jack Straw
b. 1946; Labour Party politician, Home Secretary 1997–2001

For all the lip service that the Tories pay to individual autonomy, it has been under Labour and Liberal governments, not Conservative, that most fundamental individual rights have been protected in law.

Speech, Annual Barnett Lecture, 12 May 1999

Clause Four was never intended as anything other than something to inspire party activists ... no Labour government could ever implement anything like Clause Four.

Labour Party press release, December 1994

Without ideas, there is no point in being in politics.
October 1986

I am a working politician, not a thinker.
February 1989

Markets are poor means of securing welfare and neither the only
nor the best way of allocating resources.
September 1984

Karl Marx would have supported the policy of Labour's policy
review ... for this process is genuinely dialectical. It is a great
pity that Marx's alleged disciples today can't see that.
July 1998

In answer to the McCarthyite question, 'Am I or have I ever
been a member of CND?', I can say that I used to be but have
since left.
The Times, 12 July 1991

Our vision is one of which power is returned to the citizen and
people once again feel that they have a real say and influence in
the way they are governed.
Speech, Annual Barnett Lecture, 12 May 1999

The better society that we want to build is one that fosters and
celebrates strong British values: decency; reward for hard work;
tolerance and respect for others.
Hansard, 19 May 1997

The private enterprise, free market does not work. It's anarchy
... No one can believe any longer that private enterprise can
deliver the goods ... so socialism will have to step into the
breach.
Putting Blackburn Back to Work (1983)

It's about implementing a zero tolerance strategy. It's not a magic wand. There are no magic wands about dealing with human behaviour.

The Times, 4 December 1997

As soon as I leave this briefing … I am going to find the people I think are responsible and encourage them to deal with it and to offer them some career advice.

Commenting on failings in the organisation of Britain's first major event of the European Presidency informal meeting of European foreign ministers, Newport, 1 September 2005

What I'm saying on the other side is: would those people who do wear the veil think about the implications for community relations?

Raising the issue of whether Muslim women should wear veils which cover the face, interview with BBC Radio Lancashire quoted on BBC News online, 6 October 2006

It shows how from very, very dark circumstances – and we've had to deal with terrorism year after year after year which has killed hundreds of people – it is possible to see the light, provide the process to keep going and achieve results.

Using the example of the IRA, quoted in CNN.com, 24 October 2001

I spoke last night with many of my counterparts and without exception there was overwhelming support for this action by the military coalition consisting of the United States and the United Kingdom.

Before briefing the UN Security Council, 8 October 2001

[Gates] is one of the most important business leaders of his age.

On the announcement of Bill Gates's honorary knighthood, 25 January 2004

Microsoft technology has transformed business practices and his company has had a profound impact on the British economy.

> On the announcement of Bill Gates's honorary knighthood, 25 January 2004

In this country we have a very clear tradition by which people are fully entitled to engage in all kinds of peaceful, sometimes very noisy, protest.

> Interview, BBC Radio, *Today* programme, 19 February 2001

Official brutality, which characterises boot camps in America, is inhuman and does not work.

> On Michael Howard's plans for boot camps, quoted on CNN.com, 18 September 1995

Life would be very boring if friends always agreed.

> On discussions between France and Britain on the future of Iraq, 3 October 2003

Very, very sorry.

> On the shooting of Jean Charles de Menezes, 25 July 2005

This is a negotiation. Our aim was to listen.

> On the EU budget, quoted in the *New York Times*, 7 December 2005

Will Straw
b. 1980; founder, Left Foot Forward

Laissez-faire approaches to economic policy, as favoured by the chancellor, have been the scourge of progress throughout time.

> 'Falling Behind: Why Britain Is Losing The Global Race', *Progress*, March 2013

Edith Summerskill

1901–80; Labour Party politician

The housewife is the Cinderella of the affluent state ... She is wholly dependent on the whim of the individual to give her money for the essentials of life. If she complains she is nagger – for nagging is the repetition of unpalatable truths.

Speech to the Married Women's Association, House of Commons, 14 July 1960

T

William Howard Taft
1857–1930; US Republican politician, President 1909–13

Socialism proposes no adequate substitute for the motive of enlightened selfishness that today is at the basis of all human labour and effort, enterprise and new activity.

Popular Government (1913)

Peter Tatchell
b. 1952; political and equal rights campaigner

While I remain committed to the value of political parties pushing for legislative reform, I am also convinced it is only when challenged by a troublesome and demanding lesbian and gay movement that those parties will effectively address our concerns.

Capital Gay, 26 February 1993

What happens in Bermondsey on 24 February will be a pointer to the rest of the country as far as Labour's prospects are concerned.

On the by-election eventually won by the Liberal Party candidate, Simon Hughes, 18 February 1983

His homophobic jibes help make bigotry cool and acceptable.

Speaking about Eminem, February 2001

I feel very guilty and sad that I lost a safe Labour seat.

Interview, on the Bermondsey by-election, BBC TV, *Newsnight*, 22 February 2013

Dick Taverne

b. 1928; Labour Party politician, later joined SDP

When in doubt, we should favour the small. Indeed, our guiding principle should be 'small is beautiful', that variety provides for independence, and that independence provides for greater security and freedom.

The Future of Labour (1974)

Labour was becoming entrenched as an old-style, fundamentalist socialist party.

On Labour's failure to reform, cited in T. Jones, *Remaking the Labour Party* (1996)

R. H. Tawney

1880–1962; Christian socialist and economic historian

Inequality ... leads to the misdirection of production. For, since the demand of one income of £50,000 is as powerful a magnet as the demand of 500 incomes of £100, it diverts energy from the creation of wealth to the multiplication of luxuries.

The Acquisitive Society (1921)

The characteristic virtue of Englishmen is a power of sustained practical activity, and their characteristic vice a reluctance to test the quality of that activity by reference to principles.

The Acquisitive Society (1921)

Militarism ... is fetish worship. It is the prostration of men's souls and the laceration of their bodies to appease an idol.

The Acquisitive Society (1921)

To abolish all advantages and disabilities which have their source, not in differences of personal quality, but in disparities of wealth, opportunity, social position and economic power.

The Choice before the Labour Party (1932)

Societies, like individuals, have their moral crises and their spiritual revolutions.

Religion and the Rise of Capitalism (1926)

Private property is a necessary institution, at least in a fallen world; men work more and dispute less when goods are private than when they are common. But it is to be tolerated as a concession to human frailty, not applauded as desirable in itself.

Religion and the Rise of Capitalism (1926)

In order to believe in human equality it is necessary to believe in God. It is only when one contemplates the infinitely great that human differences appear so infinitely small as to be negligible [*sic*] ... What is wrong with the modern world is that having ceased to believe in the greatness of God, and therefore, the infinite smallness (or greatness – the same thing!) of *man*, it has to invent or emphasise distinctions between men.

Diary entry, 6 March 1930

Such societies may be called Acquisitive Societies because their whole tendency and interest and preoccupation is to promote their acquisition of wealth.

The Acquisitive Society (1921)

Where the treasure is, there will the heart be also and, if men are to respect each other for what they are, they must cease to respect each other for what they own.

Equality (1931)

It does more than any other single cause, except capitalism itself, to perpetuate the division of the nation into classes of which one is almost unintelligible to the other.

On education, *Equality* (1931)

Functionless property is the great enemy of legitimate property itself. It is the parasite which kills the organism that produced it ... When property for acquisition or power and property for service or for use jostle each other freely in the market ... the latter tends normally to be absorbed by the former, because it has less resisting power.

The Acquisitive Society (1921)

The wage-earner is as much entitled as the property-owner to claim equitable consideration for his established expectations... and that workmen have precisely the same right to be satisfied that organisation and management are up to date, as management has that workmen are earning their wages.

Equality (1931)

An organised money market has many advantages. But it is not a school of social ethics or of political responsibility.

Religion and the Rise of Capitalism (1926)

Political principles resemble military tactics; they are usually designed for a war which is over.

Equality (1931)

Thank you for your letter. What harm have I ever done to the Labour Party?

Declining the offer of a peerage, letter to Ramsay MacDonald

Talk is nauseous without practice. Who will believe that the Labour Party means business so long as some of its stalwarts sit and beg for sugar-plums, like poodles in a drawing room ... To kick over an idol, you must first get off your knees.

Attacking the honours system, 1934

Nothing could be more remote from Socialist ideals than the competitive scramble of a society which pays lip-service to equality, but too often means by it merely opportunities of becoming unequal.

The Acquisitive Society (1921)

The truth is that a conception of Socialism which views it as involving the nationalisation of everything except political power, on which all else depends, is not, to speak with moderation, according to light. The question is not merely whether the State owns and controls the means of production. It is also who owns and controls the State.

[Opportunities depend] not only upon an open road, but upon an equal start.

The Acquisitive Society (1921)

A classless society, which does not mean a society without differentiated groups, but one in which varieties of individual endowments, not contrasts of property, income and access to education, are the basis of differentiation.

The Choice before the Labour Party (1931)

That is where the mere economics of social reform – Fabianism etc. – breaks down. They study the room but they open no windows in the soul.

Commonplace Book (1913)

Under present arrangements men are used not as ends but as means.

Commonplace Book (1913)

Industry creates poverty by refusing to treat men as ends or respect their personalities.

Commonplace Book (1913)

Divided, in its economic and social relations, into classes which are ends and classes which are instruments.

On society; *Equality* (1931)

The purpose of industry [should be] service, to supply men with the material means of a good life.

The Acquisitive Society (1921)

Socialism, however, is obviously a word with more than one meaning.

Attributed

[The] heart of the problem is not economic. It is a question of moral relationships. This is the citadel which must be attacked … the immoral philosophy which underlies much of modern society.

Commonplace Book (1913)

When three or four hundred years hence mankind looks back on the absurd preoccupation of our age with economic issues … the names they will reverence will be those of men who stood out against the prevalent fallacy that the most important problems were economic problems.

Commonplace Book (1913)

A. J. P. Taylor
1906–90; historian

Trotsky tells how, when he first visited England, Lenin took him around London and, pointing out the sights, exclaimed: 'That's *their* Westminster Abbey! That's *their* Houses of Parliament!' Lenin was making a class, not a national emphasis. By *them* he meant not the English, but the governing classes, the Establishment. And indeed in no other European country is the Establishment so clearly defined and so completely secure.

Essays in English History (1953)

There is nothing more agreeable in life than to make peace with the Establishment – and nothing more corrupting.

Essays in English History (1953)

The crusade against Communism was even more imaginary than the spectre of Communism.

The Origins of the Second World War (1961)

He objected to ideas only when others had them.

On Ernest Bevin

Norman Tebbit

b. 1931; Conservative Party politician

It is certainly safe, in view of the movement to the right of intellectuals and political thinkers, to pronounce the brain death of socialism.

The Times, 26 April 1988

Margaret Thatcher

1925–2013; Conservative Party politician, Prime Minister 1979–90

It glorified in planning, regulation, controls and subsidies. It had a vision of the future: Britain as a democratic socialist society, third way between east European collectivism and American capitalism.

On the Labour Party, *The Downing Street Years* (1993)

He is probably the most formidable leader we have seen since Gaitskell. I see a lot of Socialism behind their front bench but not in Mr Blair – I think he has genuinely moved.

BBC TV, 1994

Paul Theroux

b. 1941; American novelist

The ship follows Soviet custom: it is riddled with class distinctions so subtle it takes a trained Marxist to appreciate them.

The Great Railway Bazaar (1975)

J. H. Thomas

1874–1949; Labour Party politician

Poor Sidney can't put the breeches on, because his wife wears them.

On Sidney Webb

Norman Thomas

1884–1968; American socialist

Poverty, insecurity and exploitation are not the judgement of God or nature upon us, but are our own creation.

Human Exploitation (1934)

E. P. Thompson

1924–93; social historian

Will Britain founder under old habits, rotting institutions, its hull encrusted with nostalgia, drifting half-waterlogged into the twenty-second century, a bourgeois Spain among the socialist nations?

Out of Apathy (1960)

Richard Titmuss

1907–73; academic in social administration

As the social services become more complex, more specialised and subject to a finer division of labour they become less intelligible to the lay councillor or public representatives.

Essays of the Welfare State (1955)

To me, the 'Welfare State' has no meaning unless it is positively and constructively concerned with redistributive justice and social participation.

Cited in P. Anderson, *Towards Socialism* (1965)

Alexis-Charles-Henri Clérel de Tocqueville

1805–59; French politician and historian

Democracy and socialism have nothing in common but one word, equality. But notice the difference: while democracy seeks equality in liberty, socialism seeks equality in restraint and servitude.

Democracy in America (1835)

Ron Todd

1927–2005; General Secretary of the Transport and General Workers' Union 1985–92

If we don't win the return of a Labour government we can wave goodbye to all that is good in Labour's proposals.

The Independent, 2 October 1990

Leo Tolstoy

1828–1910; Russian novelist

Yes, we will do almost anything for the poor man, anything but get off his back.

Cited in J. O. S. Huntington, *Philanthropy and Morality* (1892)

Government is an association of men who do violence to the rest of us.

The Kingdom of God is Within You (1894)

Alain Touraine

b. 1925; French sociologist

Socialism is dead.

L'après socialisme (1983)

Robert Tressell

1870–1911; pseudonym of Robert Noonan, Irish house painter, member of the Social Democratic Federation, novelist

'There are many causes' answered Owen, 'but they are all part and inseparable from the system. In order to do away with poverty we must destroy the causes: to do away with the causes we must destroy the whole system.'

The Ragged Trousered Philanthropists (1914)

The present Money System prevents us from doing the necessary work, and consequently cause the majority of the population to go short of the things that can be made by work. They suffer want in the midst of the means of producing abundance. They remain idle because they are bound and fettered with a chain of gold.

The Ragged Trousered Philanthropists (1914)

Mankind, awakening from the long night of bondage and mourning and arising from the dust wherein they had lain prone so long, were at last looking upward to the light that was riving asunder and dissolving the dark clouds which had so long concealed from them the face of heaven. The light that will shine upon the world wide Fatherland and illuminate the gilded domes and glittering pinnacles of the beautiful cities of the future, where men shall dwell together in true brotherhood and goodwill and joy. The Golden Light that will be diffused throughout all the happy world from the rays of the risen sun of Socialism.

The Ragged Trousered Philanthropists (1914)

Leon Trotsky

1879–1940; Soviet revolutionary, Commissar for Foreign Affairs 1917–18

Even a successful solution of the elementary problem of food,
clothing, shelter and even of literacy, would in no way signify
a complete victory of the new historic principle, that is, of
Socialism. Only a movement of scientific thought on a national
scale and the development of a new art would signify that the
historic seed had not only grown into a plant, but had even
flowered. In this sense, the development of art is the highest test
of the vitality and significance of each epoch.

Literature and Revolution (1924)

It is fundamentally incorrect to contrast bourgeois culture
and bourgeois art with proletarian culture and proletarian art.
The latter will never exist, because the proletarian regime is
temporary and transient. The historic significance and the moral
grandeur of the proletarian revolution consist in the fact that it
is laying the foundations of a culture which is above classes and
which will be the first culture that is truly human.

Literature and Revolution (1924)

Comrades! Our Soviet Socialist Republic needs a well-organised
army.

Speech, Moscow, 19 March 1918

Old age is the most unexpected of all things that happen to a
man.

Diary in Exile, 8 May 1935

Let there be no wavering, no doubts. Work, order, perseverance,
discipline, self-sacrifice – and we shall triumph.

Speech, Moscow, 19 March 1918

The dictatorship of the Communist Party is maintained by
recourse to every form of violence.

1924

If we are, in the end, forced to go, we shall slam the door behind us in such a way that the echo will be felt throughout the world.
  1917

England is ripe for revolution.
  1925

A proletarian church is impossible.
  Literature and Revolution (1924)

Civilisation has made the peasantry its pack animal. The bourgeoisie in the long run only changed the form of the pack.
  History of the Russian Revolution (1933)

The Revolution is, above all, a city one; without the city there could have been no abolition of the nobles' estates.
  Literature and Revolution (1924)

If we had more time for discussion, we should probably have made a great many more mistakes.
The party in the last instance is always right, because it is the single historic instrument which the working class possesses for the solution of its fundamental problems ... I know that one must not be right against the party. One can be right only with the party, and through the party, because history has created no other road for the realisation of what is right.
  Speech to the Communist Party Congress, May 1924

You [the Mensheviks] are pitiful, isolated individuals; you are bankrupts; your role is played out. Go where you belong from now on – into the dustbin of history.
  History of the Russian Revolution (1933)

I will issue a few revolutionary proclamations to the people of the world and then shut up shop.
  Cited in E.H. Carr, *The Bolshevik Revolution 1917–1923* (1971)

Revolutions are as a rule not made arbitrarily. If it were possible to map out the revolutionary road beforehand and in a rational way, then it would probably also be possible to avoid the revolution altogether. Revolution is an expression of the impossibility of reconstructing class society by rational methods.

Where Is Britain Going? (1926)

Where force is necessary, there it must be applied boldly, decisively and completely. But one must know the limitations of force; one must know when to blend force with a manoeuvre, a blow with an agreement.

What Next? (1932)

It is impossible to build a socialist paradise as an oasis amid the inferno of world capitalism.

Critique of the Programme of the Third International (1928)

The dictatorship of the proletariat which has risen to power as the leader of the democratic revolution is inevitably and very quickly confronted with tasks, the fulfilment of which is bound up with deep inroads into the rights of bourgeois property. The democratic revolution grows directly into the Socialist revolution and thereby becomes a *permanent* revolution ... The completion of the socialist revolution within national limits is unthinkable ... The Socialist revolution begins in the national arena, it unfolds in the international arena, and is completed in the world arena.

The Permanent Revolution (1930)

England is nothing but the last ward of the European madhouse, and quite possibly it will prove to be the ward for particularly violent cases.

Diary in Exile, 11 April 1935

Revolutions are always verbose.

The History of the Russian Revolution (1930)

The most popular mass insurrection in history.
On the Russian Revolution, *History of the Russian Revolution* (1933)

Insurrection is an art and like all arts it has its laws.
History of the Russian Revolution (1933)

The party organisation at first substitutes itself for the party as a whole; then the central committee substitutes itself for the organisation; and finally a single 'dictator' substitutes himself for the central committee.
Our Political Tasks (1904)

All those for whom the word socialism is not a hallow sound but the content of their moral life-forward!
Speech, New York, 9 February 1937

Mao Tse-tung
1893–1976; Chinese Communist leader 1945–76

Every Communist must grasp the truth, 'Political power grows out of the barrel of a gun'.
Problems of War and Strategy (1938)

We Communists are like seeds and the people are like the soil. Wherever we go, we must unite with the people, take root and blossom among them.
Quotations from Chairman Mao Tse-tung (1966)

Communism is not love. Communism is a hammer which we use to crush the enemy.
Cited in *Time* magazine, 18 December 1950

Classes struggle, some classes triumph, others are eliminated. Such is history; such is the history of civilisation for thousands of years.
Cited in S. Karnow, *Mao and China* (1972)

Politics is war without bloodshed while war is politics with bloodshed.

Quotations from Chairman Mao Tse-tung (1966)

War can be abolished only through war, and in order to get rid of the gun it is necessary to take up the gun.

Problems of War and Strategy (1938)

We should support whatever the enemy opposes and oppose whatever the enemy supports.

Selected Works

Letting a hundred flowers blossom and a hundred schools of thought contend is the policy for promoting the progress of the arts and the sciences and a flourishing socialist culture in our land.

Speech, Peking, 27 February 1957

All the so-called powerful reactionaries are no more than paper tigers, for they are cut off from their people. Think of Hitler: was he not a paper tiger and was he not overthrown? I have said that the Tsar of Russia, the Emperor of China and the imperialism of Japan were all paper tigers. As we know, they were all overthrown. US imperialism has not yet been overthrown, and it has atomic bombs. But I believe it, too, will be overthrown. It, too, is a paper tiger.

Speech, Moscow, 18 November 1957

Let other people speak out. The heavens will not fall and you will not be thrown out. If you do not let others speak, then the day will surely come when you will be thrown out.

Speech, 30 January 1962

There may be thousands of principles of Marxism, but in the final analysis they can be summed up in one sentence: Rebellion is justified.

The Times, 31 October 1966

I am a lone monk walking the world with a leaky umbrella.
Complacency is the enemy of study. We cannot really learn
anything until we rid ourselves of complacency.

Quotations from Chairman Mao Tse-tung (1966)

If you want to know the taste of a pear, you must change the
pear by eating it yourself ... If you want to know the theory and
methods of a revolution, you must take part in a revolution. All
genuine knowledge originates in direct experience.

'On Practice' (1937)

A revolution is not a dinner party, or writing an essay, or
painting a picture, or doing embroidery, it cannot be so refined
... A revolution is an insurrection, an act of violence by which
one class overthrows another.

Quotations from Chairman Mao Tse-tung (1966)

To read too many books is harmful.

Remarks made at Spring Festival, 13 February 1964

War cannot be divorced from politics for a single moment.

Lecture, 1938

An army without culture is a dull-witted army. And a dull-
witted army cannot defeat the enemy.

Speech, 30 October 1944

U

Chuka Umunna

b. 1978; Labour Party politician, shadow Secretary of State for Business, Innovation and Skills 2011–

We have a plentiful supply of passion, but we also need to rediscover our confidence.

Speech to Compass conference, 12 June 2010

Hopefully the private sector will be strong enough to counteract the effects of Osborne's measures, Britain will enjoy an exporting and investment renaissance and workers will move near seamlessly from the public payroll to newly created jobs in industry. However, history suggests that the odds of this occurring, especially at a time of continued global economic turmoil, are not high. Osborne's lack of a Plan B could prove his undoing – unfortunately it is the British people and not the likes of Osborne who will ultimately pay the price.

'The Man's Not for Turning', *New Statesman* blog (with Duncan Weldon), 25 October 2010

At the next general election, we must be able to explain what the country will look like after five years of Labour government and what vision we offer; as Ed Miliband sets the party's direction of travel, Blue Labour has much to offer.

'One Nation Labour', Left Foot Forward, 12 May 2011

So the 'Blue Labour' label can perhaps be misleading – 'One Nation Labour' perhaps would be more appropriate, signposting Ed Miliband and Labour's determination to win back support across the country and across all demographics.

'One Nation Labour', Left Foot Forward, 12 May 2011

My father arrived here after a very long journey on a boat from Nigeria in the mid 1960s. When he arrived at Liverpool Docks he had a suitcase and no money. A random stranger leant him the cash to pay for his train fare to London where he was due to take up lodgings with friends.

Speech to Hub Westminster, 'Getting On With Business: Entrepreneurship and Social Mobility', Hub Westminster, 26 June 2012

Entrepreneurship has a key role to play here because running your own business, research suggests, can sometimes offer a better route for weakening the link between where you come from and where you end up, than being in paid employment.

Speech to Hub Westminster, 'Getting On With Business: Entrepreneurship and Social Mobility', Hub Westminster, 26 June 2012

To succeed in the future we must write the next chapter of our own national story – with aspiration at its heart, entrepreneurship as its state of mind, and community as its end. It must encourage your restlessness and inspire my young constituents. That way, together, we will create a better future for all in Britain.

Speech to Hub Westminster, 'Getting On With Business: Entrepreneurship and Social Mobility', Hub Westminster, 26 June 2012

My late father arrived in this country in the mid-1960s from Nigeria. It was the Labour Party that insisted he – and others like him – should be able to pursue their aspirations and dreams free from prejudice. My mother, who comes from an altogether different background, benefited from the right to equal pay at work after she graduated in the 1970s, again, thanks to this Labour Party. You see, this party has given me, my family – all of our families – so much. That is why we all join the Labour Party – to put something back.

Speech to Labour Party Conference, 1 October 2012

V

Eric Varley

1932–2008; Labour Party politician, Secretary of State for Energy 1973–74

Free trade unionism in Britain is an essential ingredient in
our free society and one of the safeguards to our liberties.
Cited in G. Kaufman (ed.), *Renewal: Labour's Britain in the 1980s* (1983)

Pierre Vergniaud

1753–93; French revolutionary leader

When justice has spoken, humanity must have its turn.
Speech to the National Assembly, 17 January 1793

José Antonio Viera-Gallo

b. 1943; Chilean politician

Socialism can only arrive by bicycle.
Cited in I. Illich, *Energy and Equity* (1974)

Voltaire

1694–1778; French political theorist and writer

The poor man is never free; he serves in every country.
Attributed

W

Lech Wałęsa
b. 1943; Polish trade union leader and President of Poland 1990–95

It depends on the way you measure the concept of good, bad,
better, worse, because, if you choose the example of what we
Poles have in our pockets and in our shops, then I answer that
Communism has done very little for us. If you chose the example
of what is in our souls, instead, I answer that Communism has
done very much for us. In fact our souls contain exactly the
contrary of what they wanted. They wanted us not to believe in
God and our churches are full. They wanted us to be materialistic
and incapable of sacrifices: we are anti-materialistic, capable of
sacrifice. They wanted us to be afraid of the tanks, of the guns,
and instead we don't fear them at all.

Sunday Times, 22 March 1981

G. J. Wardle
1865–1947; Labour Party politician and trade unionist, editor *Keighley
Labour Journal* 1893–97

Labour has fought where instinct and reason taught it fighting
was essential; it has bargained where it saw a reasonable chance
of success; it has entered into partnership where political
sagacity and national safety seemed alike to call for that method.
It still remains a separate party. Partnerships can be dissolved,
arguments can be revived, fighting can be resumed, each in
proper place and each at its proper time.

Labour Party Annual Conference Report (1917)

[To create] the kingdom of heaven on earth.

> On the aim of their campaigning, *Keighley Labour Journal*, 16 December 1894

Earl Warren

1891–1974; American lawyer and politician

Many people consider the things which government does for them to be social progress, but they consider the things government does for others as socialism.

> Address to National Press Club in Washington, DC, as quoted in *Freedom and Union* (1952)

Tom Watson

b. 1967; Labour Party politician, deputy chair of the Labour Party 2011–13

They lied and cheated and broke the law. They defiled the dead and mocked the murdered and Rupert Murdoch kept the change.

> Speech to Labour Party Conference on phone hacking scandal, 27 September 2011

Beatrice Webb

1858–1943; Fabian socialist

If I ever felt inclined to be timid as I was going into a room full of people, I would say to myself 'You're the cleverest member of one of the cleverest families in the cleverest class of the cleverest nation in the world, why should you be frightened?'

> Cited in B. Russell, *Portraits From Memory* VIII

To go back on the creation of a Labour Party would be to admit failure.

> *On Socialists*

I never visualised labour as separate men and women of different sorts and kinds ... labour was an abstraction, which seemed to denote an arithmetically calculable mass of human beings, each individual a repetition of the other.

My Apprenticeship (1926)

The Trade Union Movement has become, like the hereditary peerage, an avenue to political power through which stupid untrained persons may pass up to the highest office if only they have secured the suffrages of the members of a large union. One wonders when able rascals will discover this open door to remunerative power.

Diary, 7 June 1917

Hot-air propaganda in mean streets and industrial slums with chill moderation on the Treasury Bench and courtly phrases at Society functions may be the last word in political efficiency; but it is unsavoury, and leads, among the rank and file, to deep discouragement.

Diary, 15 March 1924

Are all Cabinets congeries of little autocrats with a super-autocrat presiding over them?

Diary, 7 April 1924

Permeation of one British class or party, by another, still holds the field. The *middle man governs*, however *extreme* may seem to be the men who sit on the Front Bench, in their reactionary or revolutionary opinions.

Diary, 10 November 1925

Sidney Webb
1859–1947; Fabian socialist

A body of expert representatives is the only form capable of coping with expert administrators. The only way to choose expert representatives is popular election, but that is just the worst way to obtain expert administrators.

Fabian News, 1897

Elections and parties are quite subordinate – even trivial – parts of political action. More is done in England in politics whilst ignoring elections and parties than by or with them.

Letter to H. G. Wells, 15 June 1907

First let me insist on what our opponents habitually ignore, and indeed what they seem intellectually incapable of understanding, namely the inevitable gradualness of our scheme of change.

Address to the Labour Party, 26 June 1925

The economic side of the democratic ideal is ... socialism itself.

Fabian Essays, 1889

The main principle of reform must be the substitution of Collective ownership and Control for Individual Private Property in the means of production.

Socialism: True and False (1894)

For the Labour Party, it must be plain. Socialism is rooted in political democracy; which necessarily comes us to recognise that every step towards our goal is dependent on gaining the assent and support of at least a numerical majority of the whole people.

Labour Party Annual Conference Report (1923)

Marriage is the waste-paper basket of the emotions.

Cited in B. Russell, *Autobiography* (1967)

To feel that every moment that I am acting as a member of a committee ... I aspire to act alone or for myself.

Private correspondence

No more specific than a definite repudiation of individualism.

On Socialism, *The New Constitution of the Labour Party* (1918)

The Labour Party of the future is, in short, to be a Party of the producers.

The New Constitution of the Labour Party (1918)

Sidney and Beatrice Webb
Fabian socialists

Old people are always absorbed into something, usually themselves. We prefer to be absorbed in the Soviet Union.

On themselves, cited in K. Martin, *The Webbs In Retirement* (1985)

The deliberate regulation of the condition of employment in such a way as to ward off from the manual working producers the evil effects of industrial competition.

On the object of trade unions, *Industrial Democracy* (1897)

There is no reason why the fully recognised Trade Unions should not, we do not say merely acquiesce in scientific management, but actually promote the new science.

New Statesman, 7 June 1913

The Socialist State, far from being a centralised and coercive bureaucracy, presents itself to us as a highly diversified and extremely numerous set of social groupings.

New Statesman, 21 June 1913

Who can estimate among how many different boards and committees, partnerships and combinations, in how many entirely uncoordinated centres of management, unaware of each other's proceedings and constantly in conflict or confusion the direction of ... British ... industry is dispersed.

A Constitution for the Socialist Commonwealth of Great Britain (1920)

Sidney Weighell

1922–2002; trade unionist, General Secretary of the National Union of Railwaymen 1975–83

If you want it to go out ... that you now believe in the philosophy of the pig trough – those with the biggest snouts get the largest share – I reject it.

Speech to Labour Party Conference, 6 October 1978

I don't see how we can talk with Mrs Thatcher ... I will say to the lads, come on, get your snouts in the trough.

Speech, London, 10 April 1979

H. G. Wells

1866–1946; English novelist

Crude classifications and false generalisations are the curse of the organised life.

A Modern Utopia (1905)

I see knowledge increasing and human power increasing. I see ever-increasing possibilities before life, and I see no limits set to it at all. Existence impresses me as a perpetual dawn. Our lives, as I apprehend, are great in expectations.

Mr Belloc Objects (1926)

Adapt or perish, now as ever, is nature's inexorable imperative.

The Mind at the End of its Tether (1945)

Every time I see an adult on a bicycle, I no longer despair for the future of the human race.

Attributed

No passion in the world is equal to the passion to alter someone else's draft.

Attributed

After people have repeated a phrase a great number of times,
they begin to realise it has meaning and may even be true.
  Attributed

Human history becomes more and more a race between
education and catastrophe.
  The Outline of History (1920)

In England we have come to rely upon a comfortable time-lag
of a century intervening between the perception that something
ought to be done and a serious attempt to do it.
  The Work, Wealth and Happiness of Mankind (1934)

Dame Rebecca West
1892–1983; novelist

A charming companion and a virtuoso conversationalist and not
a selfish one. He was a wonderful hand at conducting a general
conversation and could bring out the best in the shy and the
alien. But he had his handicaps. The chief of these was his failure
to tell the truth. He also had no sense of humour.
  On Richard Crossman, 1971

William Whitelaw
1918–99; Conservative Party politician

The Labour Party is going about the country stirring up apathy.
  Aimed at Harold Wilson, October 1974 general election

Gough Whitlam
b. 1916; Australian Labor Party politician, Prime Minister 1972–75

You may call me bourgeois, but not decadent.
  Comment to Francis James, Australian publisher

The time will come when you may interrupt me.

Responding to John McEwan's interruption of his maiden speech,
19 March 1953

There is a great amount of talent in the parliamentary Labor
Party, but I believe that I have the greatest amount of talent at
the present time.

1974

Oscar Wilde

1854–1900; Irish writer

As for the virtuous poor, one can pity them, of course, but one
cannot possibly admire them.

The Soul of a Man under Socialism (1891)

Marcia Williams

b. 1932; personal and political secretary to Prime Minister Harold Wilson

Primarily it was surely a matter of people switching or
abstaining as a result of the actions of the final week, particularly
that bold, crude, uncompromising promise to reduce taxation,
to halt the rise in prices and to bring unemployment down.
Nothing, not even the asset of a popular leader and his wife, was
sufficient to counter this beguiling prospect.

On Labour's defeat in 1970, *Inside Number 10* (1975)

Raymond Williams

1921–88; writer and critic

A Marxist theory of culture will recognise diversity and
complexity, will take account of continuity within change,
will allow for chance ... but, with these reservations, will
take the facts of the economic structure and the consequent

social relations as the guiding string on which a culture is to be understood.

Culture and Society 1780–1950 (1958)

It wasn't idealism that made me, from the beginning, want a more secure and rational society. It was an intellectual judgement, to which I still hold. When I was young its name was socialism. We can be deflected by names. But the need was absolute, and is still absolute.

Loyalties (1985)

The resulting controversy, between many groups and tendencies all calling themselves *socialist*, has been long, intricate and bitter.

Cited in T. Wright, *Socialisms: Old And New* (1996)

Shirley Williams

b. 1930; former Labour Party politician, Secretary of State for Education and Science 1976–79, co-founder of the SDP

Owen and Tawney are to political thought what Vaughan Williams was to music; pastoral, gentle and humane.

Politics is for People (1981)

The women's vote has reshaped the geography of politics much more fundamentally than the election of a handful of women to Parliament.

Women in Politics (1980)

Socialists need to recognise the force of the antipathy that now exists towards 'big government': the multiplication of bureaucracy, the increase in cost, the feeling that government already has too large an influence over people's individual lives.

Politics is for People (1981)

There are hazards in anything one does, but there are far greater hazards in doing nothing.
1974

The saddest illusion of revolutionary socialists is that revolution itself will transform the nature of human beings.
1977

If I got fed up with the Labour Party, I should leave politics altogether.
1979

We believe that a centre party would have no roots, no principles, no philosophy, and no values.
1980

I would not join a centre party because I feel the whole idea is wrong.
1980

There is no way I could have been anything but a socialist. It would have been a clear revolt against my whole upbringing and family background.
1980

Harold Wilson
1916–95; Labour Party politician, Prime Minister 1964–70 and 1974–76

No one should be in a political party unless he believes that party represents his own highest religious and moral ideas.
Daily Mail, 21 June 1948

The other week I read a story in the *Daily Express* that I was going to sack all junior ministers over fifty-two. Wondered where it came from, and then suddenly remembered I'd leaked it myself.

Cited by John Junor, editor of the *Sunday Express*

I haven't read Karl Marx, I got stuck on that footnote on page two.

Attributed

We are not a flag-waving party. But we are a deeply patriotic party, because we truly represent the British people.

Speech to Labour Party Conference, 1963

I want to speak to you today about the new Britain and how we intend to bring home to our people the excitement there will be in building it. Since the war, the world has been rushing forward at an unprecedented and exhilarating speed ... Yet Britain lags behind, lacking the will or the plan which can bring this future within the reach of us all. We are living in the jet-age but we are governed by an Edwardian Establishment mentality. Over the British people lies the chill frost of Tory leadership ... Tory society is a *closed* society, in which birth and wealth have priority. This is the time for a breakthrough to an exciting and wonderful period in our history ... We want the youth of Britain to storm the new frontiers of knowledge ... This is what 1964 can mean. A chance for change. More, a time for resurgence. A chance to sweep away the grouse-moor conception of Tory leadership.

The New Britain (1964)

The Labour Party gives defence of the pound the first priority. We shall need to sacrifice all other considerations to make sterling strong.

February 1958

Smethwick Conservatives can have the satisfaction of having topped the poll, of having sent a Member who, until another

election returns him to oblivion, will serve his time here as a
Parliamentary leper.

On the candidate who defeated Patrick Gordon Walker in a racist
campaign, Hansard, 4 November 1964

This is not a lightly given pledge. It is a promise. We shall
achieve the 500,000 target, and we shall not allow any
developments, any circumstances, however adverse, to deflect
us from our aim.

Speaking during the 1966 general election campaign

Since technological progress left to the mechanism of private
industry and private purpose can lead only to high profits
for a few, a high rate of employment for a few, and to mass
redundancy for many, if there had never been a case for
Socialism before, automation would have created it.

Speech to Labour Party Conference, 1963

The one lesson of the past few years is that you won't make
sterling strong by making the economy weak. We condemn
attempts to solve our export–import problem by holding
production down below the level of our industrial capacity.
The key to a strong pound lies not in Britain's finances but
in the nation's industry. Finance must be the index not the
determinant of economic strength.

The New Britain (1964)

He immatures with age.

On Tony Benn, cited in J. Adams, *Tony Benn: A Biography* (1992)

The man's a genius. He's holding up the banner of Suez for
the party to follow, and he's leading the party away from
Suez. That's what I'd like to do with the Labour Party over
nationalisation.

On Harold Macmillan, cited in P. Foot, *The Politics of Harold Wilson*
(1968)

Socialism, as I understand it, means applying a sense of purpose to our national life: economic purpose, social purpose, moral purpose. Purpose means technical skill – be it the skill of a manager, a designer, a craftsman, a nuclear physicist, or a doctor, a nurse, a social worker.

Purpose in Politics: Selected Speeches (1964)

I have no regrets at all either politically or personally.

On his resignation from the Cabinet in 1951, cited in L. Smith, *Harold Wilson* (1964)

And all these financiers, all the little gnomes of Zurich and the other financial centres about whom we keep on hearing, started to make their dispositions in regard to sterling.

Hansard, 12 November 1956

Devaluation would be regarded all over the world as an acknowledgement of defeat, a recognition that we are not on a springboard but a slide.

Speech, House of Commons, 26 July 1961

I believe that the spirit of Dunkirk will once again carry us through to success.

On handling economic difficulties, speech to Labour Party Conference, 1964

What the Tories propose [entry into the EEC at the first favourable opportunity] would mean an unacceptable increase in the cost of living ... an unacceptable increase in our imports bill ... and a total disruption of our trade with the Commonwealth.

Election campaign, March 1966

You must understand that I am running a Bolshevik Revolution with a Tsarist shadow Cabinet.

In conversation with Richard Crossman, Barbara Castle and others, 12 March 1963

The Labour Party is a moral crusade or it is nothing.
  Speech, Rothesay, 5 September 1964

We are a world power, and a world influence, or we are nothing.
  Speech, London, 16 November 1964

I'm not a Kennedy, I'm a Johnson. I fly by the seat of my pants.
  1964

A Prime Minister governs by curiosity and range of interest.
  The Observer, 24 October 1965

I hope no one is going to bring sterling into this election ...
sterling should be above politics.
  Interview, BBC TV, 10 March 1966

Every dog is allowed one bite, but a different view is taken of
a dog that goes on biting all the time ... He may not get his
licence renewed when it falls due.
  Speech to the Parliamentary Labour Party on rebellions, 2 March 1967

From now on the pound abroad is worth fourteen per cent or
so less in terms of other currencies. It does not mean, of course,
that the pound here in Britain, in your pocket or purse, or in
your bank, has been devalued.
  Speech, BBC TV, 20 November 1967 after the devaluation of Sterling

Selsdon Man is designing a system of society for the ruthless and
the pushing, the uncaring ... His message to the rest is: you're
out on your own.
  Speech, London, 21 February 1970

I have no wish to lead a party of political zombies.
  On the 'extreme left', speech to Labour Party Conference,
  30 September 1975

The monarchy is a labour-intensive industry.
  1962

If I had the choice between smoked salmon and tinned salmon,
I'd have it tinned with vinegar.
  November 1962

However tired people may be of me, I think most people in the
country will regard me as the lesser of two evils. I always put
these things in a modest way.
  During the 1970 election campaign

If I go on TV and look grim, they say the situation must be even
worse; if I smile at all, it's complacency.
  1975

I think that probably the attacks on me in the press and in
politics have been worse than any other Prime Minister, even
Lloyd George.
  1969

Few politicians are masochists.
  1978

After a half of century of democratic advance the whole process
has ground to a halt with the Fourteenth Earl.
  On the new Prime Minister, Lord Home. Lord Home replied, 'As far
  as the 14th Earl is concerned I suppose that Mr Wilson, when you come
  to think of it, is the fourteenth Mr Wilson.'

A shiver looking for a spine to run up.
  On Edward Heath, 1970

The Rt Hon. Gentleman has inherited the streak if charlatantry
in Disraeli without his vision, and the self-righteousness of
Gladstone without his dedication to principle.
  On Harold Macmillan

Strikes against the national interest are always to be condemned; strikes of capital are no less, and in certain circumstances infinitely more, damaging.

The Labour Governments 1963–70 (1971)

I don't mind running a green Cabinet but I'm buggered if I'm going to run a yellow.

During the 'In Place of Strife' debate, cited in P. Ziegler, *Wilson* (1993)

All along I have believed that my duty was to be the custodian of party unity.

Cited in B. Castle, *Fighting All the Way* 1993

The Cabinet was clearly taken by surprise.

On his resignation as Prime Minister, *Final Term* (1979)

We were being asked to take Genesis out of the Bible; you don't have to be fundamentalist in your religious approach to say that Genesis is part of the Bible.

On Gaitskell's plans for Clause IV, BBC Radio interview, February 1964

Socialism must be harnessed to science and science to socialism.

Speech to Labour Party Conference, 1960

It is not enough to reject the organised conservatism of the Tory Party. We cannot afford to perpetuate any form of dinosaur-type thinking in our own Party ... We cannot afford to fight the problems of the sixties with the attitudes of the Social Democratic Federation, nor, in looking for a solution to those problems, seek vainly to find the answer in Highgate cemetery.

Speech to Labour Party Conference, 1966

Hugh [Gaitskell] wanted to fight, I wanted to set the Party on a new path.

Cited in T. Jones, *Remaking the Labour Party* (1996)

A tightly-knit group of politically motivated men, who, as the last general election showed, utterly failed to secure acceptance of their views by the electorate, but who are now determined to exercise backstage pressures. endangering the security of the industry and the economic welfare of the nation.

On the seamen's strike, Hansard, 1966

We do not wish to give the impression that every constituency was ... badly organised ... In many constituencies, especially marginal seats where a keen contest was fought, efficient organisation and fighting enthusiasm went hand in hand. But the fact remains that compared to our opponents, we are still at the penny-farthing stage in a jet-propelled era, and our machine, at that, is getting rusty and deteriorating with age.

An NEC investigation into the organisation of the Labour Party, presented to the conference of 1955

There are two kinds of Prime Minister I will never be a Ramsay MacDonald or a Dubček.
I see myself as a deep-lying half-back feeding the ball forward to the chaps who score the goals.

1974

If I were a football manager, on present form I would be more worried about job security than I am as Prime Minister.

April 1970 (he lost the following election)

People rather like all the talk of cliff-hanging. It makes politics more interesting.

1965

Everyone seemed to want an election.

Announcing the date of the general election, 1970

Memories don't last as long as you people in the media think.

1975

We are redefining and we are restating our Socialism in terms of the scientific revolution. But that revolution cannot become a reality unless we are prepared to make far-reaching changes in economic and social attitudes which permeate our whole system of society. The Britain that is going to be forged in the white heat of this revolution will be no place for restrictive practices or for outdated methods on either side of industry.

Speech to Labour Party Conference, Scarborough, 1 October 1963

The Labour Party is like a stage-coach. If you rattle along at great speed everybody is too exhilarated or too seasick to cause any trouble. But if you stop everybody gets out and argues about where to go next.

Harold Wilson: The Authentic Portrait (1964)

Hence the practised performances of latter-day politicians in the game of musical daggers: never be left holding the dagger when the music stops.

The Governance of Britain (1976)

[Labour] is the natural party of government.

Speaking in 1965, cited in A. Sampson, *The Changing Anatomy of Britain* (1982)

A week is a long time in politics.

Cited in N. Rees, *Sayings of the Century* (1984)

Mary Wilson

b. 1916; poet, wife of Harold Wilson

Although Harold gets great happiness in family matters, there's no doubt that what excites him most is politics.

Cited in L. Smith, *Harold Wilson* (1964)

Woodrow Wilson
1856–1924; American Democratic politician, President 1913–21

High society is for those who stopped working and no longer
have anything important to do.
> Speech, 24 February 1915

Walter Wolfgang
b. 1923; political activist

'Nonsense…'
> Heckling Jack Straw's speech at the Labour Party Conference, 28
> September 2005. Wolfgang was responding to Straw's claim that 'We
> are in Iraq for one reason only: to help the elected Iraqi government
> build a secure, democratic and stable nation', for which he was
> removed from the conference hall

Barbara Wootton
1897–1988; political economist

[Parliament is] at best an assembly, not of experts on everything
from cost counting to material morality … but of guardians of
common human interest.
> *Plan or No Plan* (1934)

[There is] nothing in the nature of the price mechanism which
would prevent it from functioning in an egalitarian society.
> *Plan or No Plan* (1934)

Tony Wright

b. 1948; Labour Party politician, Parliamentary Private Secretary to the
Lord Chancellor 1997–98

The growth of big government has outstripped the ability of
representative institutions to keep up.

Citizens and Subjects (1994)

In the relationship that is governing, the citizen is a participant
while the subject is a recipient.

Citizens and Subjects (1994)

A unitary dogma of sovereignty, traditionally buttressed by the
ideological dispositions of the main twentieth century political
traditions, has blocked the path to secure forms of shared and
devolved power. Yet it is precisely this which is needed and
demanded.

Citizens and Subjects (1994)

The main point is that Labour in government should
demonstrate an innovative zeal in its approach to institutional
reform and democratic renewal.

Who Wins Dares (1997)

The Blairite revolution, converting Socialism into 'social-ism'
and constructing a liberal communitarianism anchored in a
broad intellectual inheritance of the left centre, succeeded
where the putative revisionism of a generation earlier had failed.
The means and ends of socialism had finally been disentangled,
not through evasion or obfuscation but through a direct and
explicit process of theoretical reconstruction.

Cited in T. Wright, *Socialisms: Old and New* (1996)

One of the great achievements of Labour's new thinking has
been to enable it to reclaim the public service principle, badly

in néed of restoration and restatement, while not confusing this with old models of public service organisation and delivery.

Why Vote Labour? (1997)

Out of the contradictions of market individualism, there is the promise of a new politics of community. Out of an antique constitution, there is the promise of a new way of governing. But for the promise to become achievement, political creativity and audacity are essential.

Who Wins Dares (1997)

The English have been the silent and uninvited guests at the devolutionary feast.

The Independent, 23 April 1999

Y

Sun Yat-sen

1866–1925; Chinese revolutionary leader

The civilisation of Europe and America is completely materialistic. There is nothing more vulgar, more brutal, more evil. We Chinese call that barbarism. Our inferiority as a power derives from the fact that we have always scorned and avoided it. The Chinese Way is the way of mankind and morals. Our ancient books call this system the royal Way.

Cited in A. Peyrefitte, *The Chinese: Portrait of a People* (1977)

In the construction of a country, it is not the practical workers, but the planners and idealists that are difficult to find.

Chung-shan Ch'üan-shu (*Zhongshan Quanshu*), Volume II (1936)

Boris Yeltsin

1931–2007; Russian politician, President 1991–99

It would have been better if the experiment had been conducted in some small country to make it clear that it was a Utopian idea.

On Communism, September 1991

Let's talk about Communism. Communism was just an idea, just pie in the sky.

The Independent, 13 September 1989 Hugo Young

1938–2003; British journalist

James Callaghan, living proof that the short-term schemer and the frustrated bully can be manifest in one man.

1980

Z

Grigory Zinoviev

1883–1936; Soviet politician

Armed warfare must be preceded by a struggle against the inclinations to compromise which are embedded among the majority of British workmen, against ideas of evolution and peaceful extermination of capitalism. Only then will it be possible to count upon complete success of an armed insurrection.

Letter to the British Communist Party, 15 September 1924, purportedly from Zinoviev

Index

Abbott, Diane 1–2
Abse, Leo 2
Acton, First Baron 2
Adonis, Andrew 3–4
Allen, Clifford 4
Allende, Salvador 4
Anderson, Joe 4
Anonymous 5
Anthony, Susan B. 6
Aristotle 6
Ashton, Joe 6
Attlee, Clement 6–10
    Tony Benn 34
    Aneurin Bevan 45
    Winston Churchill 104–5
    Douglas Jay 208
    George Orwell 295

Bagehot, Walter 11
Bakunin, Mikhail 11–13
Baldwin, Stanley 13
Balls, Ed 14–17
Balogh, Thomas 17
Banks, Tony 17–23
Barnett, Joel 23
Barratt Brown, Michael 23–4
Barry, Brian 24
Basnett, David 24
Bauer, Otto 25
Beaverbrook, Lord Max 26
Bebel, August 26
Beckett, Margaret 26–7
Bell, Daniel 27
Benn, Tony 27–34
    Anthony Crosland 131

    Richard Crossman 133
    Hugh Gaitskell 162
    Roy Hattersley 189
    Peter Shore 326
    Harold Wilson 373
Bennett, Alan 35
Bernstein, Eduard 35–6
Besant, Annie 36
Bevan, Aneurin 36–46
    Clement Attlee 8
    Max Beaverbrook 26
    Ernest Bevin 48
    Winston Churchill 104
    Lord Ralf Dahrendorf 136
    Jennie Lee 234
    Harold Macmillan 251
    Herbert Morrison 284
Beveridge, William 46–7
Bevin, Ernest 47–9
    Michael Foot 155
    A. J. P. Taylor 349
Bickerstaffe, Rodney 49
Bidault, Georges 49
Biko, Steve 50
Blair, Tony 50–75
    Diane Abbott 1
    Leo Abse 2
    Gordon Brown 86, 89
    Ken Coates 110
    Robin Cook 120
    Tam Dalyell 138
    Michael Foot 155
    Roy Hattersley 188
    Denis MacShane 251
    Peter Mandelson 254, 255

Blair, Tony *cont.*
   Mo Mowlam 286
   John Prescott 303
   Margaret Thatcher 349
Blanc, Louis 76
Blatchford, Robert 76
Blum, Léon 76–7
Blunkett, David 77–9
Bobbio, Norberto 79
Bonham Carter, Lady Violet 79
Boothby, Robert 41
Bottomore, Tom 79
Bradshaw, Ben 80
Brailsford, H. N. 80
Brandt, Willy 81
Brezhnev, Leonid 81
Brown, George 81–2
Brown, Gordon 82–90
   Ed Balls 15
   Tony Blair 74, 75
   Charles Clarke 106
   Tom Harris 187
   George Howarth 203
   Peter Mandelson 255, 257
   David Miliband 272
   James Purnell 308
Burnham, Andy 90
Burrows, Sir Fred 91
Byers, Stephen 91
Byrne, Liam 91

Callaghan, Jim 92–5
   Tony Benn 32
   Richard Crossman 133
   Peter Jenkins 210
   Hugo Young 384
Câmara, Dom Hélder 95
Campbell, Alastair 96–8
   Tony Blair 75
   Peter Mandelson 254

Camus, Albert
capitalism
   Clement Attlee 7–8
   Stanley Baldwin 13
   Michael Barratt Brown 23
   Tony Benn 29
   Aneurin Bevan 38–9, 45
   Tony Blair 50, 59–60
   H. N. Brailsford 80
   Maureen Colquhoun 115–16
   Stafford Cripps 124
   Anthony Crosland 125
   Friedrich Engels 150–51
   J. K. Galbraith 162–3, 164
   Bryan Gould 171
   Peter Hain 180
   Thomas Hodgskin 198
   Geoff Hodgson 199
   Stuart Holland 200
   Jean Jaurès 208
   John Maynard Keynes 218
   Neil Kinnock 220
   Labour Party 229
   Vladimir Ilyich Lenin 236
   Pope Leo XIII 240
   Karl Liebknecht 241
   Abraham Lincoln 241
   Ken Loach 245
   Rosa Luxemburg 246
   David Marquand 260
   Karl Marx 262–3, 264, 266, 267
   Bertrand Russell 317
   Leon Trotsky 355
Carlyle, Thomas 98
Carpenter, Edward 99
Castle, Barbara 99–101
   Alastair Campbell 97
Castle, Ted 101
Castro, Fidel 101–2

Chamberlain, Neville
    Aneurin Bevan 41, 45
Chávez, Hugo 103
Churchill, Winston 104–5
    Clement Attlee 7, 8, 9
    Aneurin Bevan 41, 42, 46
Clarke, Charles 106
class
    Diane Abbott 1, 2
    First Baron Acton 2
    Clement Attlee 7–8
    Michael Barratt Brown 24
    Otto Bauer 25
    Daniel Bell 27
    Tony Benn 31
    Alan Bennett 35
    Aneurin Bevan 37
    Ernest Bevin 48
    Louis Blanc 76
    Gordon Brown 86–7
    Albert Camus 98
    G. D. H. Cole 112, 113
    Calvin Coolidge 121
    Stafford Cripps 123
    Anthony Crosland 127, 129
    Eugene Debs 142–3
    E. J. Dionne 145
    Frank Dobson 146
    Terence Duffy 155
    Evan Durbin 148
    Frank Field 154–5
    Hugh Gaitskell 161
    Oliver Goldsmith 168
    André Gorz 169–70
    Antonio Gramsci 172–3
    Peter Hain 179–80
    Keir Hardie 183, 184, 185–6
    Roy Hattersley 189
    Patricia Hewitt 196
    Clive Jenkins 210

    John Maynard Keynes 218
    Vladimir Ilyich Lenin 235, 236, 237, 238–9
    Tom Mann 259
    Karl Marx 262, 263–4, 266, 267
    George Mikes 271
    William Morris 282
    Stanley Orme 293
    Tony Parsons 299
    Plato 302
    John Prescott 307
    Jean-Paul Sartre 318
    Arthur Scargill 319
    Joseph Stalin 337
    R. H. Tawney 347
    A. J. P. Taylor 348
    Leon Trotsky 353
    Mao Tse-tung 356
Clegg, Nick 88
Clemitson, Ivor 106
Clinton, Bill 106–9
Clough, Brian 109
Clynes, John 110
Coates, Ken 110
Cole, G. D. H. 110–15
Colquhoun, Maureen 115–16
communism
    Anonymous 5
    Clement Attlee 9
    Aneurin Bevin 42
    Albert Camus 98
    Maxim Gorky 169
    John F. Kennedy 217
    Robert F. Kennedy 217
    John Maynard Keynes 219
    Nikita Khrushchev 226, 227, 228
    Vladimir Ilyich Lenin 235, 237
    Karl Marx 262, 263
    William Morris 282, 283
    George Orwell 293

communism *cont.*

    Pierre Joseph Proudhon 307

    Will Rogers 314

    George Bernard Shaw 322

    Joseph Stalin 336

    A. J. P. Taylor 348

    Mao Tse-tung 356

    Lech Wałesa 362

    Boris Yeltsin 383

community

    Tony Blair 51, 54, 57–8, 63

    David Blunkett 78

    Gordon Brown 82

    Alistair Darling 138

    Will Hutton 204

    Neil Kinnock 220–21

    David Lammy 231–2

    Charles Leadbeater 234

    Ramsay MacDonald 247

    David Marquand 260

    Raymond Plant 301–2

    Jack Straw 340

Connell, James M. 116

Connolly, James 116–17

Conservative Party

    Aneurin Bevan 36–7, 38, 39

    Robin Cook 118

    Yvette Cooper 121

    Anthony Crosland 127

    Hugh Dalton 137

    Anthony Giddens 167

    Bryan Gould 171

constitution

    Tony Blair 55, 70

constituency work

    Tony Banks 21

    Tony Benn 28

Cook, Arthur 117

Cook, Robin 117–21

    Gordon Brown 86

Coolidge, Calvin 121

Cooper, Yvette 121

Corbyn, Jeremy 122

corruption

    First Baron Acton 2

    Tony Banks 19, 23

    Stephen Byers 91

Cousins, Frank 122

Creasy, Stella 124–5

Crick, Bernard 123

Cripps, Stafford 123–4

    Lady Violet Bonham Carter 79

    Winston Churchill 105

Crosland, Anthony 125–31

Crossman, Richard 131–5

    Rebecca West 368

Cunningham, Jack 135

Dahrendorf, Lord Ralf 136

Dalton, Hugh 136–7

Dalyell, Tam 137–8

Darling, Alistair 138–40

Davies, Denzil 140

Davies, Ernest 140

Deakin, Arthur 141

De Beauvoir, Simone 141

De Cervantes Saavedra, Miguel 141

De Condorcet, Marquis 142

De Gaulle, Charles 142

Debs, Eugene 142–3

democracy

    Tony Benn 30

    Aneurin Bevan 38–9, 42

    David Blunkett 77

    Gordon Brown 84

    Hugo Chávez 103

    Bill Clinton 107

    G. D. H. Cole 113, 114

    Stafford Cripps 124

    Will Hutton 204

democracy *cont.*
  Neil Kinnock 222
  Vladimir Ilyich Lenin 237, 238
  Ramsay MacDonald 247
  John Mackintosh 250
  Chris Mullin 287
  George Bernard Shaw 323
  Hartley Shawcross 325
  Alexis-Charles-Henri Clérel de
    Tocqueville 351
Desmond, Shaw 143
Dewar, Donald 144–5
Diana, Princess of Wales
  Tony Blair 66
Dicks, Terry 20
Dobson, Frank 146
Draper, Derek 146
Driberg, Tom 147
Dubček, Alexander 147
Duffy, Gillian 88
Duffy, Terence 155
Dunn, John 148
Durbin, Evan 148–9

Eden, Anthony 46
Edmonds, John 150
education
  Diane Abbott 2
  Andrew Adonis 3–4
  Tony Blair 55, 61, 66
  David Blunkett 78
  Gordon Brown 86–7
  Alastair Campbell 97
  Anthony Crosland 131
  François Hollande 201
  Tony Parsons 299
Engels, Frederick 150–53
environment
  Margaret Beckett 26, 27
  William Morris 283

equality
  Susan B. Anthony 6
  Aristotle 6
  Mikhail Bakunin 12, 13
  Tony Blair 57
  Gordon Brown 83, 84
  Winston Churchill 104
  Anthony Crosland 126, 127, 129
  Richard Crossman 134
  Friedrich Engels 151
  Frank Field 155–6
  Hugh Gaitskell 162
  Anthony Giddens 166–7
  Roy Hattersley 188, 189
  Leonard Hobhouse 197
  François Hollande 201
  Will Hutton 204, 205
  Douglas Jay 208
  Neil Kinnock 224–5
  Labour Party 229
  David Marquand 260
  George Orwell 294
  R. H. Tawney 344, 346
  Alexis-Charles-Henri Clérel de
    Tocqueville 351
  Barbara Wootton 380
Europe
  Clement Attlee 9
  Ed Balls 15–16
  Tony Banks 20
  Tony Benn 30
  Tony Blair 51, 52, 69
  Ben Bradshaw 80
  Jim Callaghan 93
  Robin Cook 117, 118
  Hugh Gaitskell 160
  François Hollande 201
  John Monks 280
  Jack Straw 340, 341
  Harold Wilson 374

Evans, Moss 153

Feather, Vic 154
Ferguson, Sir Alex 154
Field, Frank 154–5
Foot, Michael 155–7
   John Major 251
   Chris Patten 299
Ford, Isabella 157
Foucault, Michael 157
Fourier, Charles 158

Gaitskell, Hugh 159–62
   James Griffiths 175
   Harold Wilson 377
Galbraith, J. K. 162–4
Galloway, George 165
Gandhi, Mahatma 165–6
gender
   Susan B. Anthony 6
   August Bebel 26
   Barbara Castle 99
   Maureen Colquhoun 115
   Yvette Cooper 121
   Simone De Beauvoir 141
   Isabella Ford 157
   Charles Fourier 158
   Julia Gillard 167–8
   Germaine Greer 175
   Keir Hardie 182, 184
   Harriet Harman 186
   David Lammy 231
   Karl Marx 264
   Christabel Pankhurst 298
   Emmeline Pankhurst 298–9
   George Bernard Shaw 321
   Edith Summerskill 342
   Shirley Williams 370
Giddens, Anthony 166–7
Gillard, Julia 167–8

Goldsmith, Oliver 168
Gorbachev, Mikhail 168
Gordon Walker, Patrick 169
Gorky, Maxim 169
Gormley, Joe 169
Gorz, André 169–70
Gould, Bryan 170–72
Gould, Philip 172
Gramsci, Antonio 172–3
Gray, John 173–4
Grayson, Victor 174
Greene, Graham 174
Greer, Germaine 175
Griffiths, James 175
Guevara, Ernesto 'Che' 176–7

Habermas, Jürgen 178
Hague, William
   Tony Banks 21
   Tony Blair 65
Hailsham, Lord 178
Hain, Peter 178–81
Hall, Stuart 181
Halsey, A. H. 182
Hancock, Matthew 14–15
Hardie, Keir 182–6
Harman, Harriet 186
Harris, Tom 186–7
Hattersley, Roy 187–9
   David Owen 297
Hawke, Bob 190
Hayek, Friedrich 190
Haywood, Ron 190
Healey, Denis 190–94
Heath, Edward
   Harold Wilson 376
Heffer, Eric 194–5
   Robert Kilroy-Silk 219
Heseltine, Michael 195
Hewitt, Patricia 195–6

Hilferding, Rudolf 196–7
Hill, Joe 197
Hobhouse, Leonard 197
Hobsbawm, Eric 197
Hobson, J. A. 198
Hobson, S. G. 198–9
Hodgskin, Thomas 198
Hodgson, Geoff 199
Holland, Stuart 200
Hollande, François 200–202
Hoon, Geoff 202
House of Lords
   Clement Attlee 10
   Tony Banks 22
   Tony Benn 31
   George Brown 81
   Michael Foot 156
   Austin Mitchell 278
   Emanuel Shinwell 325
Howarth, George 203
Howe, Geoffrey 190
Howells, Kim 203
Hugo, Victor 203
Hunt, Tristram 203
hunting
   Tony Banks 19
Hutton, Will 204–5
Hyndman, H. M. 206

Ibárruri, Dolores 207
immigration
   Neal Lawson 234
   John Reid 311
Iraq war
   Ed Balls 15
   Tony Blair 67–8
   Robin Cook 118, 119

Jaurès, Jean 208
Jay, Douglas 208–9

Jenkins, Clive 210
Jenkins, Peter 210
Jenkins, Roy 210–12
Johnson, Alan 213
Jones, Jack 213
Jowell, Tessa 213–14

Kaufman, Gerald 215–16
Kautsky, Karl 216–17
Kennedy, John F. 217
Kennedy, Robert F. 217
Keynes, John Maynard 218–19
Khrushchev, Nikita 226–8
Kilroy-Silk, Robert 219
Kinnock, Neil 219–26
   Tony Banks 18
   Eric Heffer 194–5
   Michael Heseltine 195
   Ken Livingstone 243

Labour Party 229–31
   Clement Attlee 7
   Ed Balls 14
   Tony Benn 29, 31, 32, 33
   Aneurin Bevan 40, 44, 45
   Tony Blair 51, 53, 54, 55, 56,
      58, 59, 61, 62–3, 65, 66, 68,
      72, 74
   David Blunkett 77
   Gordon Brown 82, 90
   Jim Callaghan 95
   Barbara Castle 100
   Winston Churchill 104
   Charles Clarke 106
   John Clynes 110
   Jeremy Corbyn 122
   Anthony Crosland 125–6, 128,
      129, 131
   Richard Crossman 132, 133
   Hugh Dalton 137

Labour Party *cont.*

Alistair Darling 138, 139

John Edmonds 150

Michael Foot 155, 156, 157

Hugh Gaitskell 159, 160, 161, 162

Patrick Gordon Walker 169

Bryan Gould 171

Lord Hailsham 178

Peter Hain 180

Stuart Hall 181

Keir Hardie 182, 183, 185

Harriet Harman 186

Tom Harris 186–7

Roy Hattersley 187, 188, 189

Denis Healey 193, 194

Patricia Hewitt 195–6

Eric Hobsbawm 197

J. A. Hobson 198

Kim Howells 203

Will Hutton 204

Roy Jenkins 210, 211, 212

Gerald Kaufman 215–16

John Maynard Keynes 218, 219

Neil Kinnock 221, 222, 223, 224, 225

Harold Lever 240

Ken Livingstone 242, 243

Ramsay MacDonald 249

Denis MacShane 251

Peter Mandelson 252, 253, 254, 256

David Marquand 260–61

Ian Mikardo 270–71

Ed Miliband 274

Ralph Miliband 277–8

Austin Mitchell 278, 279

Mo Mowlam 285

David Owen 296

Morgan Phillips 301

Laurens van der Post 302

John Prescott 303, 304

Giles Radice 309

Bill Rodgers 313, 314

Dora Russell 317

Clare Short 327

Robert Skidelsky 328

John Smith 332

Philip Snowden 333

Jack Straw 338, 339

Dick Taverne 344

R. H. Tawney 346

Margaret Thatcher 349

Chuka Umunna 359

G. J. Wardle 362

Beatrice Webb 363, 364

Sidney Webb 366

Willie Whitelaw 368

Harold Wilson 372, 375, 377, 378, 379

Tony Wright 381–2

Lafontaine, Oscar 231

Lammy, David 231–2

Lansbury, George 48, 49, 232

Laski, Harold 232–4

Lawson, Neal 234

Leadbeater, Charles 234

Lee, Jennie 234

Lenin, Vladimir Ilyich 235–40

Leo XIII, Pope 240

Lestor, Joan 240

Lever, Harold 240

Levin, Bernard 241

Liebknecht, Karl 241

Lincoln, Abraham 98, 241

Litterick, Tom 241

Livingstone, Ken 242–5

Dennis Skinner 329

Loach, Ken 245

Lovett, William 245

Luxemburg, Rosa 246
MacDonald, Ramsay 247–50
    Winston Churchill 105
    James Maxton 269
Mackintosh, John 250
Macmillan, Harold 251
    Harold Wilson 373, 376
MacShane, Denis 251
Major, John 251
    Tony Banks 21–2
    Tony Blair 66
    John Smith 333
Mandela, Nelson 252
Mandelson, Peter 252–8
    Tony Blair 72, 75
    Gordon Brown 85
    John Prescott 306
Mann, Thomas 258
Mann, Tom 258–9
Marquand, David 260–61
Marquis, Don 261
Marx, Karl 262–8
    Tony Banks 17
    Tony Benn 30, 31, 33–4
    Friedrich Engels 151–2
    André Gorz 170
    William Morris 282–3
    Bertrand Russell 316–17
    Joseph Schumpeter 320
    John Strachey 337–8
    Harold Wilson 372
Mauroy, Pierre 268
Maxton, James 269
McDonagh, Margaret 269
McGovern, Jimmy 269
Meacher, Michael 269–70
Mikardo, Ian 270–71
Mikes, George 271
Miliband, David 271–3
    Ed Miliband 274–5

Miliband, Ed 273–7
    David Miliband 271–2
Miliband, Ralph 277–8
    Ed Miliband 274, 276
miners' strike
    Tony Banks 17
    Arthur Cook 117
    Moss Evans 153
    Peter Hain 179, 180
    Arthur Scargill 319
    Dennis Skinner 329
Minkin, Lewis 278
Mitchell, Austin 278–9
Mitterrand, François 279
Monks, John 280
Montgomery, Bernard Law 280
Moore, Jo 280
Morgan, Rhodri 280
Morris, Bill 280
Morris, Estelle 281
Morris, William 281–4
Morrison, Herbert 284
Mosley, Oswald 284–5
Mowlam, Mo 285–6
    John Reid 311
Muggeridge, Malcolm 286
Mulgan, Geoff 286–7
Mullin, Chris 287
Murphy, Jim 288
Murray, Len 288

National Health Service
    Aneurin Bevan 43
    Andy Burnham 90
    Patricia Hewitt 196
New Labour
    Leo Abse 2
    Ed Balls 16
    Tony Banks 17, 18

New Labour *cont.*
   Tony Benn 34
   Tony Blair 53, 54, 55, 56, 58, 61,
     62–3
   Barbara Castle 100, 101
   Jack Cunningham 135
   Alistair Darling 138
   Anthony Giddens 166–7
   Philip Gould 172
   Roy Hattersley 188, 189
   Patricia Hewitt 195–6
   Will Hutton 205
   Peter Mandelson 253, 254, 255, 258
   Margaret McDonagh 269
   Ed Miliband 275
   John Prescott 305
   Arthur Scargill 319
   Tony Wright 381–2
Northern Ireland
   Tony Blair 67
   Jim Callaghan 93
   Peter Hain 180
   Peter Mandelson 256
   Mo Mowlam 285, 286
nuclear weapons
   Clement Attlee 10
   Tony Banks 18
   Tony Benn 28–9
   Aneurin Bevan 42
   Ernest Bevin 49
   Robin Cook 118
   Jeremy Corbyn 122
   Alistair Darling 139
   Denzil Davies 140
   Hugh Gaitskell 159, 160
   Bryan Gould 170
   Peter Hain 179
   Stuart Hall 181
   Roy Hattersley 187
   Neil Kinnock 220, 221

   Joan Ruddock 316
Obama, Barack 289–93
Orme, Stanley 293
Orwell, George 293–5
Osborne, George 17
   Chuka Umunna 359
Owen, David 295–7
Owen, Robert 297

Pankhurst, Christabel 298
Pankhurst, Emmeline 298–9
Parsons, Tony 299
Patten, Chris 299
Penty, Arthur 300
Perón, Eva 300
Perón, Juan 300–301
Phillips, Morgan 301
Plant, Raymond 301–2
Plato 302
Portillo, Michael 22
Post, Laurens van der 302
Pottier, Eugene 302–3
poverty
   Aristotle 6
   Walter Bagehot 11
   Aneurin Bevan 38–9
   G. D. H. Cole 110, 111
   Miguel De Cervantes Saavedra 141
   Oliver Goldsmith 168
   Tristram Hunt 203
   Douglas Jay 208
   Roy Jenkins 212
   Ramsay MacDonald 248
   Eva Perón 300
   George Bernard Shaw 321
   Oscar Wilde 369
power
   First Baron Acton 3
   Mikhail Bakunin 11
   Tony Benn 28

power *cont.*
    Aneurin Bevan 40
    Tony Blair 72
    Fidel Castro 102
    Denis Healey 191–2, 193
    Karl Marx 264
Prescott, John 303–7
    Tony Blair 73
    Peter Mandelson 254
property
    Mikhail Bakunin 13
    Pierre Joseph Proudhon 306
    R. H. Tawney 345–6
Proudhon, Pierre Joseph 306–7
public ownership
    Clement Attlee 10
    Thomas Balogh 17
    Tony Benn 29
    Aneurin Bevan 43
    Ernest Bevin 47, 48
    Edward Carpenter 99
    Frank Cousins 122
    Anthony Crosland 130–31
    Richard Crossman 132
    Alistair Darling 139
    Hugh Gaitskell 159, 161, 162
    Patrick Gordon Walker 169
    Douglas Jay 209
    Roy Jenkins 211, 212
    Neil Kinnock 222
    Labour Party 229
    James Meade 270
    John Prescott 304
    Peter Shore 326
    John Strachey 338
Purnell, James 308

racism
    Diane Abbott 1
    August Bebel 26
    Steve Biko 50
    David Lammy 231
    Karl Marx 265
Radice, Giles 309
Rawls, John 310
Redmond, Phil 310
Rees, Merlyn 310
Reeves, Rachel 311
referendums
    Clement Attlee 8
    Ed Balls 15–16
Reid, John 311–12
religion
    Mikhail Bakunin 12
    Karl Marx 263, 268
    Ed Miliband 274
Renard, Jules 312
Ricardo, David 313
Robespierre, Maximilien de 313
Rodgers, Bill 313–14
Rogers, Will 314
Roosevelt, Franklin D. 314–15
Rousseau, Jean Jacques 315
Ruddock, Joan 316
Ruskin, John 316
Russell, Bertrand 316–17
Russell, Dora 317

Salmond, Alex
    Alistair Darling 139
Sartre, Jean-Paul 318
Scanlon, Hugh 318–19
Scargill, Arthur 319–20
Schumpeter, Joseph 320
Scotland
    Gordon Brown 84
    Tam Dalyell 138
    Alistair Darling 139
    Donald Dewar 144–5
    James Maxton 269

Shankly, Bill 321
Shaw, George Bernard 321–4
Shawcross, Hartley 325
Shinwell, Emanuel 325
Shore, Peter 326
Short, Clare 326–7
Skidelsky, Robert 328
Skinner, Dennis 328–9
Smith, Adam 330
Smith, Chris 330–31
Smith, John 331–3
    Tony Blair 54
Snowden, Ethel 333
Snowden, Philip 333–4
Soames, Nicholas 21
socialism
    Clifford Allen 4
    Anonymous 5
    Clement Attlee 7–8, 10
    Mikhail Bakunin 13
    Stanley Baldwin 13
    Tony Banks 19, 20
    Michael Barratt Brown
        23–4
    Otto Bauer 25
    Daniel Bell 27
    Tony Benn 32, 33
    Eduard Bernstein 35–6
    Annie Besant 36
    Aneurin Bevan 37–8, 40, 41, 42,
        43, 44, 45
    Tony Blair 51, 52, 64, 65
    Robert Blatchford 76
    Léon Blum 77
    Tom Bottomore 79
    Leonid Brezhnev 81
    Gordon Brown 82–3, 84
    Hugo Chávez 103
    Winston Churchill 104
    Brian Clough 109

    G. D. H. Cole 111–12, 113, 114,
        115
    James Connelly 116–17
    Frank Cousins 122
    Bernard Crick 123
    Anthony Crosland 125, 126–7,
        128, 129–31
    Richard Crossman 131–2, 134–5
    Lord Ralf Dahrendorf 136
    Hugh Dalton 137
    Ernest Davies 140
    Alexander Dubček 147
    John Dunn 148
    Evan Durbin 148–9
    Michael Foot 155, 157
    Hugh Gaitskell 159
    Joe Gormley 169
    André Gorz 169–70
    Bryan Gould 171
    Ernesto 'Che' Guevara 176
    Peter Hain 179
    Keir Hardie 182, 183–4, 185
    Roy Hattersley 187, 188
    Rudolf Hilferding 196–7
    Eric Hobsbawm 197
    J. A. Hobson 198
    Will Hutton 205
    Douglas Jay 208, 209
    Gerald Kaufman 215
    Karl Kautsky 216–17
    Neil Kinnock 220–21, 224
    Labour Party 230, 231
    Vladimir Ilyich Lenin 235, 236,
        237, 238
    Rosa Luxemburg 246
    Ramsay MacDonald 248, 249,
        250
    Thomas Mann 258
    Tom Mann 258–9
    Jimmy McGovern 269

socialism *cont.*
    Michael Meacher 269, 270
    François Mitterrand 279
    William Morris 282
    Herbert Morrison 284
    Oswald Mosley 285
    George Orwell 295
    Raymond Plant 301
    John Prescott 303
    Jules Renard 312
    Joseph Schumpeter 320
    Bill Shankly 321
    George Bernard Shaw 321, 322,
        323
    Chris Smith 330–31
    John Smith 333
    Philip Snowden 334
    Joseph Stalin 335, 336
    William Howard Taft 343
    R. H. Tawney 346, 347, 348
    Norman Tebbit 349
    Alexis-Charles-Henri Clérel de
        Tocqueville 351
    Alain Touraine 352
    Leon Trotsky 353, 355
    José Antonio Viera-Gallo 361
    Earl Warren 363
    Beatrice Webb 364, 366
    Sidney Webb 365, 366
    Raymond Williams 370
    Shirley Williams 370, 371
    Harold Wilson 374, 377, 379
    Tony Wright 381
SPD 335
Stalin, Joseph 335–7
    Nikita Khrushchev 226
    Vladimir Ilyich Lenin 237,
        239–40
Strachey, John 337–8
Straw, Jack 338–41

Straw, Will 341
Summerskill, Edith 342

Taft, William Howard 343
Tatchell, Peter 343
Taverne, Dick 344
Tawney, R. H. 344–8
    Hugh Gaitskell 162
taxation
    Gordon Brown 83–4
    Ivor Clemitson 106
    Clare Short 326
Taylor, A. J. P. 348–9
Tebbit, Norman 349
    Michael Foot 156
terrorism
    Tony Blair 67, 69
    Robin Cook 118–19
    George Galloway 165
    Ken Livingstone 244
    John Reid 311, 312
    Jack Straw 340
Thatcher, Margaret 349
    Tony Banks 18, 21
    Tony Benn 28, 29, 30–31
    Gordon Brown 87
    Jim Callaghan 92–3
    Barbara Castle 99
    Tam Dalyell 137
    Frank Dobson 146
    Michael Foot 156
    Bryan Gould 171
    Roy Hattersley 188
    Denis Healey 191, 192, 194
    Neil Kinnock 220–21, 222
    Joan Lestor 240
    Ken Livingstone 242, 245
    Michael Meacher 270
    David Owen 296
    Arthur Scargill 320

Theroux, Paul 349
Thomas, J. H. 350
Thomas, Norman 350
Thompson, E. P. 350
Titmuss, Richard 350–51
Tocqueville, Alexis-Charles-Henri
  Clérel de 351
Todd, Ron 351
Tolstoy, Leo 351
Touraine, Alain 352
trade unions
  Joel Barnett 23
  David Basnett 24
  Ernest Bevin 49
  Tony Blair 53, 59
  Jim Callaghan 94
  Barbara Castle 100
  Ted Castle 101
  Ken Coates 110
  G. D. H. Cole 112, 113, 114
  Terence Duffy 147
  John Edmonds 150
  Friedrich Engels 150–51
  Denis Healey 193
  S. G. Hobson 198
  Alan Johnson 213
  Jack Jones 213
  John Maynard Keynes 218
  Ramsay MacDonald 248–9
  Bill Rodgers 314
  Franklin D. Roosevelt 315
  Hugh Scanlon 318–19
  John Smith 332
  Eric Varley 361
  Beatrice Webb 364, 366
  Sidney Webb 366
transport
  Andrew Adonis 3
  Stephen Byers 91
  John Prescott 305

Tressell, Robert 352
Trotsky, Leon 353–6
Tse-tung, Mao 356–8

Umunna, Chuka 359–60

Varley, Eric 361
Vergniaud, Pierre 361
Viera-Gallo, José Antonio 361
Voltaire 361

Wales
  Gordon Brown 84
  Kim Howells 203
Wałesa, Lech 362
war
  Anonymous 5
  Ed Balls 15
  August Bebel 26
  Tony Benn 30
  Tony Blair 66, 68
  Fidel Castro 102
  Keir Hardie 185
  Jean Jaurès 208
  Harold Laski 234
  Vladimir Ilyich Lenin 236, 239
  Mao Tse-tung 357, 358
Wardle, G. J. 362–3
Warren, Earl 363
Watson, Tom 363
  James Purnell 308
Webb, Beatrice 363–4, 365–6
Webb, Sidney 364–6
  J. H. Thomas 350
Weighell, Sidney 367
welfare state
  William Beveridge 46–7
  Tony Blair 54, 58, 63, 64
  Gordon Brown 84
  Maureen Colquhoun 116

welfare state *cont.*

    Ernest Davies 140

    Frank Field 154, 155

    Richard Titmuss 350–51

Wells, H. G. 367–8

West, Rebecca 368

whips

    Joe Ashton 6

Whitelaw, Willie 368

Whitlam, Gough 368–9

Wilde, Oscar 369

Williams, Marcia 369

Williams, Raymond 369–70

Williams, Shirley 370–71

Wilson, Harold 371–9

    Willy Brandt 81

    George Brown 82

    Barbara Castle 100–101

    Richard Crossman 134

    Roy Jenkins 212

    Harold Macmillan 251

    Peter Shore 326

    Willie Whitelaw 368

    Mary Wilson 379

Wilson, Mary 379

Wilson, Woodrow 380

Wolfgang, Walter 380

women *see* gender

Wootton, Barbara 380

Wright, Tony 381–2

Yat-sen, Sun 383

Yeltsin, Boris 383

Young, Hugo 384

Zinoviev, Grigory 385

Available now from Biteback Publishing

THE DICTIONARY OF CONSERVATIVE QUOTATIONS
Iain Dale

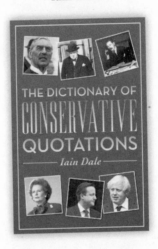

You'll need this thoughtful and entertaining assembly of conservative quotations if you're at all keen on politics. With more than 2,000 key quotes, this authoritative collection contains all the best conservatives and their sayings, whether they were standing up for what's right or standing up to the left, showing off their wit or showing that their foes were witless. It's got all the big names: everyone from Aquinas to Bagehot, Churchill to Cameron, Shakespeare to Thatcher. In *The Dictionary of Conservative Quotations* you'll find humour (Quayle) and inspiration (Burke), political punches (Hague) and ancient wisdom (Aristotle), all wrapped up into one slick, easy-to-use compendium.

416pp paperback, £12.99
Available from all good bookshops or order from
www.bitebackpublishing.com

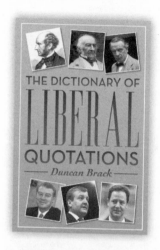

Available now from Biteback Publishing

THE MARGARET THATCHER BOOK
OF QUOTATIONS
Edited by Iain Dale and Grant Tucker

Margaret Thatcher is the most quoted British political leader
since Winston Churchill, and in this unique collection Iain Dale
and Grant Tucker have picked out her most memorable remarks.
Never far from emitting a scathing rebuke, she possesses a
facility for the spoken word rivalled by few others. Some quotes
are funny, many are inspirational, most are thoughtful – but they
are all unforgettable.

352pp paperback, £12.99
Available from all good bookshops or order from
www.bitebackpublishing.com